STAR WARS

HAN SOLO

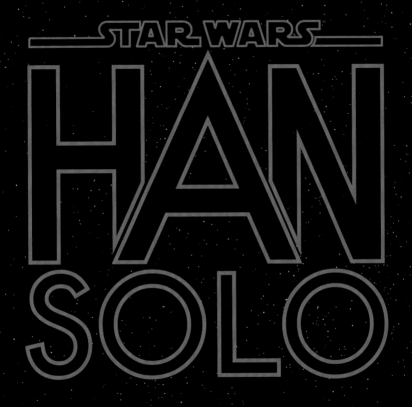

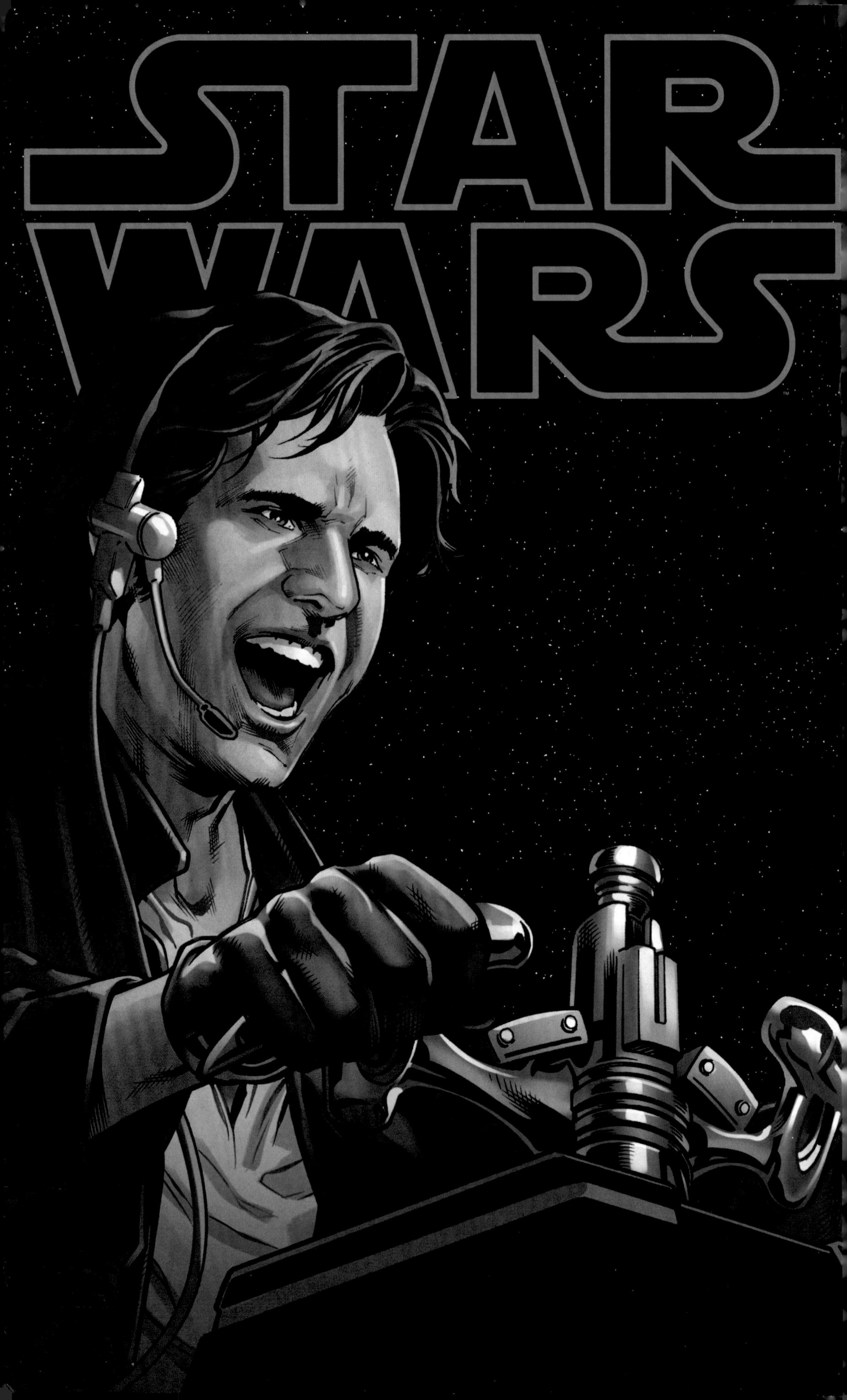
STAR WARS

HAN SOLO

Writer	**MARJORIE LIU**
Penciler	**MARK BROOKS**
Inkers	**MARK BROOKS** (#1, #4-5) &
	DEXTER VINES (#2-3)
Colorists	**SONIA OBACK** WITH **MATT MILLA** (#4)
Letterer	**VC's JOE CARAMAGNA**
Cover Art	**LEE BERMEJO** (#1, #3), **TULA LOTAY** (#2),
	OLIVIER COIPEL (#4) &
	KAMOME SHIRAHAMA (#5)
Assistant Editor	**HEATHER ANTOS**
Editor	**JORDAN D. WHITE**
Executive Editor	**C.B. CEBULSKI**
Editor in Chief	**AXEL ALONSO**
Chief Creative Officer	**JOE QUESADA**
Publisher	**DAN BUCKLEY**

For Lucasfilm:

Senior Editors	**FRANK PARISI**
Creative Director	**MICHAEL SIGLAIN**
Lucasfilm Story Group	**RAYNE ROBERTS, PABLO HIDALGO,**
	LELAND CHEE, MATT MARTIN

Collection Editor	JENNIFER GRÜNWALD
Associate Managing Editor	KATERI WOODY
Associate Editor	SARAH BRUNSTAD
Editor, Special Projects	MARK D. BEAZLEY
VP Production & Special Projects	JEFF YOUNGQUIST
SVP Print, Sales & Marketing	DAVID GABRIEL
Book Designer	ADAM DEL RE

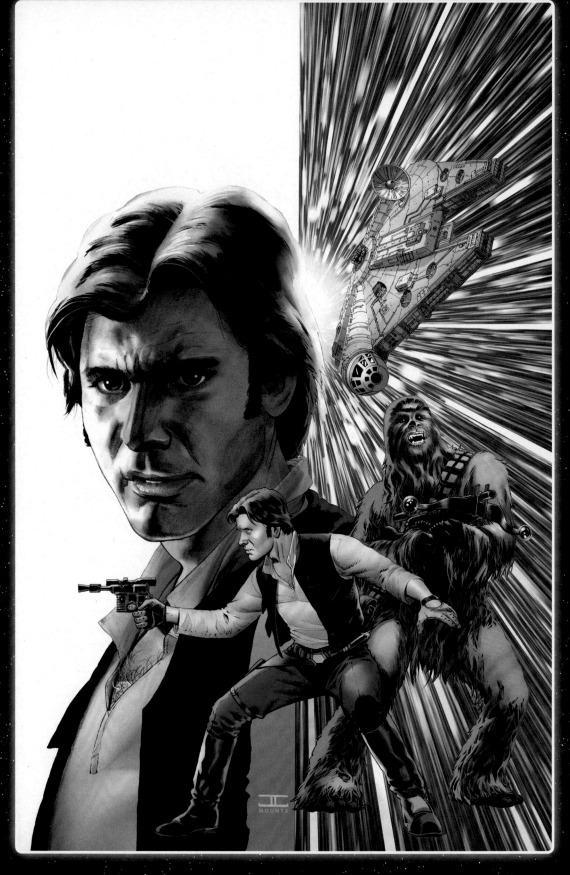

STAR WARS: HAN SOLO 1 Variant
by **JOHN CASSADAY & PAUL MOUNTS**

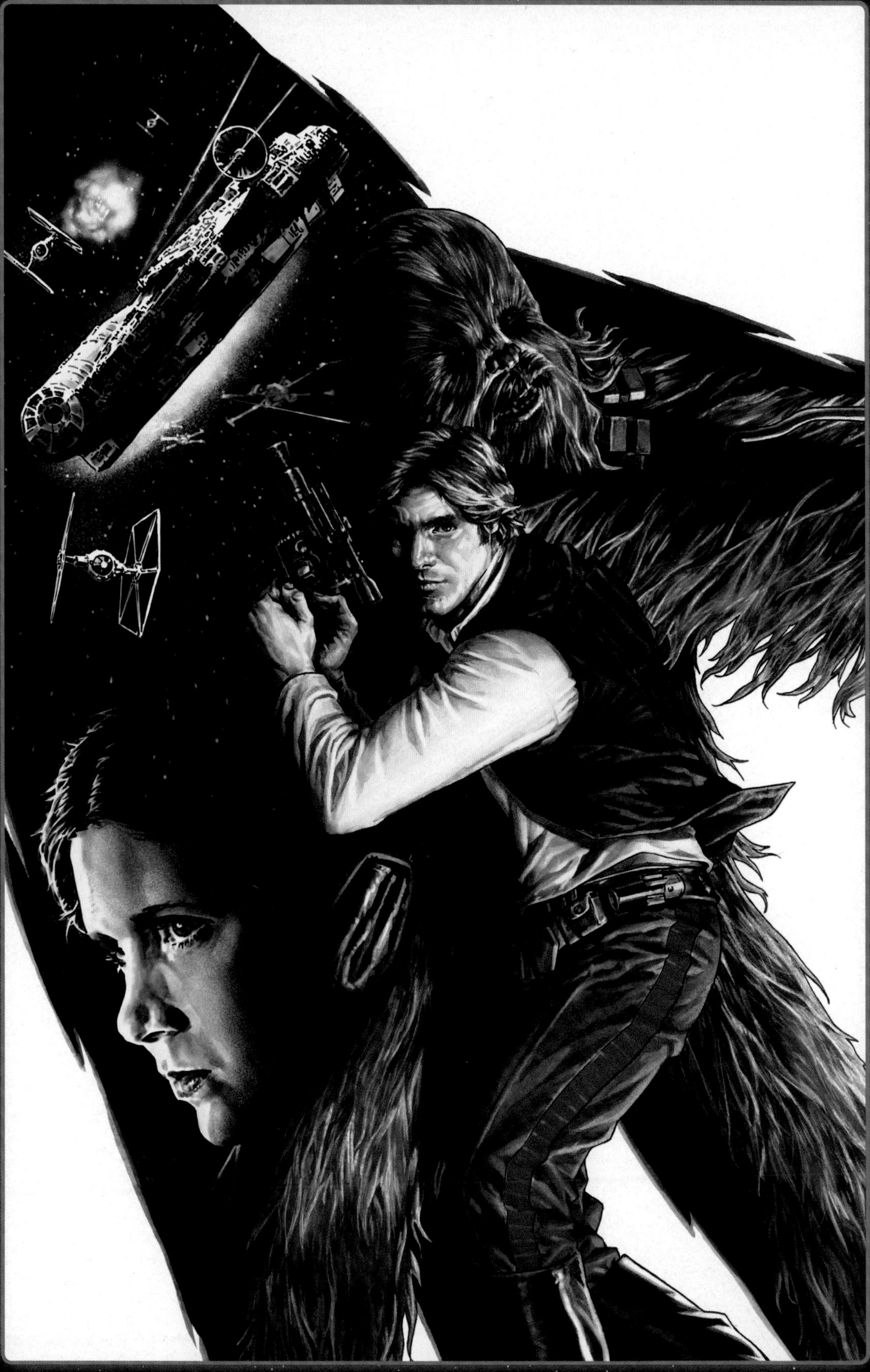

1

HAN SOLO

It is a period of unrest. In a galaxy oppressed by the Empire's unrelenting brutality, there is little hope for change. Nonetheless, rebels have banded together to fight back against such corruption.

While the Rebellion grows in power, Imperials fight to crush any hope for an overthrow. With the Empire's hands full, the opportunities for crime are endless.

HAN SOLO has taken a step back from the rebel cause, returning his focus to what he does best - smuggling. Untrusting by nature, he's skeptical of any who cross his path. Unfortunately for him, he cannot stay under the radar forever....

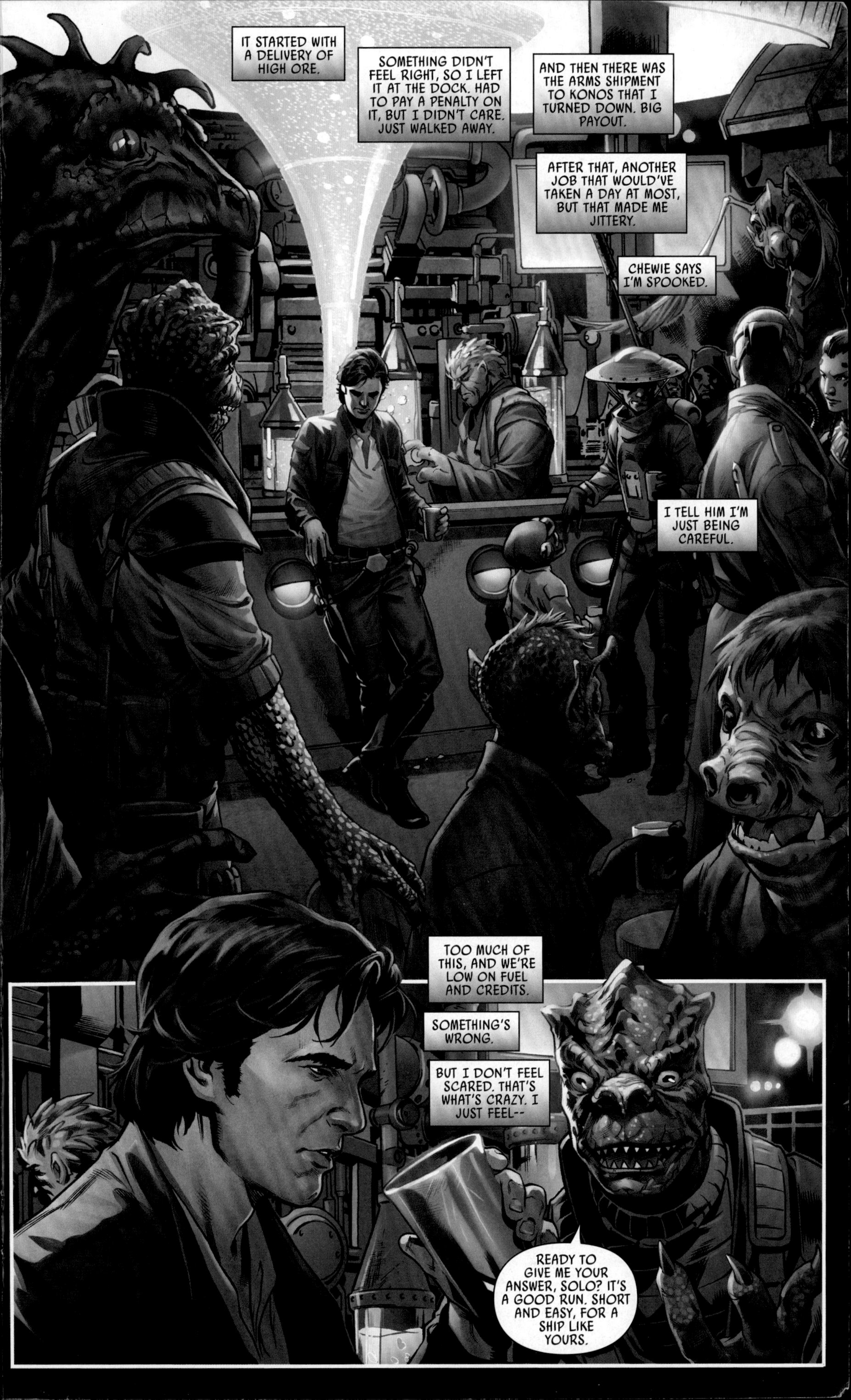
IT STARTED WITH A DELIVERY OF HIGH ORE.
SOMETHING DIDN'T FEEL RIGHT, SO I LEFT IT AT THE DOCK. HAD TO PAY A PENALTY ON IT, BUT I DIDN'T CARE. JUST WALKED AWAY.
AND THEN THERE WAS THE ARMS SHIPMENT TO KONOS THAT I TURNED DOWN. BIG PAYOUT.
AFTER THAT, ANOTHER JOB THAT WOULD'VE TAKEN A DAY AT MOST, BUT THAT MADE ME JITTERY.
CHEWIE SAYS I'M SPOOKED.
I TELL HIM I'M JUST BEING CAREFUL.
TOO MUCH OF THIS, AND WE'RE LOW ON FUEL AND CREDITS.
SOMETHING'S WRONG.
BUT I DON'T FEEL SCARED. THAT'S WHAT'S CRAZY. I JUST FEEL--
READY TO GIVE ME YOUR ANSWER, SOLO? IT'S A GOOD RUN. SHORT AND EASY, FOR A SHIP LIKE YOURS.

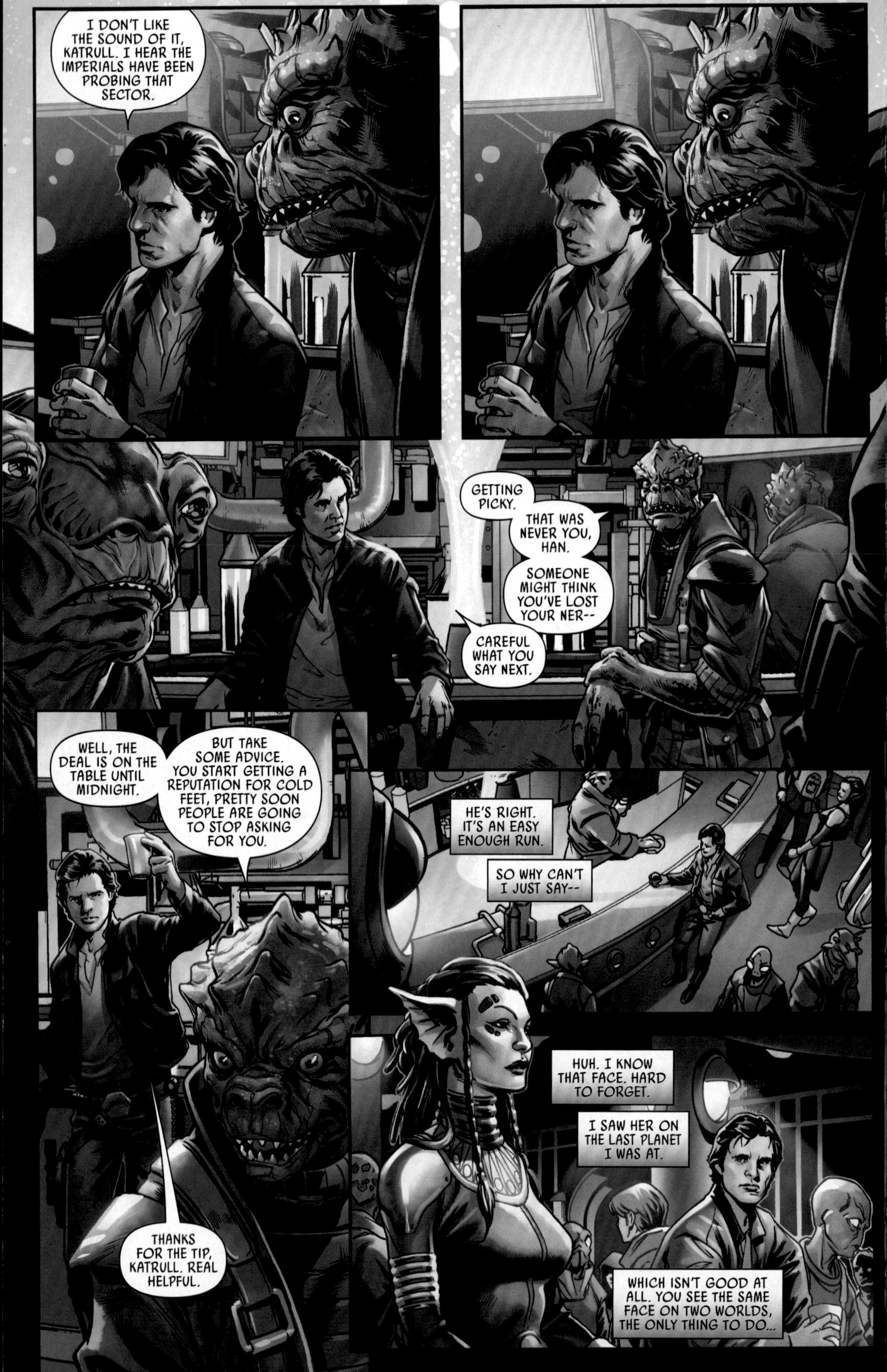
I DON'T LIKE THE SOUND OF IT, KATRULL. I HEAR THE IMPERIALS HAVE BEEN PROBING THAT SECTOR.
GETTING PICKY.
THAT WAS NEVER YOU, HAN.
SOMEONE MIGHT THINK YOU'VE LOST YOUR NER--
CAREFUL WHAT YOU SAY NEXT.
WELL, THE DEAL IS ON THE TABLE UNTIL MIDNIGHT.
BUT TAKE SOME ADVICE. YOU START GETTING A REPUTATION FOR COLD FEET, PRETTY SOON PEOPLE ARE GOING TO STOP ASKING FOR YOU.
THANKS FOR THE TIP, KATRULL. REAL HELPFUL.
HE'S RIGHT. IT'S AN EASY ENOUGH RUN.
SO WHY CAN'T I JUST SAY--
HUH. I KNOW THAT FACE. HARD TO FORGET.
I SAW HER ON THE LAST PLANET I WAS AT.
WHICH ISN'T GOOD AT ALL. YOU SEE THE SAME FACE ON TWO WORLDS, THE ONLY THING TO DO...

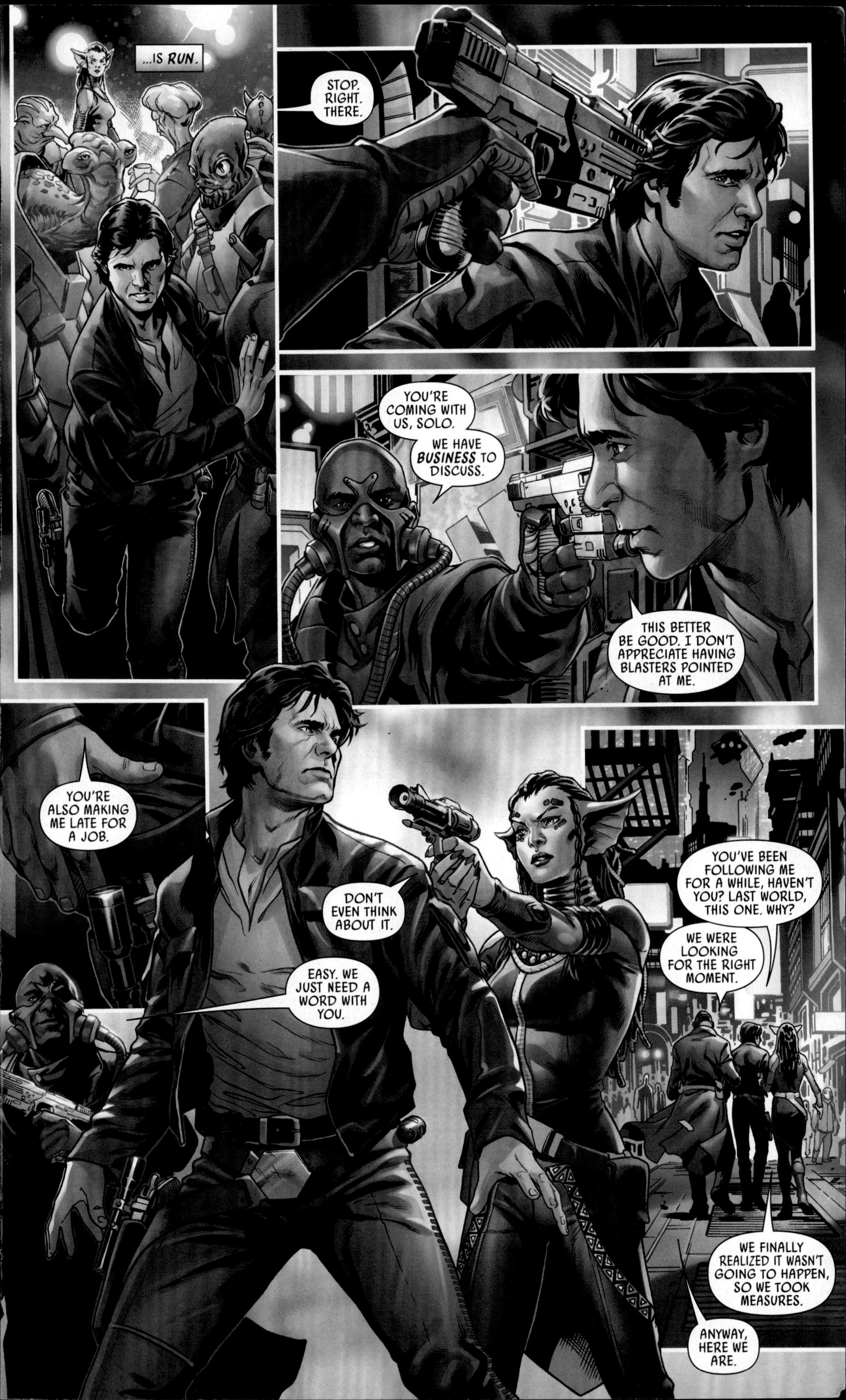
...IS RUN.
STOP. RIGHT. THERE.
YOU'RE COMING WITH US, SOLO.
WE HAVE BUSINESS TO DISCUSS.
THIS BETTER BE GOOD. I DON'T APPRECIATE HAVING BLASTERS POINTED AT ME.
YOU'RE ALSO MAKING ME LATE FOR A JOB.
DON'T EVEN THINK ABOUT IT.
EASY. WE JUST NEED A WORD WITH YOU.
YOU'VE BEEN FOLLOWING ME FOR A WHILE, HAVEN'T YOU? LAST WORLD, THIS ONE. WHY?
WE WERE LOOKING FOR THE RIGHT MOMENT.
WE FINALLY REALIZED IT WASN'T GOING TO HAPPEN, SO WE TOOK MEASURES.
ANYWAY, HERE WE ARE.

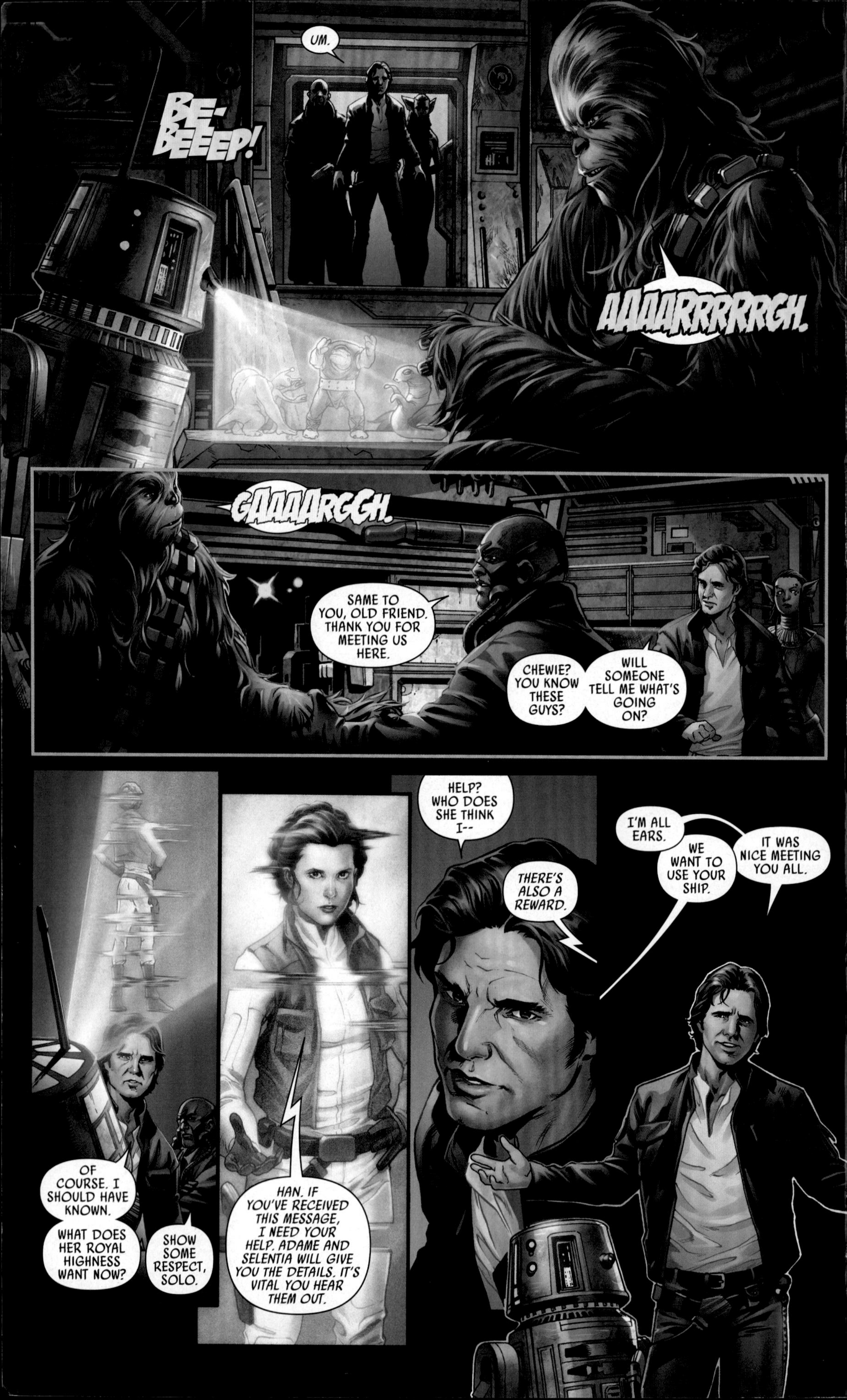
UM.
BE-BEEEP!
AAAARRRRRGH.
GAAAARGGH.
SAME TO YOU, OLD FRIEND. THANK YOU FOR MEETING US HERE.
CHEWIE? YOU KNOW THESE GUYS?
WILL SOMEONE TELL ME WHAT'S GOING ON?
OF COURSE. I SHOULD HAVE KNOWN.
WHAT DOES HER ROYAL HIGHNESS WANT NOW?
SHOW SOME RESPECT, SOLO.
HAN. IF YOU'VE RECEIVED THIS MESSAGE, I NEED YOUR HELP. ADAME AND SELENTIA WILL GIVE YOU THE DETAILS. IT'S VITAL YOU HEAR THEM OUT.
HELP? WHO DOES SHE THINK I--
THERE'S ALSO A REWARD.
I'M ALL EARS.
WE WANT TO USE YOUR SHIP.
IT WAS NICE MEETING YOU ALL.

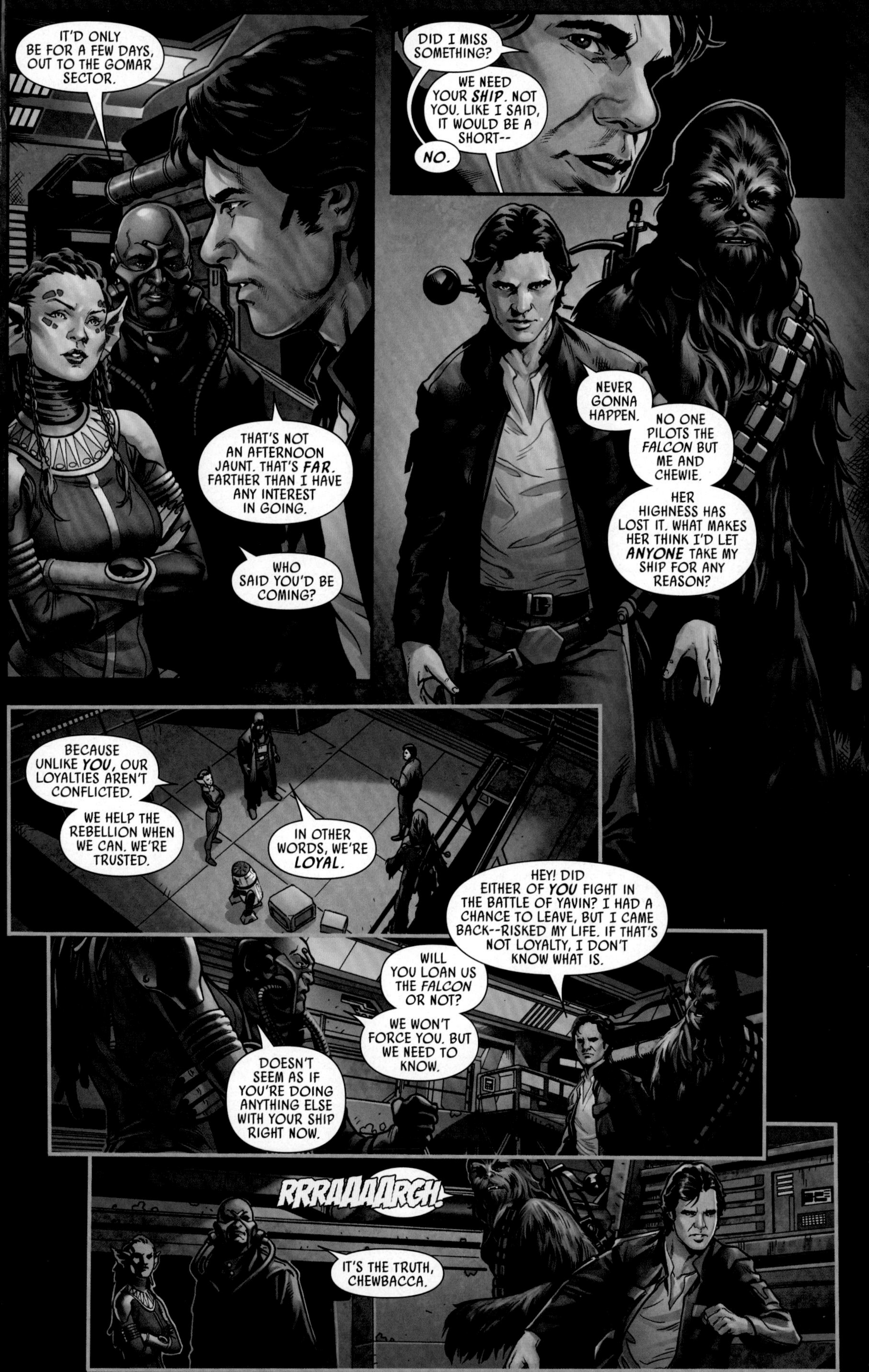
IT'D ONLY BE FOR A FEW DAYS, OUT TO THE GOMAR SECTOR.
THAT'S NOT AN AFTERNOON JAUNT. THAT'S FAR. FARTHER THAN I HAVE ANY INTEREST IN GOING.
WHO SAID YOU'D BE COMING?
DID I MISS SOMETHING?
WE NEED YOUR SHIP. NOT YOU. LIKE I SAID, IT WOULD BE A SHORT--
NO.
NEVER GONNA HAPPEN.
NO ONE PILOTS THE FALCON BUT ME AND CHEWIE.
HER HIGHNESS HAS LOST IT. WHAT MAKES HER THINK I'D LET ANYONE TAKE MY SHIP FOR ANY REASON?
BECAUSE UNLIKE YOU, OUR LOYALTIES AREN'T CONFLICTED.
WE HELP THE REBELLION WHEN WE CAN. WE'RE TRUSTED.
IN OTHER WORDS, WE'RE LOYAL.
HEY! DID EITHER OF YOU FIGHT IN THE BATTLE OF YAVIN? I HAD A CHANCE TO LEAVE, BUT I CAME BACK--RISKED MY LIFE. IF THAT'S NOT LOYALTY, I DON'T KNOW WHAT IS.
WILL YOU LOAN US THE FALCON OR NOT?
WE WON'T FORCE YOU. BUT WE NEED TO KNOW.
DOESN'T SEEM AS IF YOU'RE DOING ANYTHING ELSE WITH YOUR SHIP RIGHT NOW.
RRRAAAAARGH!
IT'S THE TRUTH, CHEWBACCA.

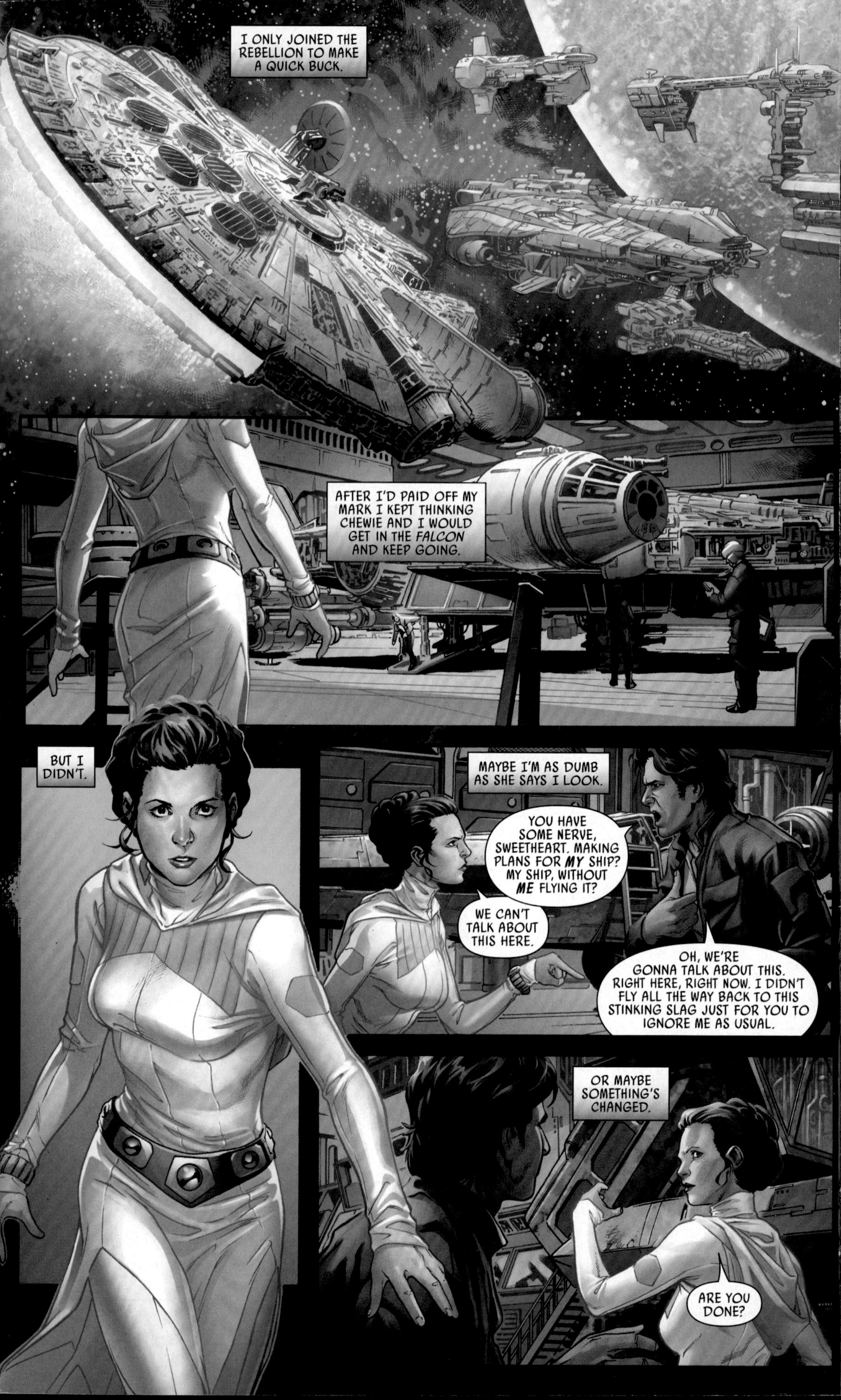

I ONLY JOINED THE REBELLION TO MAKE A QUICK BUCK.
AFTER I'D PAID OFF MY MARK I KEPT THINKING CHEWIE AND I WOULD GET IN THE *FALCON* AND KEEP GOING.
BUT I DIDN'T.
MAYBE I'M AS DUMB AS SHE SAYS I LOOK.
YOU HAVE SOME NERVE, SWEETHEART. MAKING PLANS FOR **MY** SHIP? MY SHIP, WITHOUT **ME** FLYING IT?
WE CAN'T TALK ABOUT THIS HERE.
OH, WE'RE GONNA TALK ABOUT THIS. RIGHT HERE, RIGHT NOW. I DIDN'T FLY ALL THE WAY BACK TO THIS STINKING SLAG JUST FOR YOU TO IGNORE ME AS USUAL.
OR MAYBE SOMETHING'S CHANGED.
ARE YOU DONE?

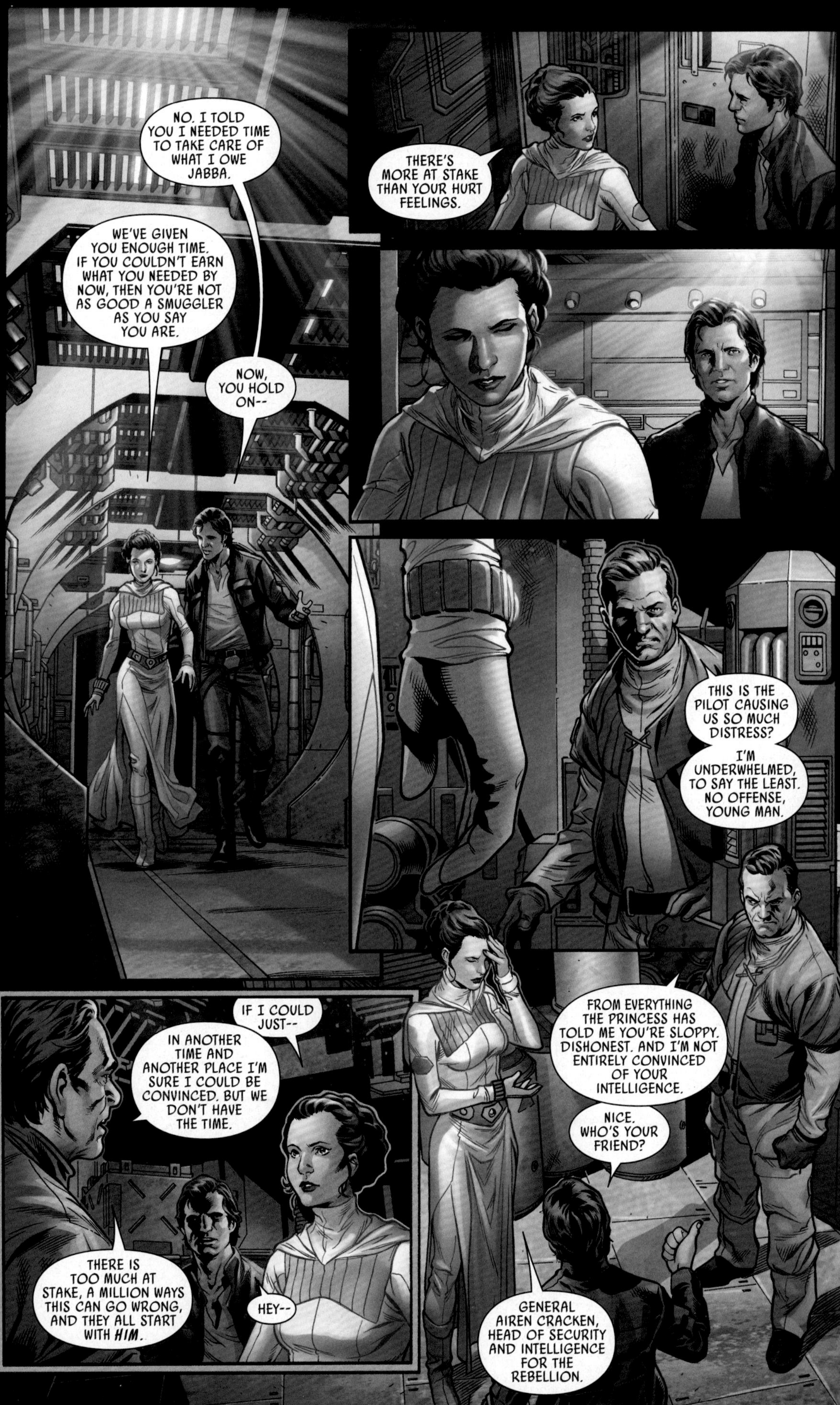
NO. I TOLD YOU I NEEDED TIME TO TAKE CARE OF WHAT I OWE JABBA.
WE'VE GIVEN YOU ENOUGH TIME. IF YOU COULDN'T EARN WHAT YOU NEEDED BY NOW, THEN YOU'RE NOT AS GOOD A SMUGGLER AS YOU SAY YOU ARE.
NOW, YOU HOLD ON--
THERE'S MORE AT STAKE THAN YOUR HURT FEELINGS.
THIS IS THE PILOT CAUSING US SO MUCH DISTRESS?
I'M UNDERWHELMED, TO SAY THE LEAST. NO OFFENSE, YOUNG MAN.
FROM EVERYTHING THE PRINCESS HAS TOLD ME YOU'RE SLOPPY. DISHONEST. AND I'M NOT ENTIRELY CONVINCED OF YOUR INTELLIGENCE.
NICE. WHO'S YOUR FRIEND?
GENERAL AIREN CRACKEN, HEAD OF SECURITY AND INTELLIGENCE FOR THE REBELLION.
IF I COULD JUST--
IN ANOTHER TIME AND ANOTHER PLACE I'M SURE I COULD BE CONVINCED. BUT WE DON'T HAVE THE TIME.
THERE IS TOO MUCH AT STAKE, A MILLION WAYS THIS CAN GO WRONG, AND THEY ALL START WITH HIM.
HEY--

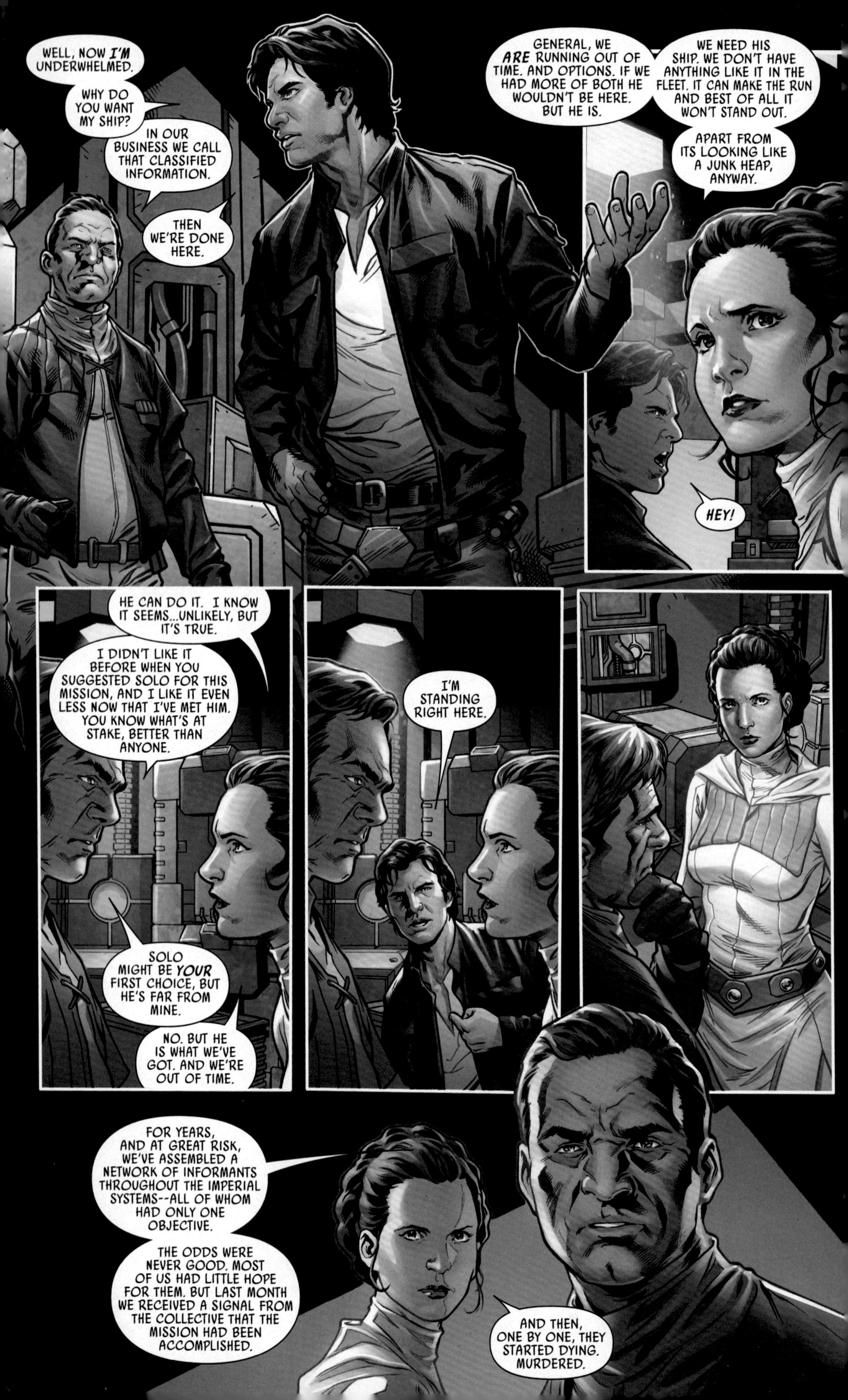
WELL, NOW I'M UNDERWHELMED.
WHY DO YOU WANT MY SHIP?
IN OUR BUSINESS WE CALL THAT CLASSIFIED INFORMATION.
THEN WE'RE DONE HERE.
GENERAL, WE ARE RUNNING OUT OF TIME. AND OPTIONS. IF WE HAD MORE OF BOTH HE WOULDN'T BE HERE. BUT HE IS.
WE NEED HIS SHIP. WE DON'T HAVE ANYTHING LIKE IT IN THE FLEET. IT CAN MAKE THE RUN AND BEST OF ALL IT WON'T STAND OUT.
APART FROM ITS LOOKING LIKE A JUNK HEAP, ANYWAY.
HEY!
HE CAN DO IT. I KNOW IT SEEMS...UNLIKELY, BUT IT'S TRUE.
I DIDN'T LIKE IT BEFORE WHEN YOU SUGGESTED SOLO FOR THIS MISSION, AND I LIKE IT EVEN LESS NOW THAT I'VE MET HIM. YOU KNOW WHAT'S AT STAKE, BETTER THAN ANYONE.
SOLO MIGHT BE YOUR FIRST CHOICE, BUT HE'S FAR FROM MINE.
NO. BUT HE IS WHAT WE'VE GOT. AND WE'RE OUT OF TIME.
I'M STANDING RIGHT HERE.
FOR YEARS, AND AT GREAT RISK, WE'VE ASSEMBLED A NETWORK OF INFORMANTS THROUGHOUT THE IMPERIAL SYSTEMS--ALL OF WHOM HAD ONLY ONE OBJECTIVE.
THE ODDS WERE NEVER GOOD. MOST OF US HAD LITTLE HOPE FOR THEM. BUT LAST MONTH WE RECEIVED A SIGNAL FROM THE COLLECTIVE THAT THE MISSION HAD BEEN ACCOMPLISHED.
AND THEN, ONE BY ONE, THEY STARTED DYING. MURDERED.

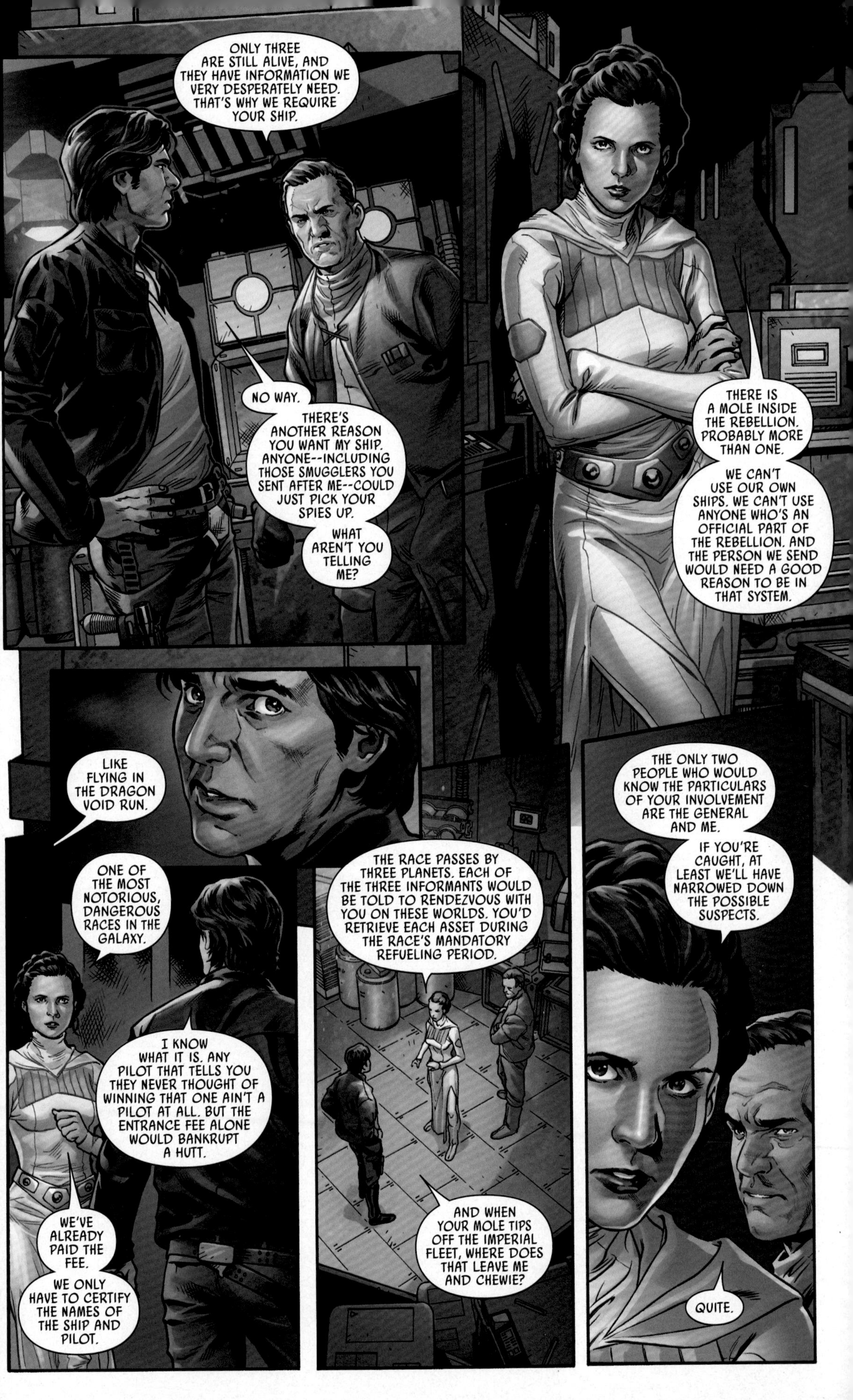
ONLY THREE ARE STILL ALIVE, AND THEY HAVE INFORMATION WE VERY DESPERATELY NEED. THAT'S WHY WE REQUIRE YOUR SHIP.
NO WAY.
THERE'S ANOTHER REASON YOU WANT MY SHIP. ANYONE--INCLUDING THOSE SMUGGLERS YOU SENT AFTER ME--COULD JUST PICK YOUR SPIES UP.
WHAT AREN'T YOU TELLING ME?
THERE IS A MOLE INSIDE THE REBELLION. PROBABLY MORE THAN ONE.
WE CAN'T USE OUR OWN SHIPS. WE CAN'T USE ANYONE WHO'S AN OFFICIAL PART OF THE REBELLION. AND THE PERSON WE SEND WOULD NEED A GOOD REASON TO BE IN THAT SYSTEM.
LIKE FLYING IN THE DRAGON VOID RUN.
ONE OF THE MOST NOTORIOUS, DANGEROUS RACES IN THE GALAXY.
I KNOW WHAT IT IS. ANY PILOT THAT TELLS YOU THEY NEVER THOUGHT OF WINNING THAT ONE AIN'T A PILOT AT ALL. BUT THE ENTRANCE FEE ALONE WOULD BANKRUPT A HUTT.
WE'VE ALREADY PAID THE FEE.
WE ONLY HAVE TO CERTIFY THE NAMES OF THE SHIP AND PILOT.
THE RACE PASSES BY THREE PLANETS. EACH OF THE THREE INFORMANTS WOULD BE TOLD TO RENDEZVOUS WITH YOU ON THESE WORLDS. YOU'D RETRIEVE EACH ASSET DURING THE RACE'S MANDATORY REFUELING PERIOD.
AND WHEN YOUR MOLE TIPS OFF THE IMPERIAL FLEET, WHERE DOES THAT LEAVE ME AND CHEWIE?
THE ONLY TWO PEOPLE WHO WOULD KNOW THE PARTICULARS OF YOUR INVOLVEMENT ARE THE GENERAL AND ME.
IF YOU'RE CAUGHT, AT LEAST WE'LL HAVE NARROWED DOWN THE POSSIBLE SUSPECTS.
QUITE.

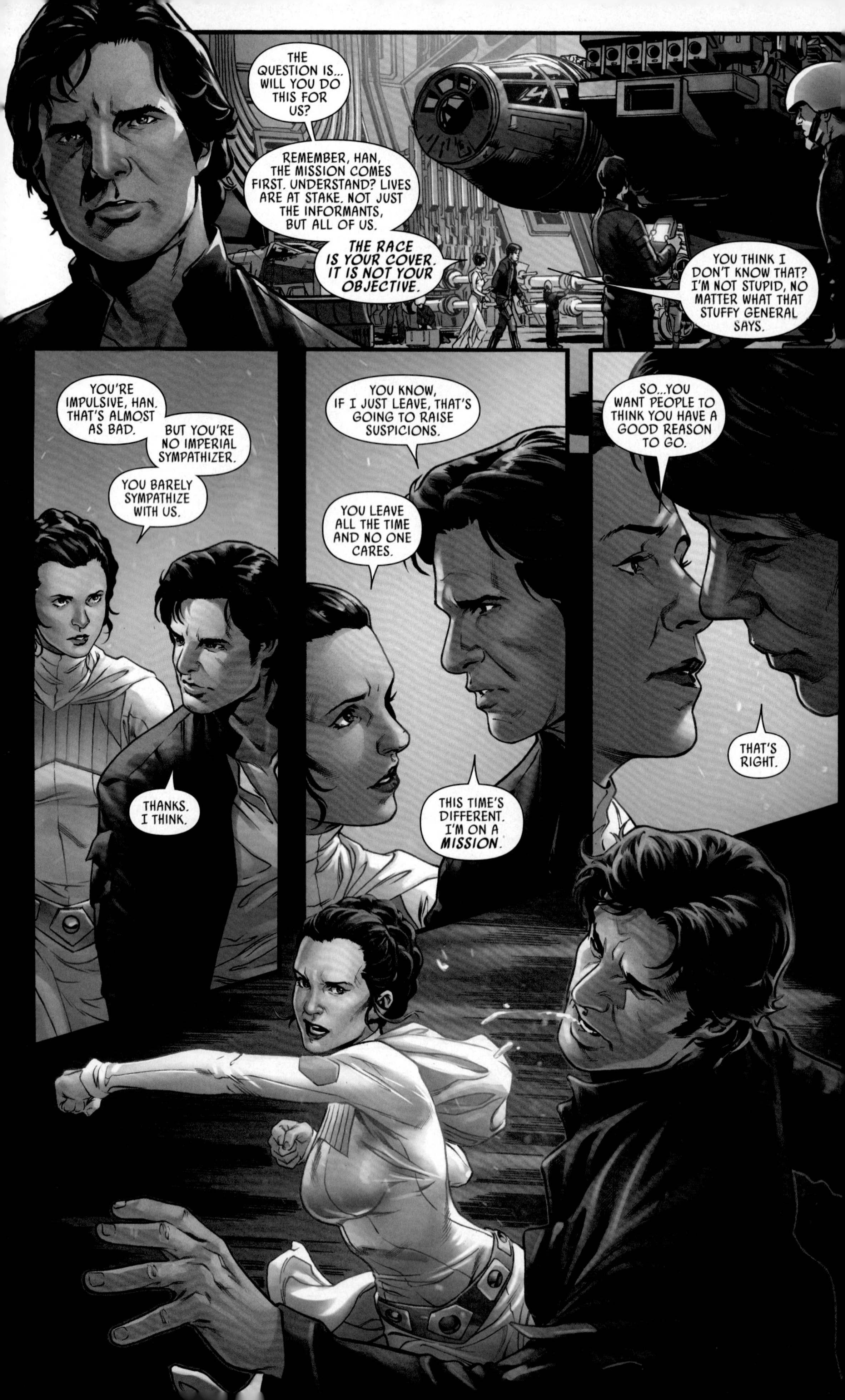

THE QUESTION IS... WILL YOU DO THIS FOR US?
REMEMBER, HAN, THE MISSION COMES FIRST. UNDERSTAND? LIVES ARE AT STAKE. NOT JUST THE INFORMANTS, BUT ALL OF US.
THE RACE IS YOUR COVER. IT IS NOT YOUR OBJECTIVE.
YOU THINK I DON'T KNOW THAT? I'M NOT STUPID, NO MATTER WHAT THAT STUFFY GENERAL SAYS.
YOU'RE IMPULSIVE, HAN. THAT'S ALMOST AS BAD.
BUT YOU'RE NO IMPERIAL SYMPATHIZER.
YOU BARELY SYMPATHIZE WITH US.
THANKS. I THINK.
YOU KNOW, IF I JUST LEAVE, THAT'S GOING TO RAISE SUSPICIONS.
YOU LEAVE ALL THE TIME AND NO ONE CARES.
THIS TIME'S DIFFERENT. I'M ON A MISSION.
SO...YOU WANT PEOPLE TO THINK YOU HAVE A GOOD REASON TO GO.
THAT'S RIGHT.

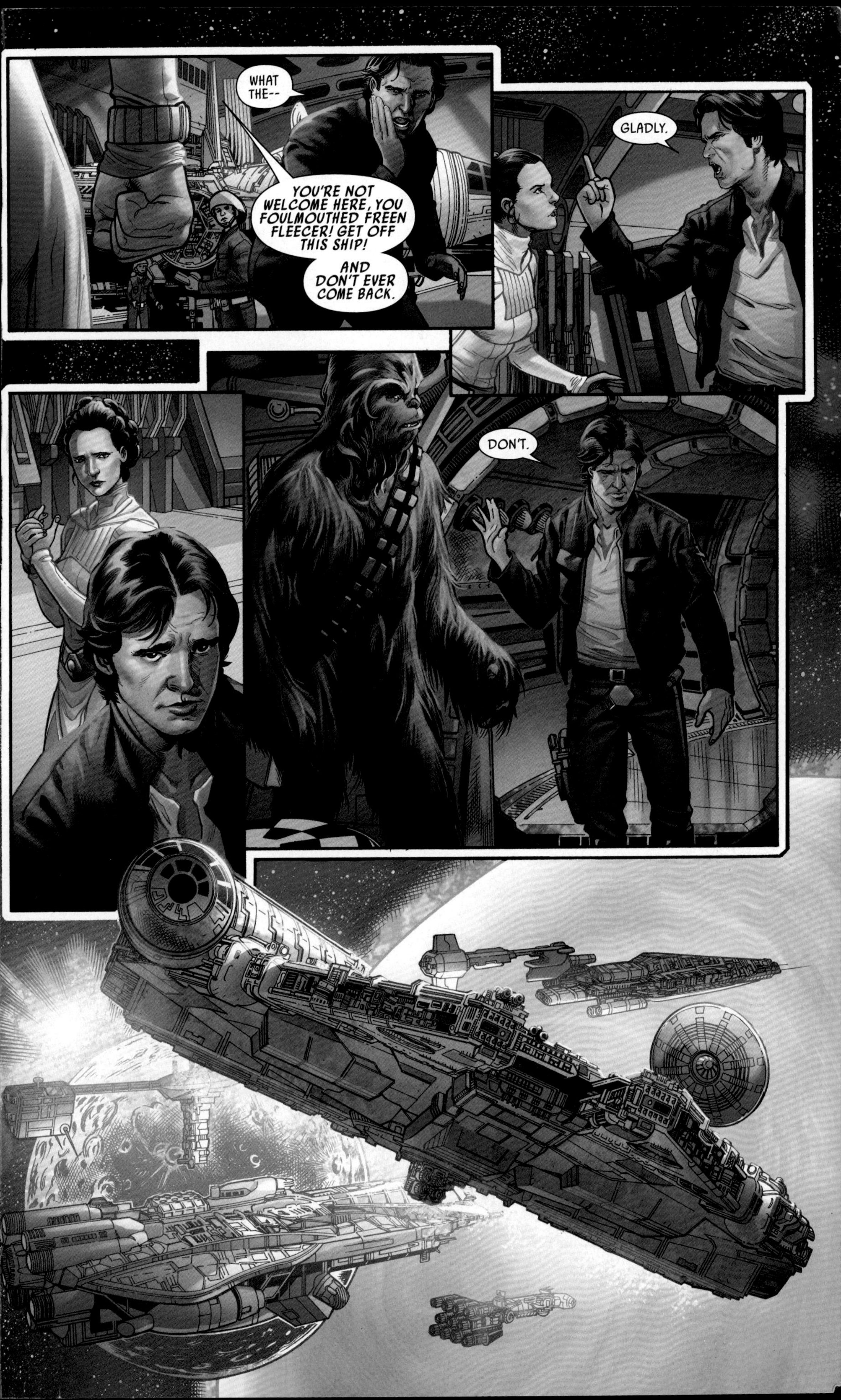
WHAT THE--
YOU'RE NOT WELCOME HERE, YOU FOULMOUTHED FREEN FLEECER! GET OFF THIS SHIP!
AND DON'T EVER COME BACK.
GLADLY.
DON'T.

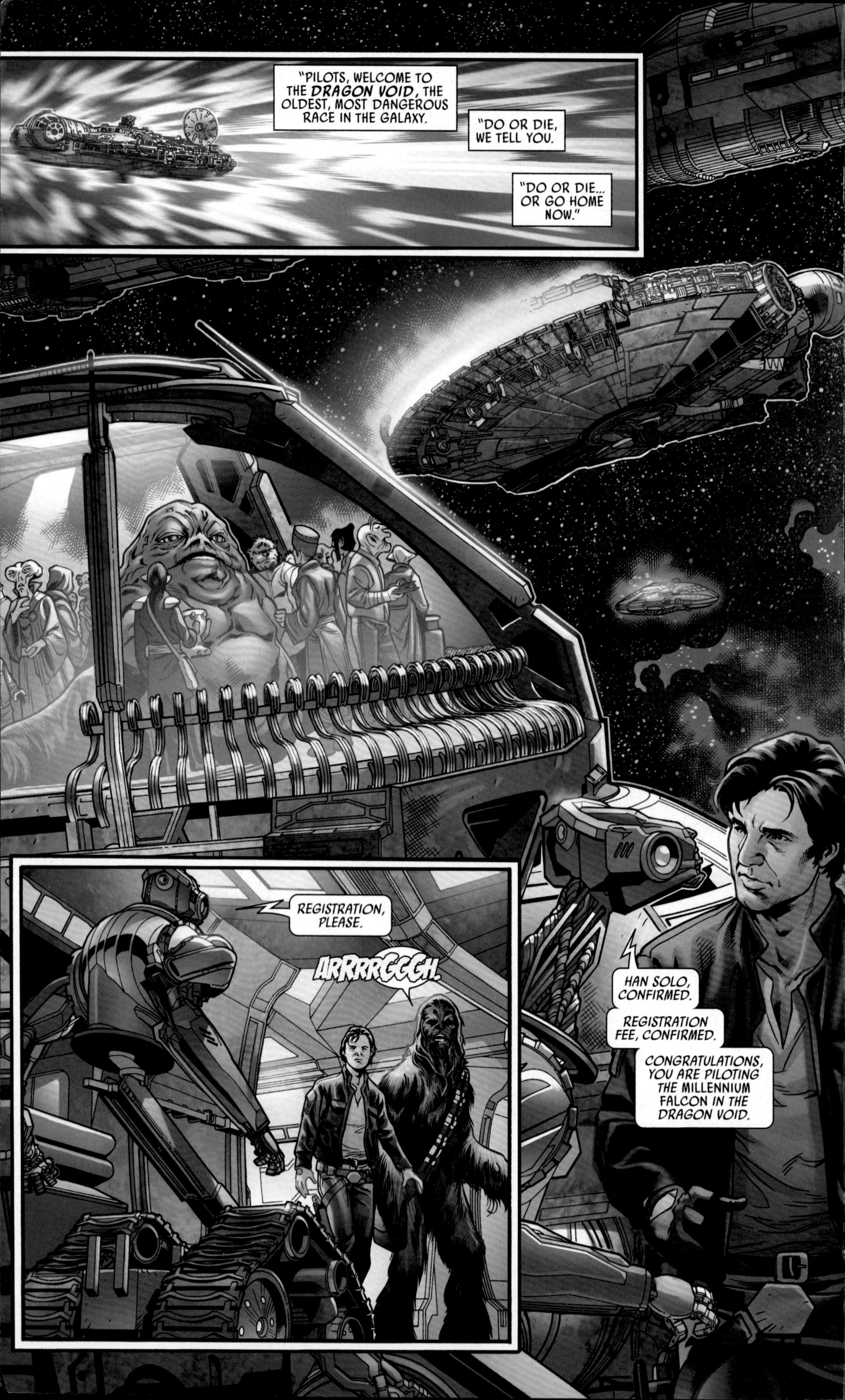
"PILOTS, WELCOME TO THE DRAGON VOID, THE OLDEST, MOST DANGEROUS RACE IN THE GALAXY.
"DO OR DIE, WE TELL YOU.
"DO OR DIE... OR GO HOME NOW."
REGISTRATION, PLEASE.
ARRRRGGGH.
HAN SOLO, CONFIRMED.
REGISTRATION FEE, CONFIRMED.
CONGRATULATIONS, YOU ARE PILOTING THE MILLENNIUM FALCON IN THE DRAGON VOID.

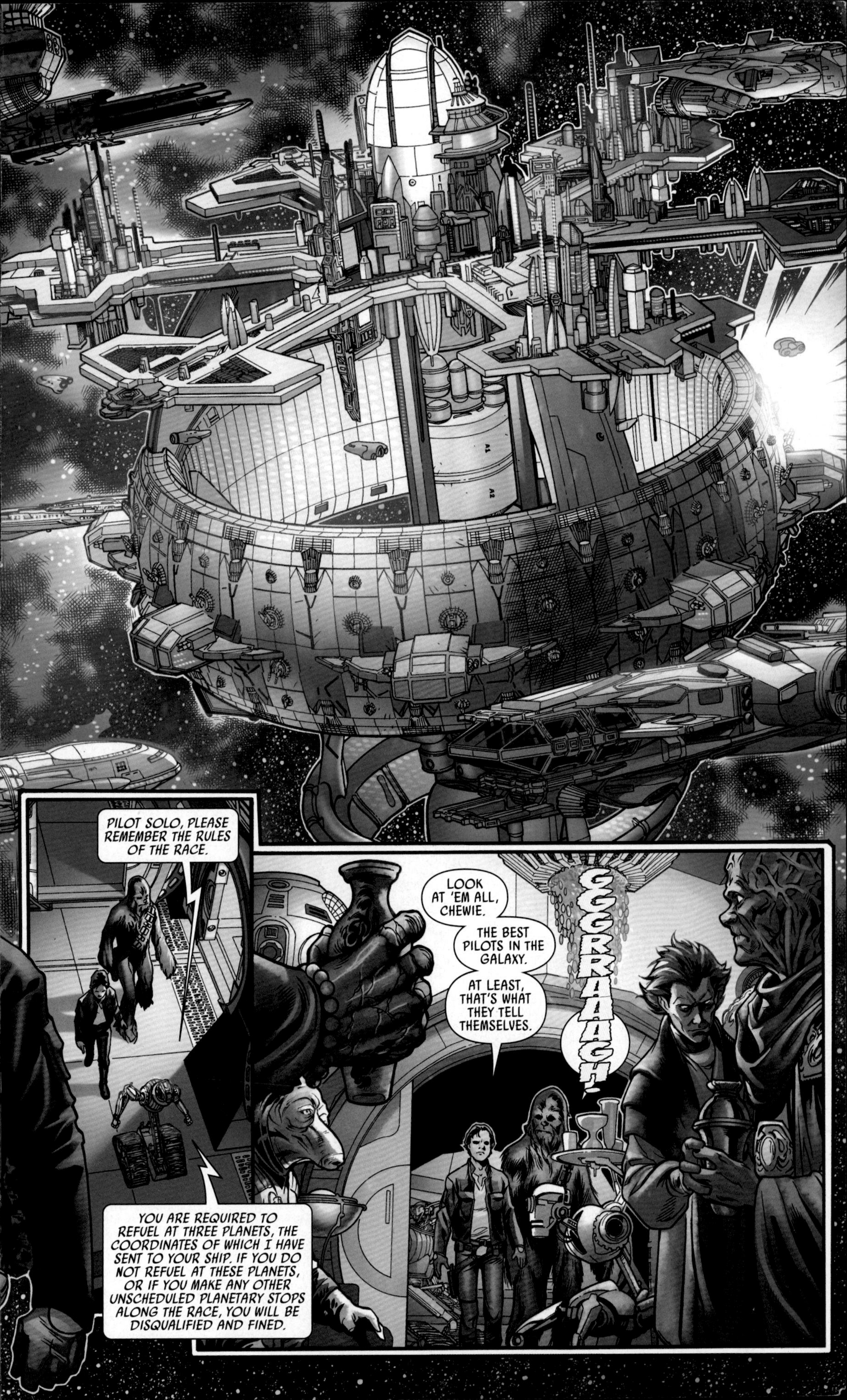

PILOT SOLO, PLEASE REMEMBER THE RULES OF THE RACE.
YOU ARE REQUIRED TO REFUEL AT THREE PLANETS, THE COORDINATES OF WHICH I HAVE SENT TO YOUR SHIP. IF YOU DO NOT REFUEL AT THESE PLANETS, OR IF YOU MAKE ANY OTHER UNSCHEDULED PLANETARY STOPS ALONG THE RACE, YOU WILL BE DISQUALIFIED AND FINED.
LOOK AT 'EM ALL, CHEWIE.
THE BEST PILOTS IN THE GALAXY.
AT LEAST, THAT'S WHAT THEY TELL THEMSELVES.
GGGRRAAAAGH!

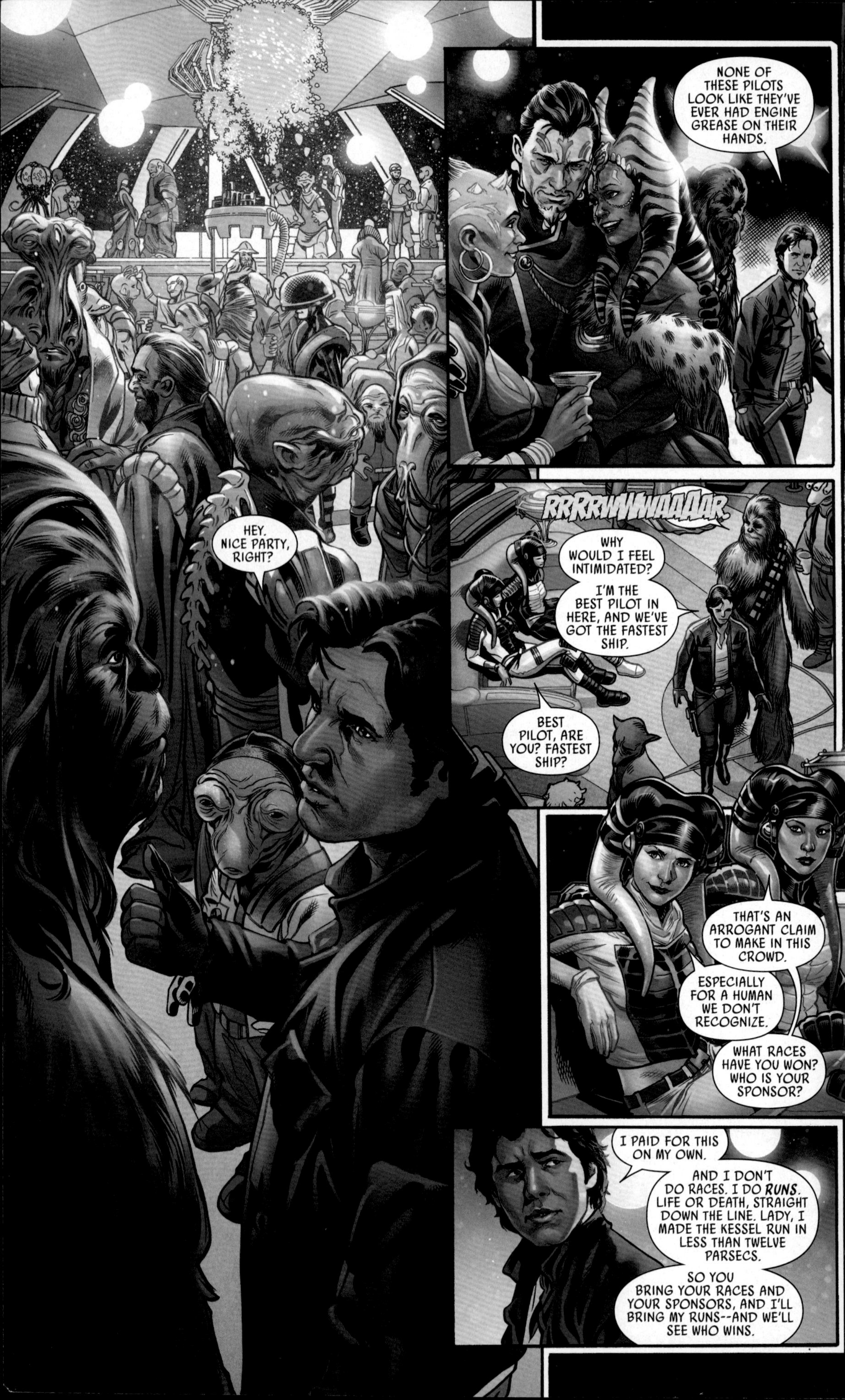
NONE OF THESE PILOTS LOOK LIKE THEY'VE EVER HAD ENGINE GREASE ON THEIR HANDS.
HEY. NICE PARTY, RIGHT?
RRRRWWWAAAAR.
WHY WOULD I FEEL INTIMIDATED?
I'M THE BEST PILOT IN HERE, AND WE'VE GOT THE FASTEST SHIP.
BEST PILOT, ARE YOU? FASTEST SHIP?
THAT'S AN ARROGANT CLAIM TO MAKE IN THIS CROWD.
ESPECIALLY FOR A HUMAN WE DON'T RECOGNIZE.
WHAT RACES HAVE YOU WON? WHO IS YOUR SPONSOR?
I PAID FOR THIS ON MY OWN.
AND I DON'T DO RACES. I DO **RUNS**. LIFE OR DEATH, STRAIGHT DOWN THE LINE. LADY, I MADE THE KESSEL RUN IN LESS THAN TWELVE PARSECS.
SO YOU BRING YOUR RACES AND YOUR SPONSORS, AND I'LL BRING MY RUNS--AND WE'LL SEE WHO WINS.

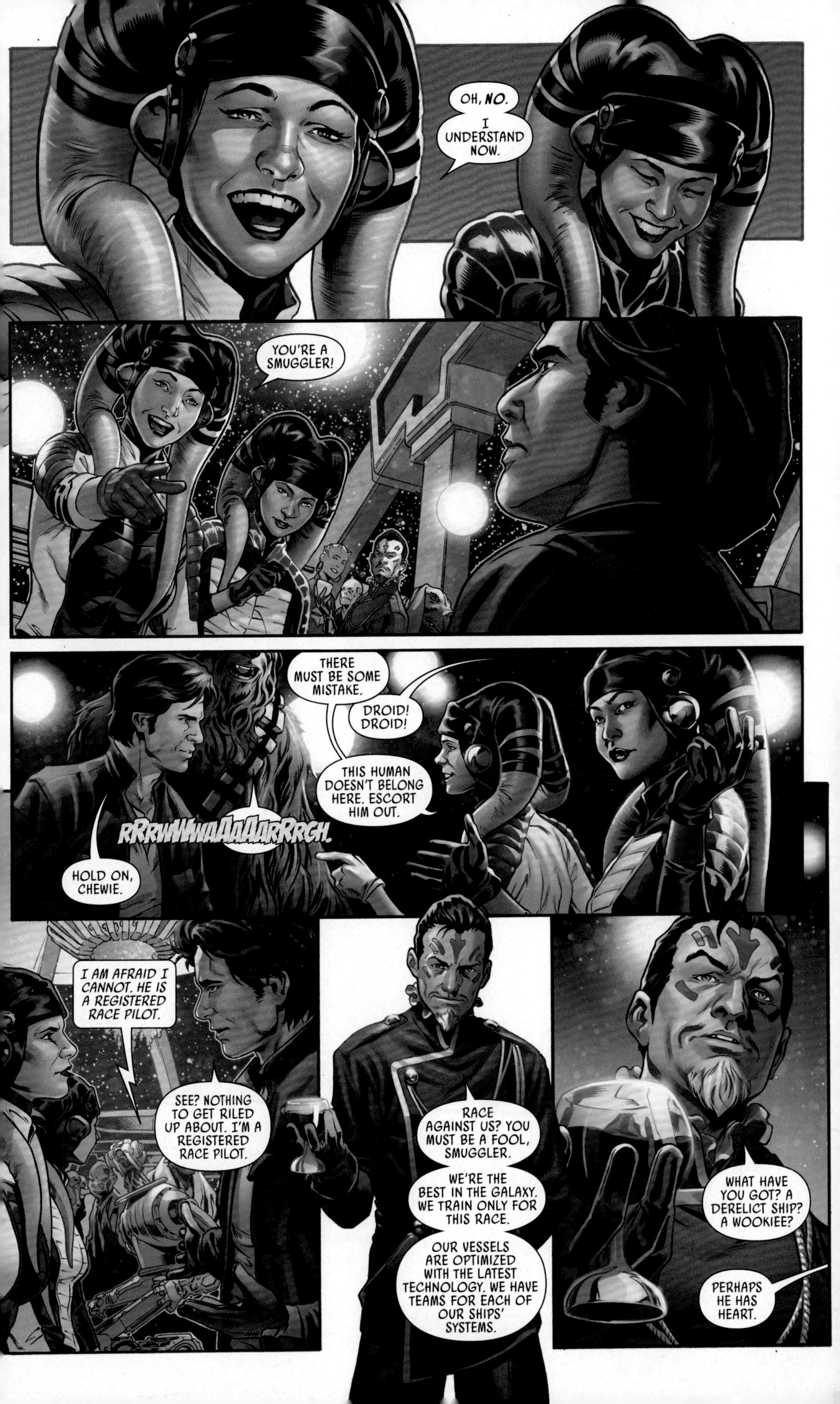
OH, NO.
I UNDERSTAND NOW.
YOU'RE A SMUGGLER!
THERE MUST BE SOME MISTAKE.
DROID! DROID!
THIS HUMAN DOESN'T BELONG HERE. ESCORT HIM OUT.
RRRWWWAAAARRRGH.
HOLD ON, CHEWIE.
I AM AFRAID I CANNOT. HE IS A REGISTERED RACE PILOT.
SEE? NOTHING TO GET RILED UP ABOUT. I'M A REGISTERED RACE PILOT.
RACE AGAINST US? YOU MUST BE A FOOL, SMUGGLER.
WE'RE THE BEST IN THE GALAXY. WE TRAIN ONLY FOR THIS RACE.
OUR VESSELS ARE OPTIMIZED WITH THE LATEST TECHNOLOGY. WE HAVE TEAMS FOR EACH OF OUR SHIPS' SYSTEMS.
WHAT HAVE YOU GOT? A DERELICT SHIP? A WOOKIEE?
PERHAPS HE HAS HEART.

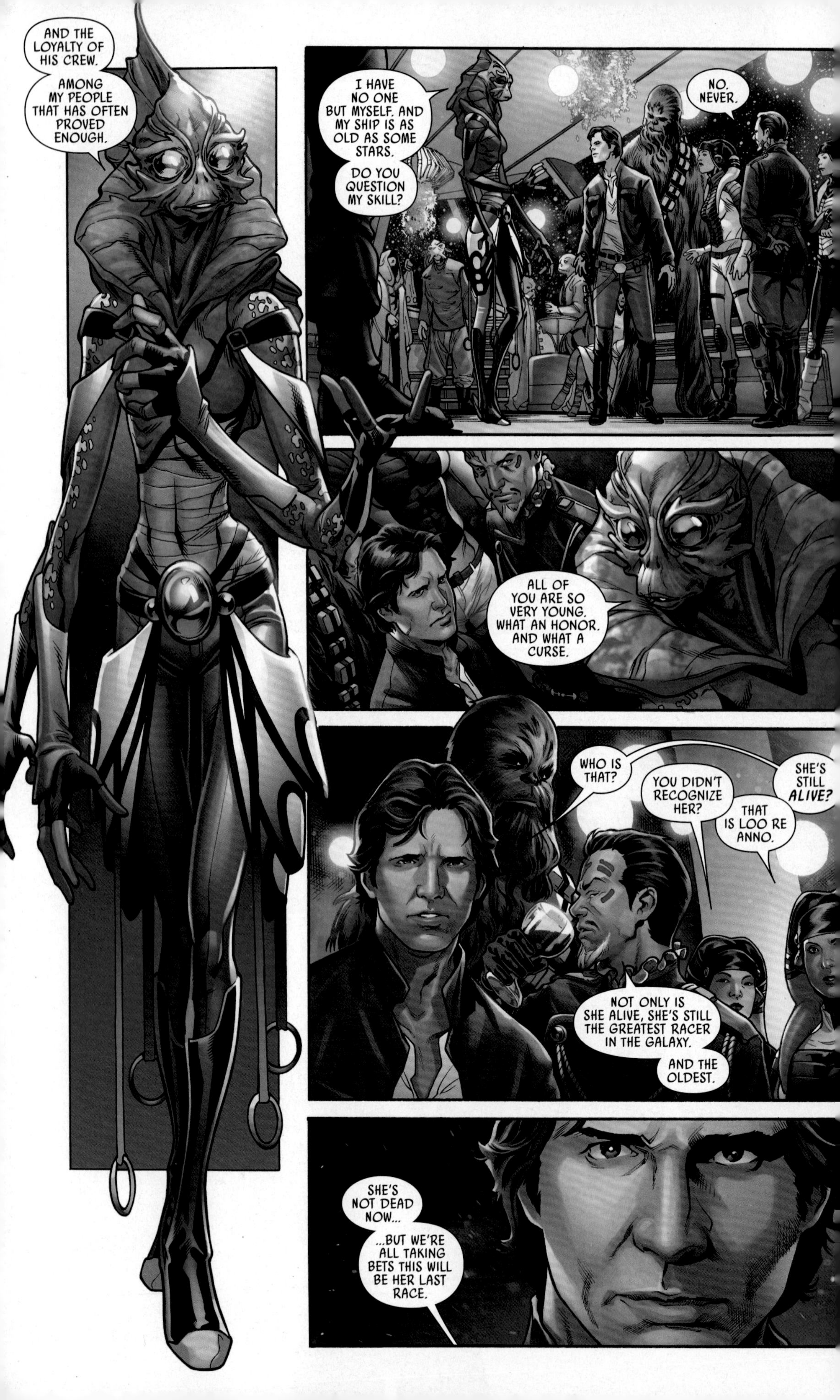
AND THE LOYALTY OF HIS CREW.
AMONG MY PEOPLE THAT HAS OFTEN PROVED ENOUGH.
I HAVE NO ONE BUT MYSELF. AND MY SHIP IS AS OLD AS SOME STARS.
DO YOU QUESTION MY SKILL?
NO. NEVER.
ALL OF YOU ARE SO VERY YOUNG. WHAT AN HONOR. AND WHAT A CURSE.
WHO IS THAT?
YOU DIDN'T RECOGNIZE HER?
THAT IS LOO RE ANNO.
SHE'S STILL ALIVE?
NOT ONLY IS SHE ALIVE, SHE'S STILL THE GREATEST RACER IN THE GALAXY.
AND THE OLDEST.
SHE'S NOT DEAD NOW...
...BUT WE'RE ALL TAKING BETS THIS WILL BE HER LAST RACE.

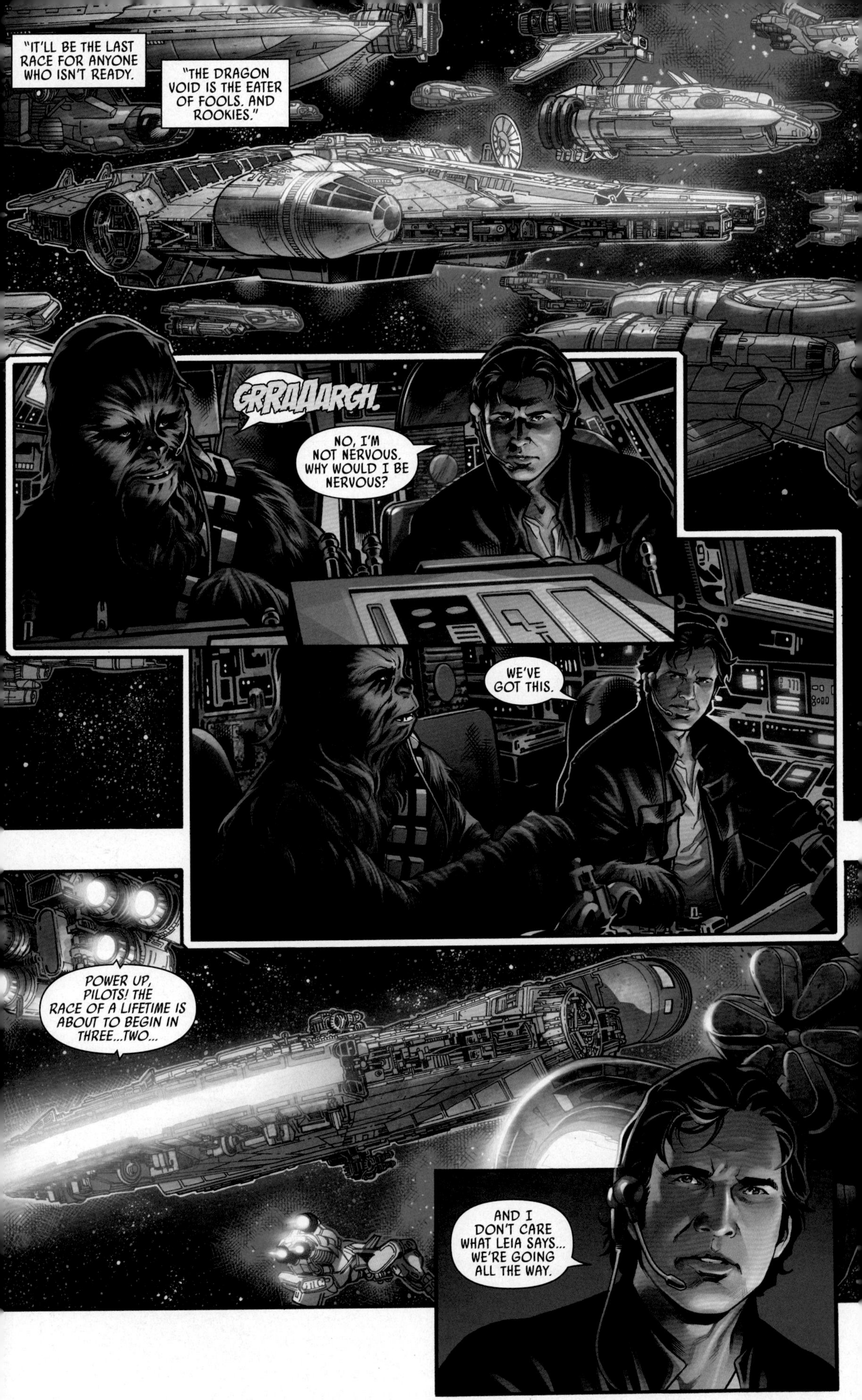
"IT'LL BE THE LAST RACE FOR ANYONE WHO ISN'T READY.
"THE DRAGON VOID IS THE EATER OF FOOLS. AND ROOKIES."
GRRAAARGH.
NO, I'M NOT NERVOUS. WHY WOULD I BE NERVOUS?
WE'VE GOT THIS.
POWER UP, PILOTS! THE RACE OF A LIFETIME IS ABOUT TO BEGIN IN THREE...TWO...
AND I DON'T CARE WHAT LEIA SAYS... WE'RE GOING ALL THE WAY.

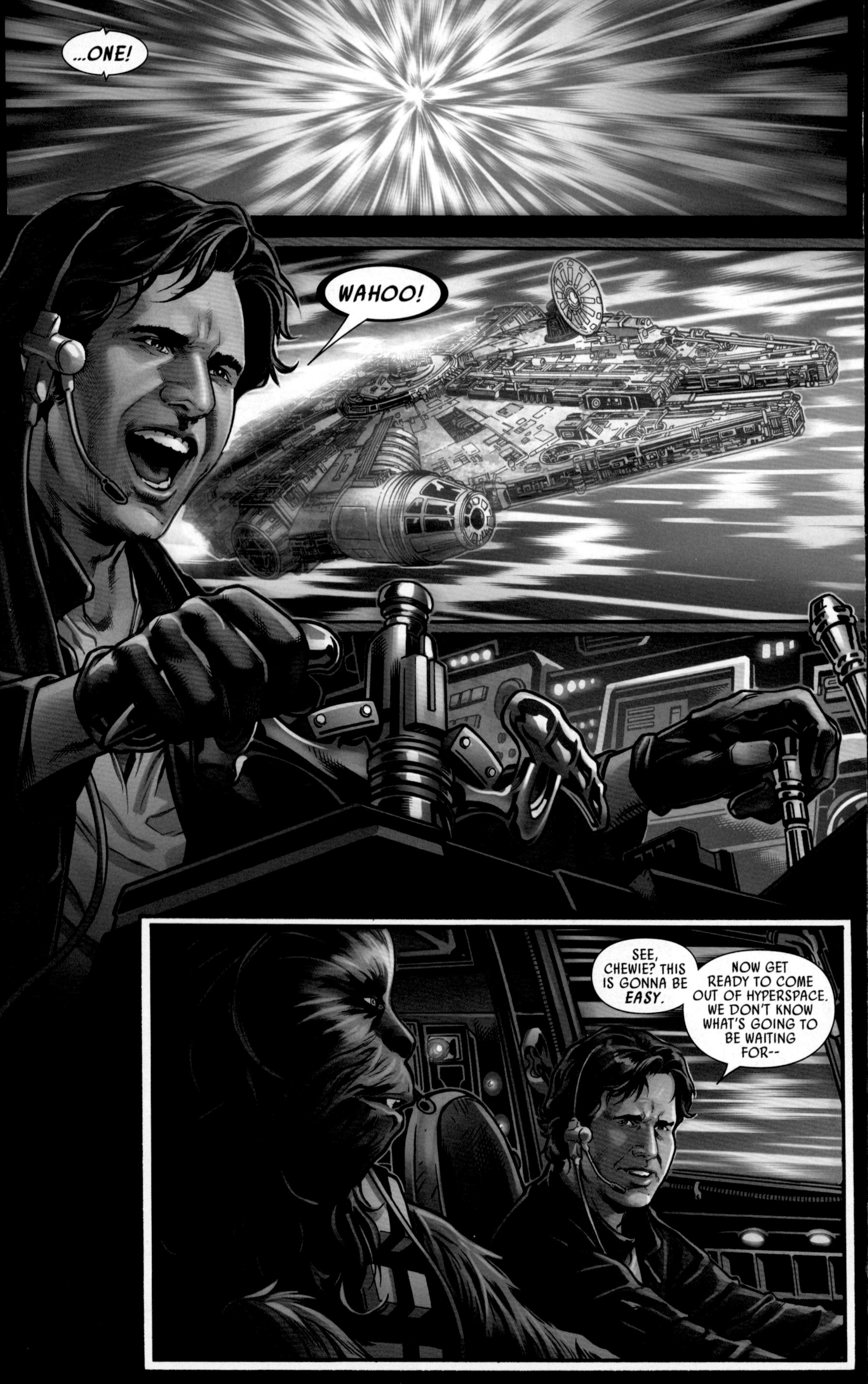
...ONE!
WAHOO!
SEE, CHEWIE? THIS IS GONNA BE *EASY*.
NOW GET READY TO COME OUT OF HYPERSPACE. WE DON'T KNOW WHAT'S GOING TO BE WAITING FOR--

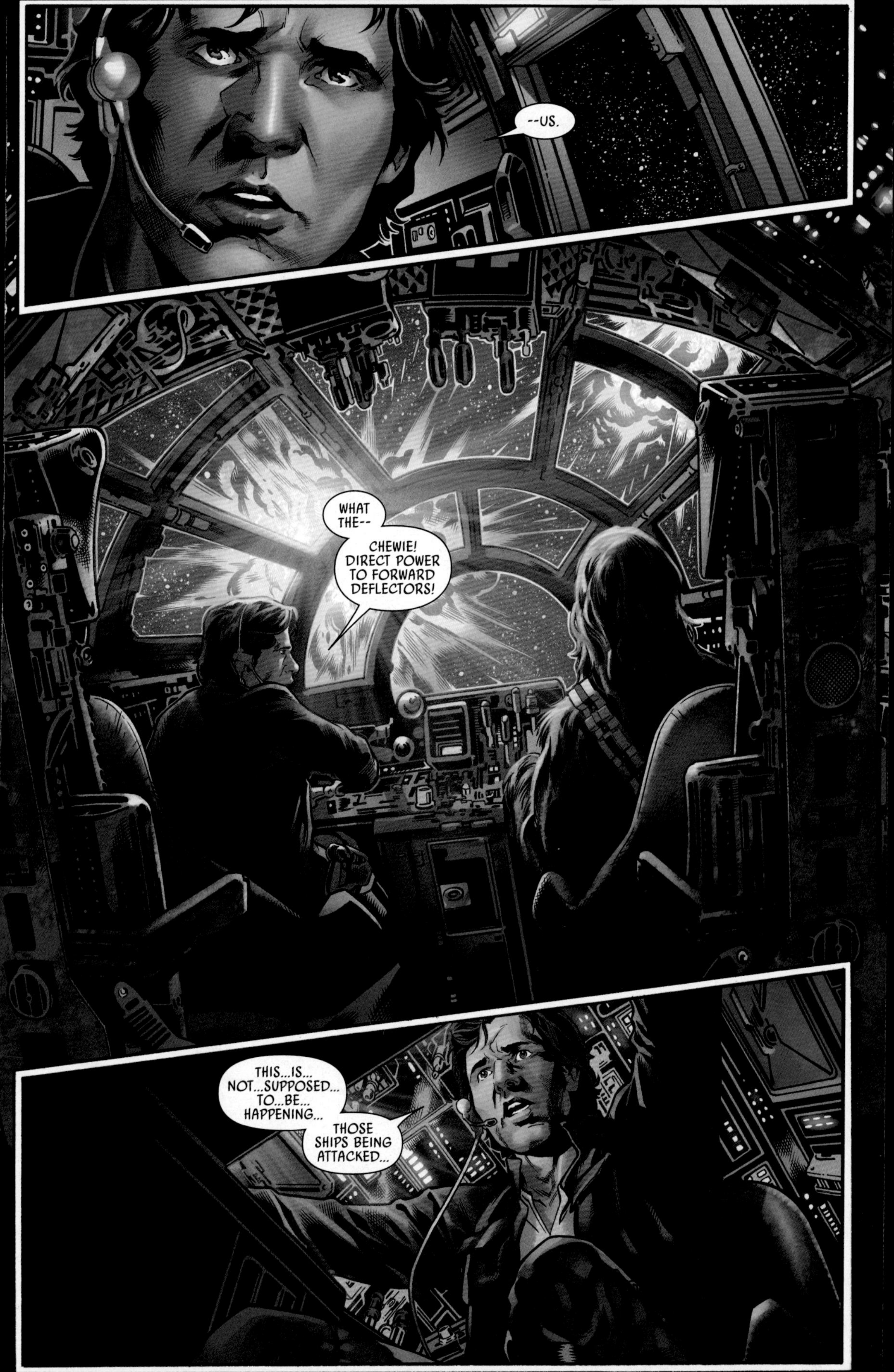
--US.
WHAT THE--
CHEWIE! DIRECT POWER TO FORWARD DEFLECTORS!
THIS...IS... NOT...SUPPOSED... TO...BE... HAPPENING...
THOSE SHIPS BEING ATTACKED...

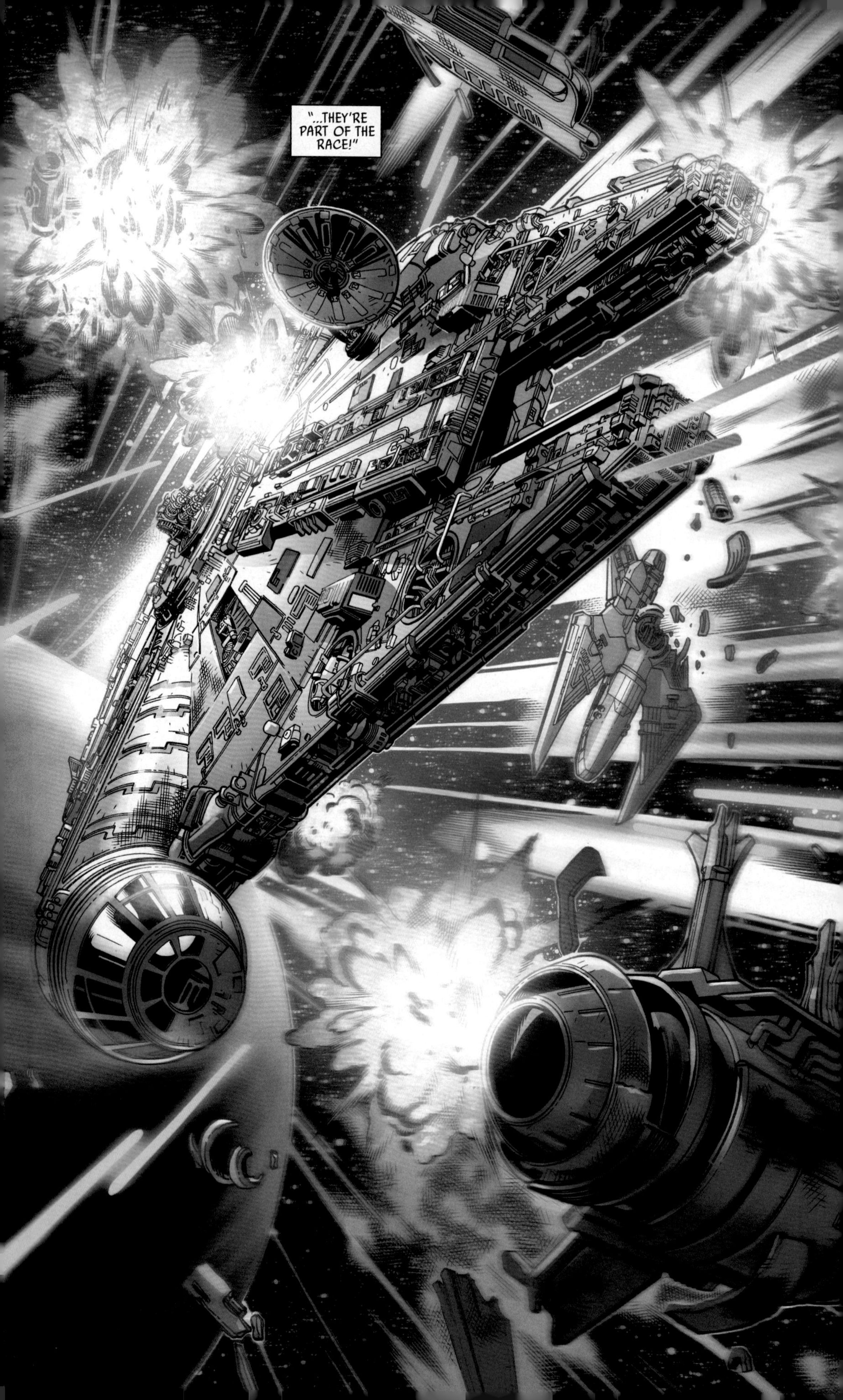
"...THEY'RE PART OF THE RACE!"

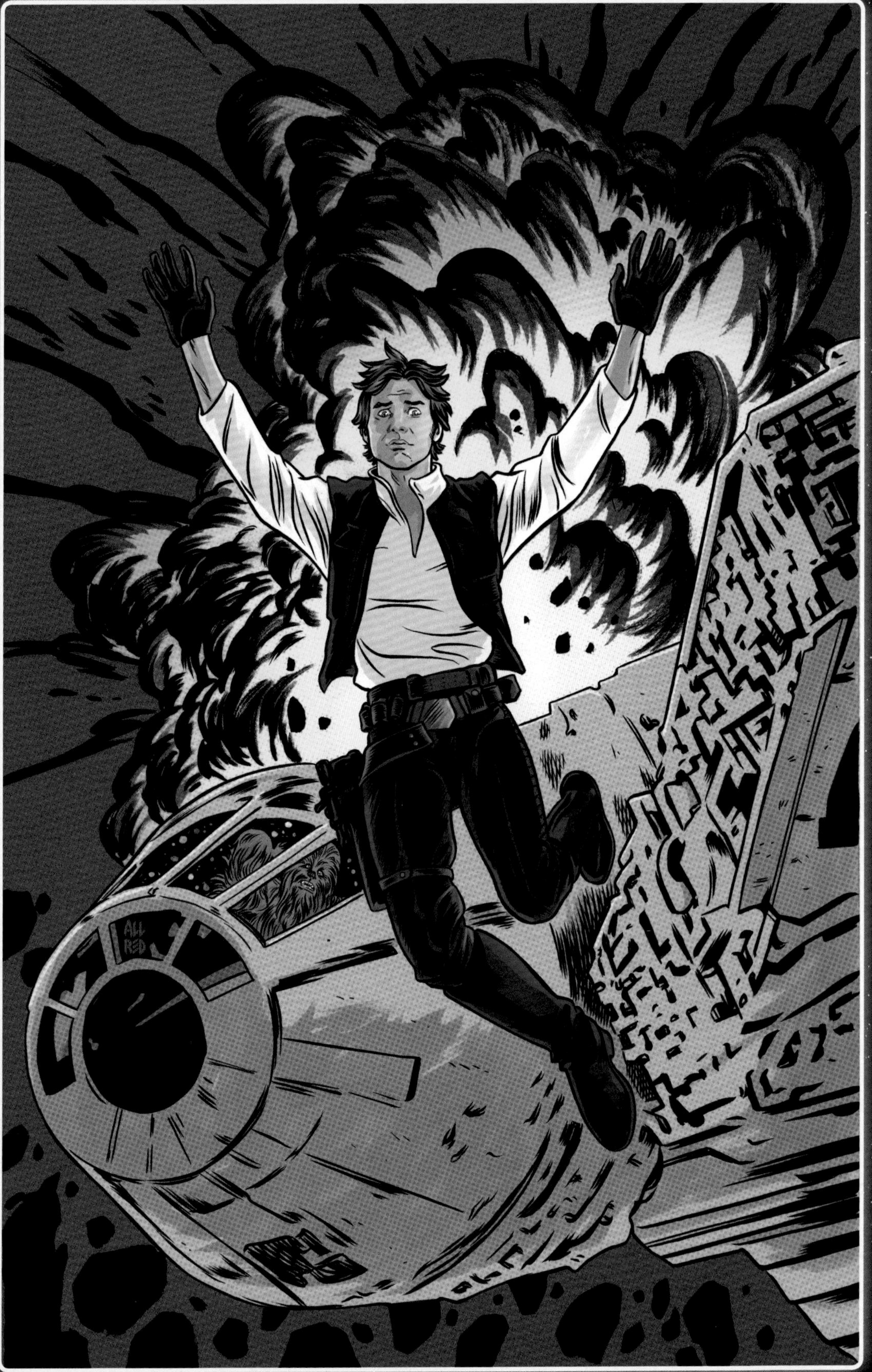
ALL RED

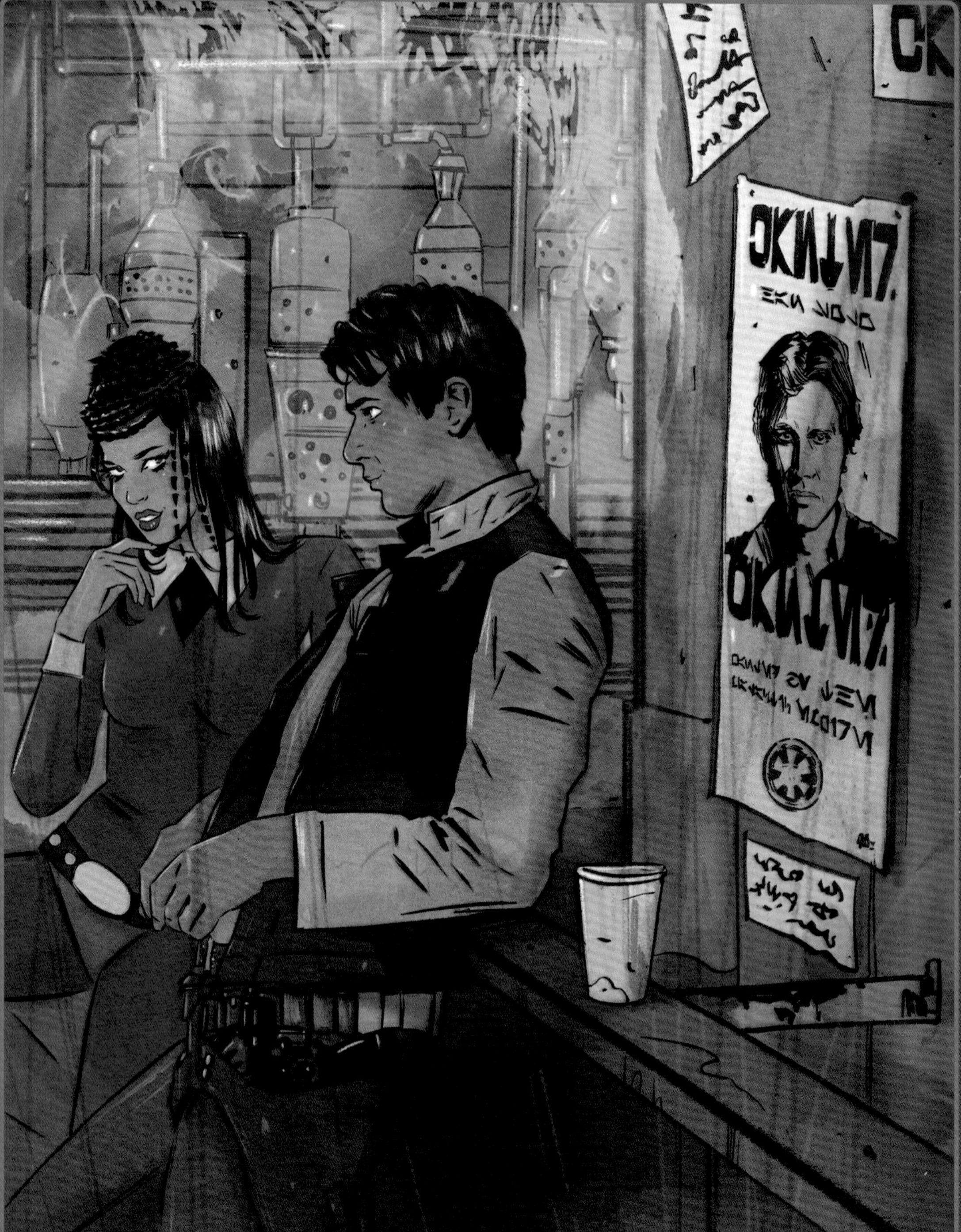

2

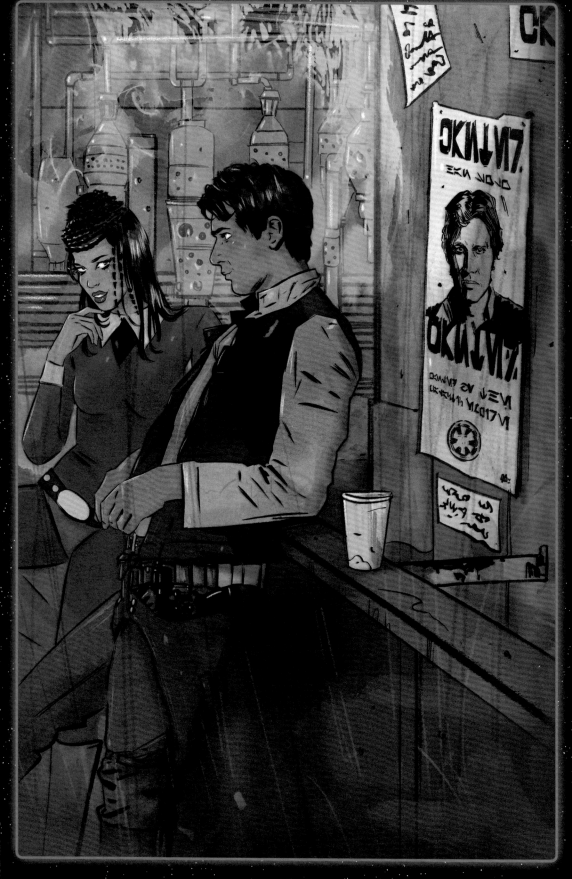

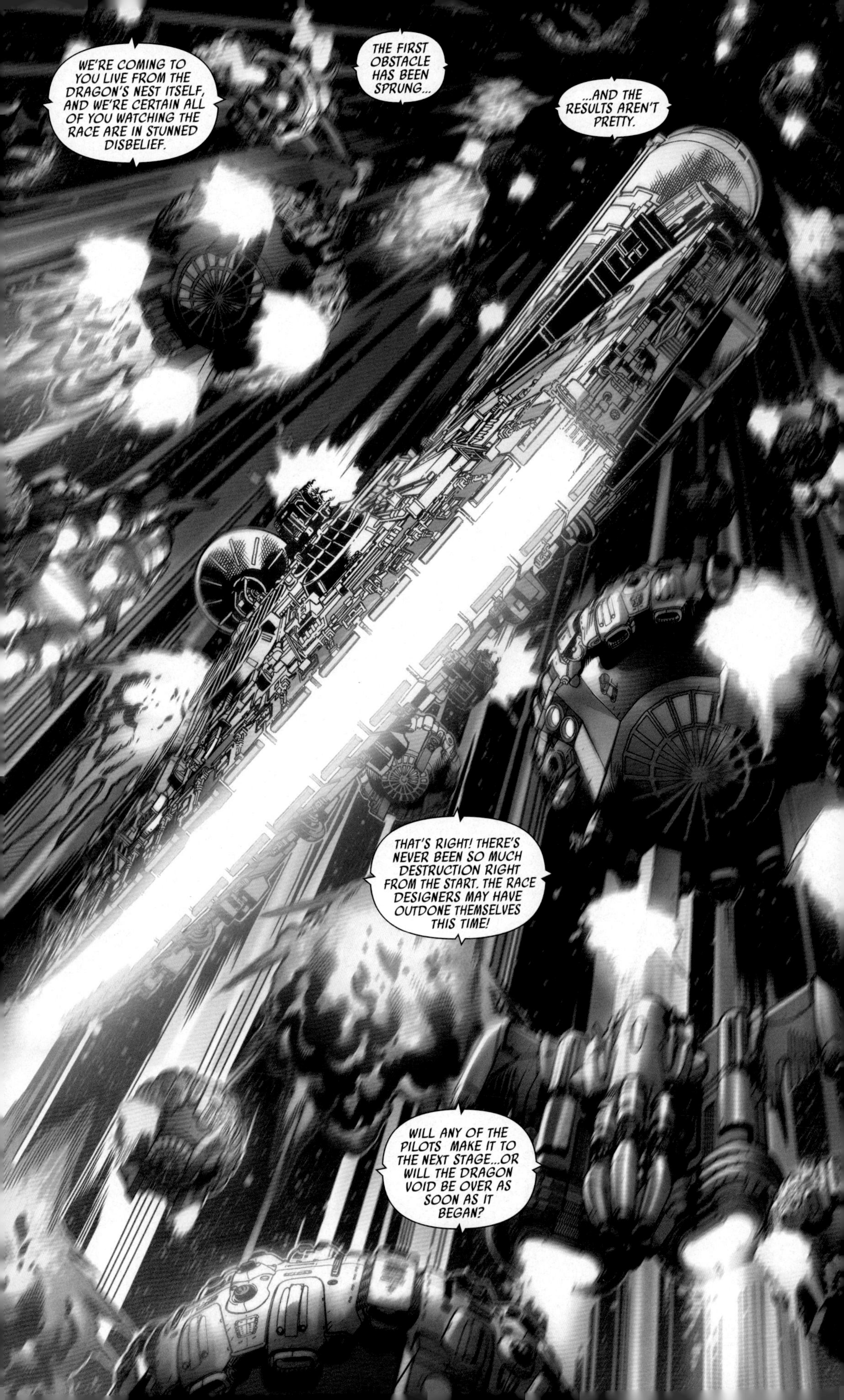
WE'RE COMING TO YOU LIVE FROM THE DRAGON'S NEST ITSELF, AND WE'RE CERTAIN ALL OF YOU WATCHING THE RACE ARE IN STUNNED DISBELIEF.
THE FIRST OBSTACLE HAS BEEN SPRUNG...
...AND THE RESULTS AREN'T PRETTY.
THAT'S RIGHT! THERE'S NEVER BEEN SO MUCH DESTRUCTION RIGHT FROM THE START. THE RACE DESIGNERS MAY HAVE OUTDONE THEMSELVES THIS TIME!
WILL ANY OF THE PILOTS MAKE IT TO THE NEXT STAGE...OR WILL THE DRAGON VOID BE OVER AS SOON AS IT BEGAN?

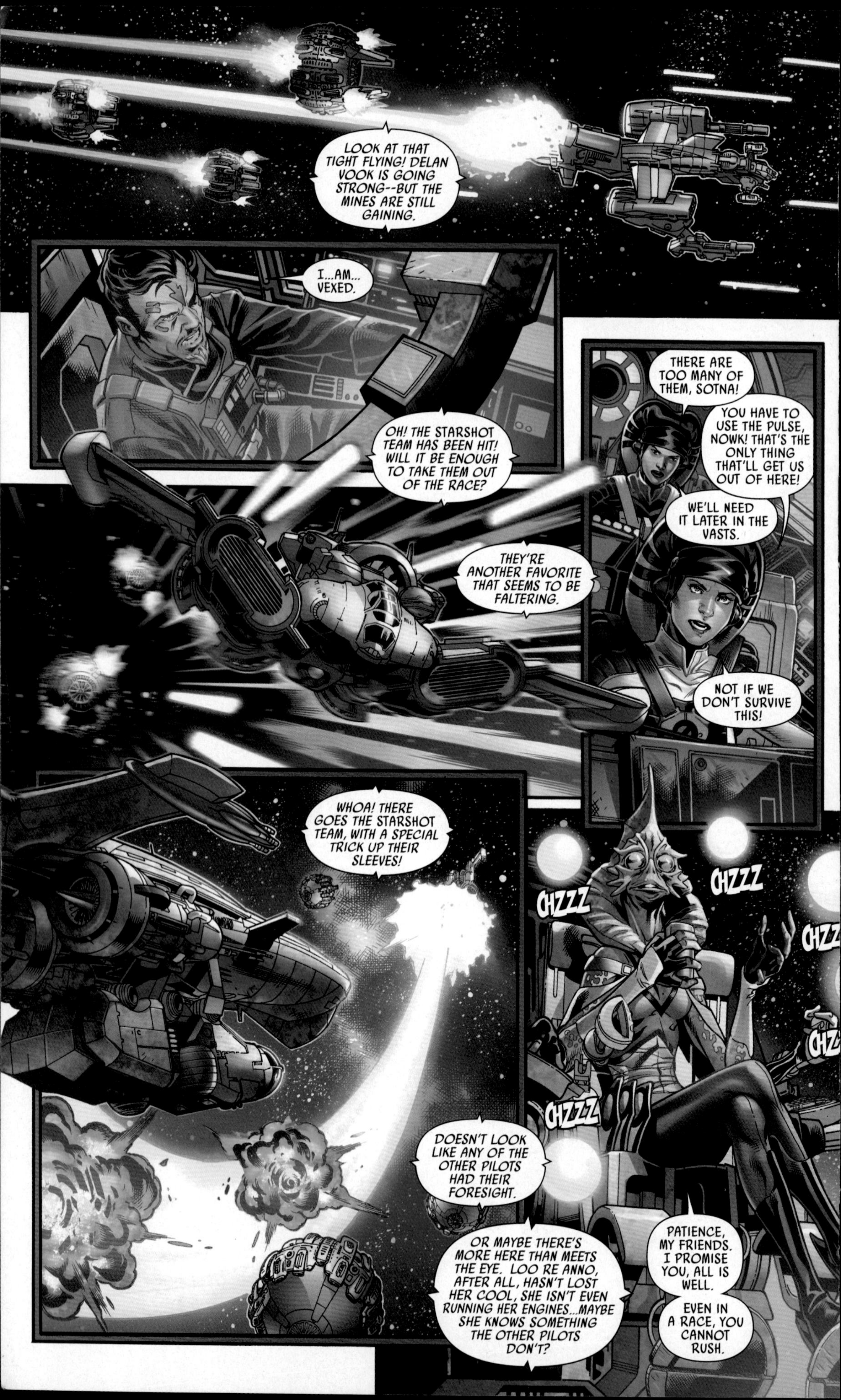
LOOK AT THAT TIGHT FLYING! DELAN VOOK IS GOING STRONG--BUT THE MINES ARE STILL GAINING.
I...AM... VEXED.
OH! THE STARSHOT TEAM HAS BEEN HIT! WILL IT BE ENOUGH TO TAKE THEM OUT OF THE RACE?
THEY'RE ANOTHER FAVORITE THAT SEEMS TO BE FALTERING.
THERE ARE TOO MANY OF THEM, SOTNA!
YOU HAVE TO USE THE PULSE, NOWK! THAT'S THE ONLY THING THAT'LL GET US OUT OF HERE!
WE'LL NEED IT LATER IN THE VASTS.
NOT IF WE DON'T SURVIVE THIS!
WHOA! THERE GOES THE STARSHOT TEAM, WITH A SPECIAL TRICK UP THEIR SLEEVES!
CHZZZ
CHZZZ
CHZZ
CHZZZ
DOESN'T LOOK LIKE ANY OF THE OTHER PILOTS HAD THEIR FORESIGHT.
OR MAYBE THERE'S MORE HERE THAN MEETS THE EYE. LOO RE ANNO, AFTER ALL, HASN'T LOST HER COOL, SHE ISN'T EVEN RUNNING HER ENGINES...MAYBE SHE KNOWS SOMETHING THE OTHER PILOTS DON'T?
PATIENCE, MY FRIENDS. I PROMISE YOU, ALL IS WELL.
EVEN IN A RACE, YOU CANNOT RUSH.

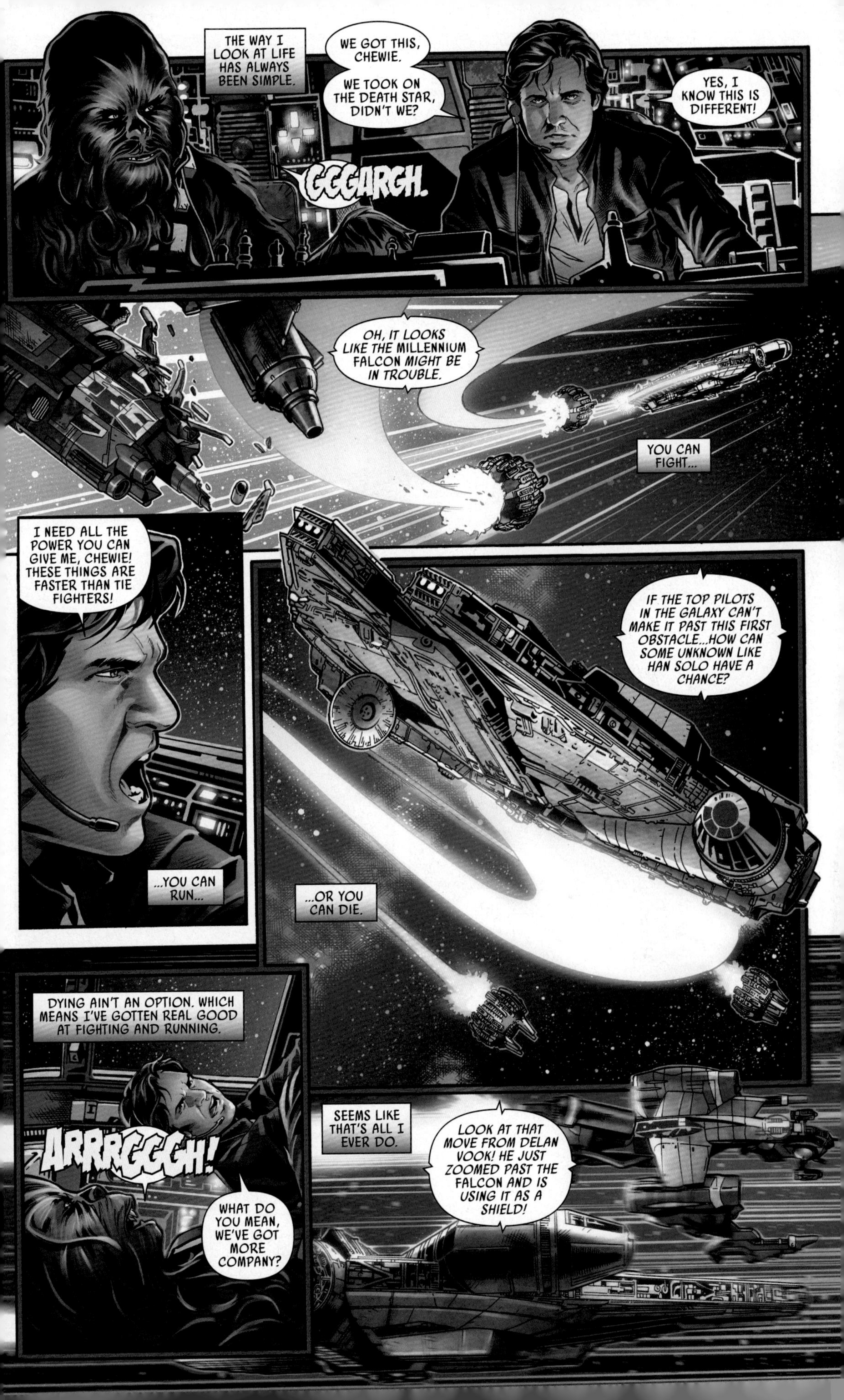
THE WAY I LOOK AT LIFE HAS ALWAYS BEEN SIMPLE.
WE GOT THIS, CHEWIE.
WE TOOK ON THE DEATH STAR, DIDN'T WE?
GGGARGH.
YES, I KNOW THIS IS DIFFERENT!
OH, IT LOOKS LIKE THE MILLENNIUM FALCON MIGHT BE IN TROUBLE.
YOU CAN FIGHT...
I NEED ALL THE POWER YOU CAN GIVE ME, CHEWIE! THESE THINGS ARE FASTER THAN TIE FIGHTERS!
...YOU CAN RUN...
IF THE TOP PILOTS IN THE GALAXY CAN'T MAKE IT PAST THIS FIRST OBSTACLE...HOW CAN SOME UNKNOWN LIKE HAN SOLO HAVE A CHANCE?
...OR YOU CAN DIE.
DYING AIN'T AN OPTION. WHICH MEANS I'VE GOTTEN REAL GOOD AT FIGHTING AND RUNNING.
ARRRGGGH!
WHAT DO YOU MEAN, WE'VE GOT MORE COMPANY?
SEEMS LIKE THAT'S ALL I EVER DO.
LOOK AT THAT MOVE FROM DELAN VOOK! HE JUST ZOOMED PAST THE FALCON AND IS USING IT AS A SHIELD!

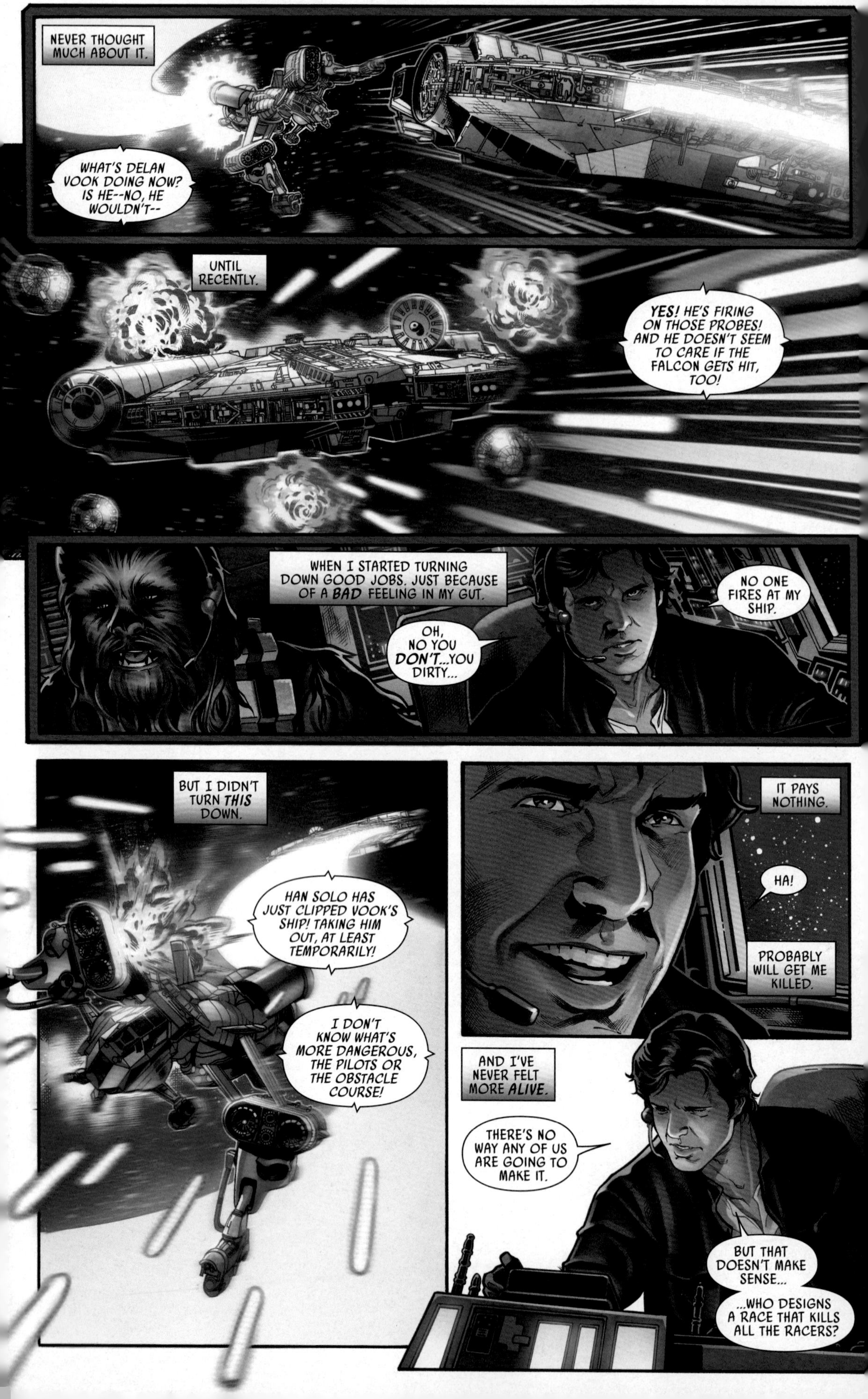
NEVER THOUGHT MUCH ABOUT IT.
WHAT'S DELAN VOOK DOING NOW? IS HE--NO, HE WOULDN'T--
UNTIL RECENTLY.
YES! HE'S FIRING ON THOSE PROBES! AND HE DOESN'T SEEM TO CARE IF THE FALCON GETS HIT, TOO!
WHEN I STARTED TURNING DOWN GOOD JOBS. JUST BECAUSE OF A BAD FEELING IN MY GUT.
OH, NO YOU DON'T...YOU DIRTY...
NO ONE FIRES AT MY SHIP.
BUT I DIDN'T TURN THIS DOWN.
HAN SOLO HAS JUST CLIPPED VOOK'S SHIP! TAKING HIM OUT, AT LEAST TEMPORARILY!
I DON'T KNOW WHAT'S MORE DANGEROUS, THE PILOTS OR THE OBSTACLE COURSE!
IT PAYS NOTHING.
HA!
PROBABLY WILL GET ME KILLED.
AND I'VE NEVER FELT MORE ALIVE.
THERE'S NO WAY ANY OF US ARE GOING TO MAKE IT.
BUT THAT DOESN'T MAKE SENSE...
...WHO DESIGNS A RACE THAT KILLS ALL THE RACERS?

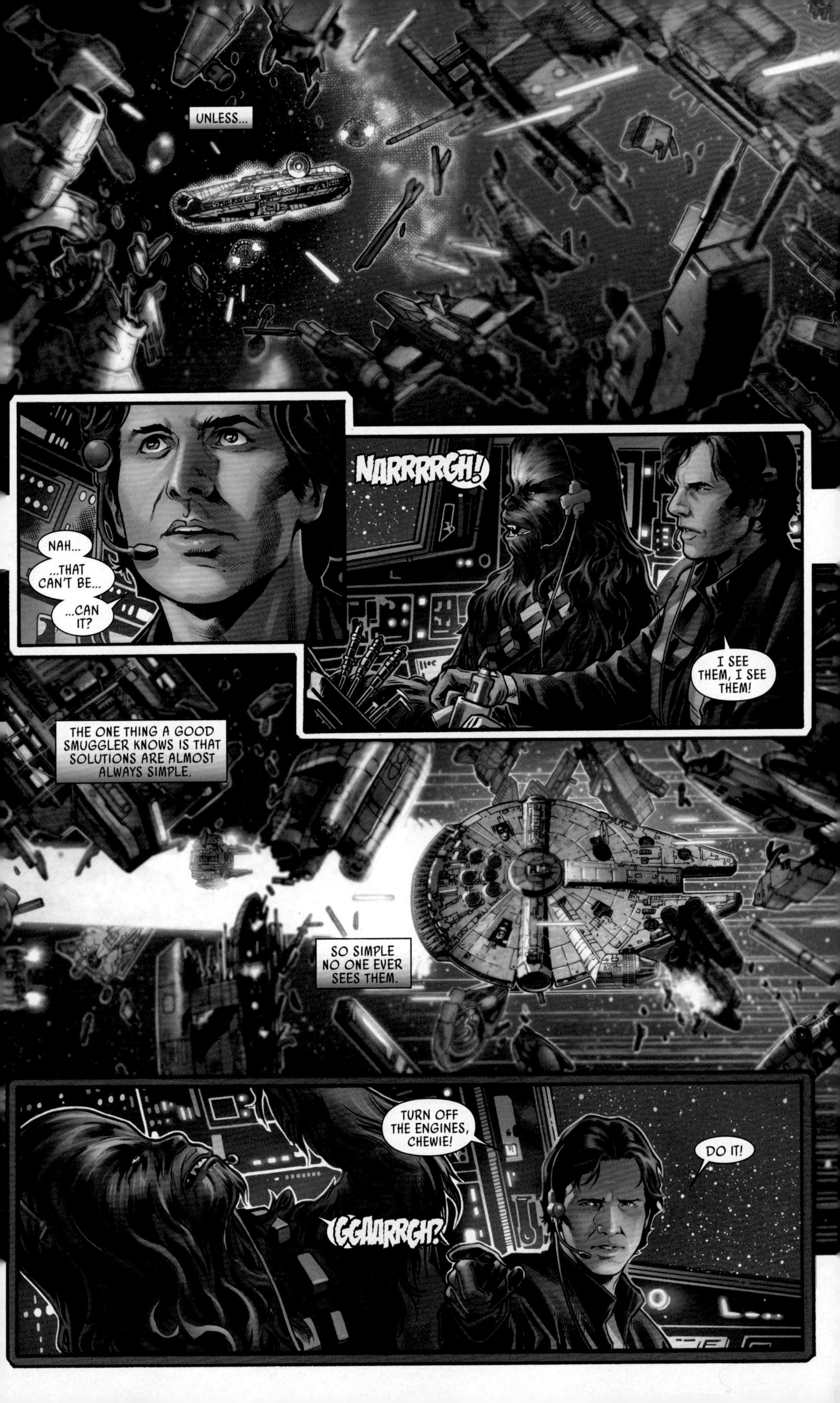
UNLESS...
NAH...
...THAT CAN'T BE...
...CAN IT?
NARRRRGH!
I SEE THEM, I SEE THEM!
THE ONE THING A GOOD SMUGGLER KNOWS IS THAT SOLUTIONS ARE ALMOST ALWAYS SIMPLE.
SO SIMPLE NO ONE EVER SEES THEM.
TURN OFF THE ENGINES, CHEWIE!
DO IT!
RGGAARRGH?!

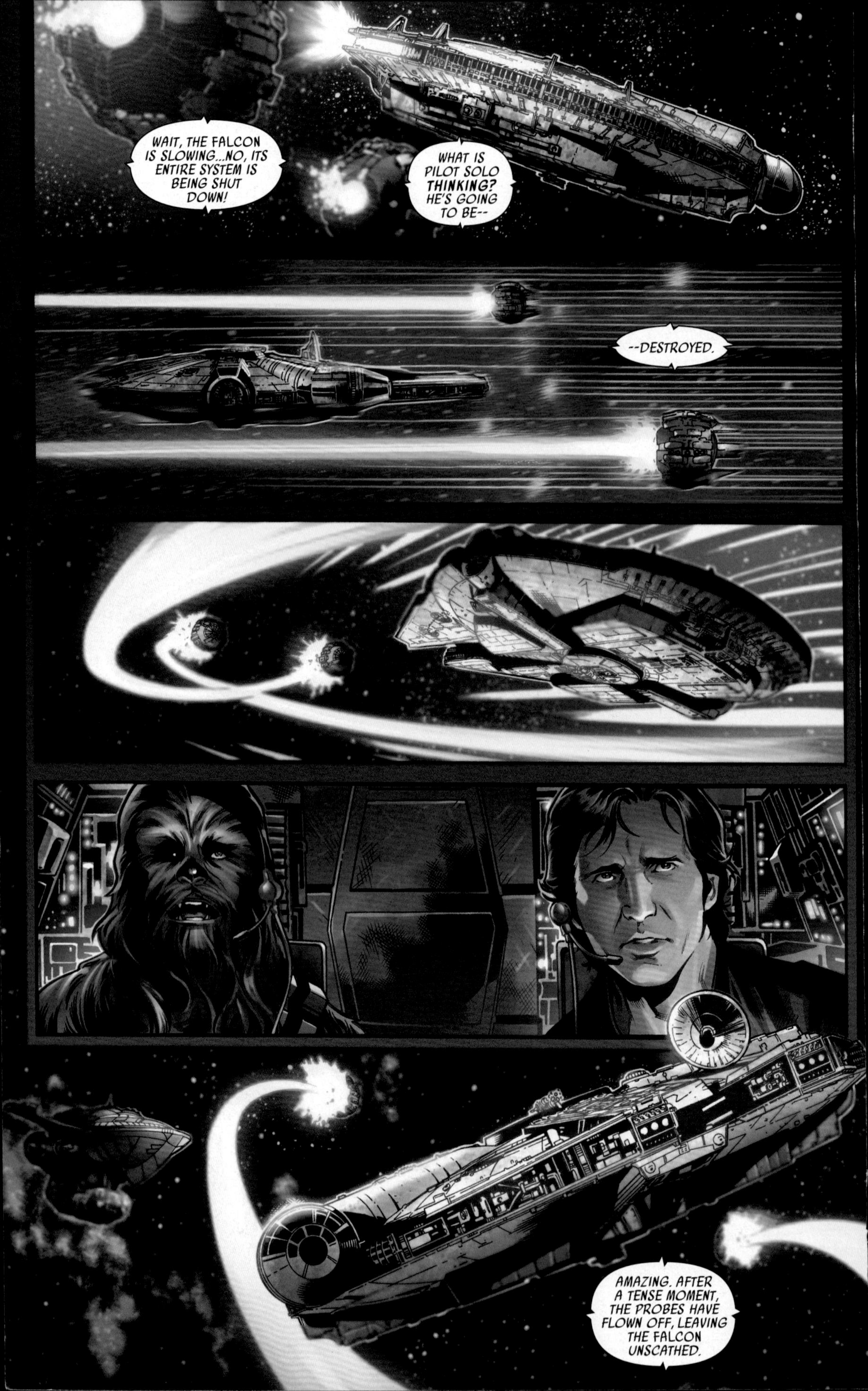
WAIT, THE FALCON IS SLOWING...NO, ITS ENTIRE SYSTEM IS BEING SHUT DOWN!
WHAT IS PILOT SOLO THINKING? HE'S GOING TO BE--
--DESTROYED.
AMAZING. AFTER A TENSE MOMENT, THE PROBES HAVE FLOWN OFF, LEAVING THE FALCON UNSCATHED.

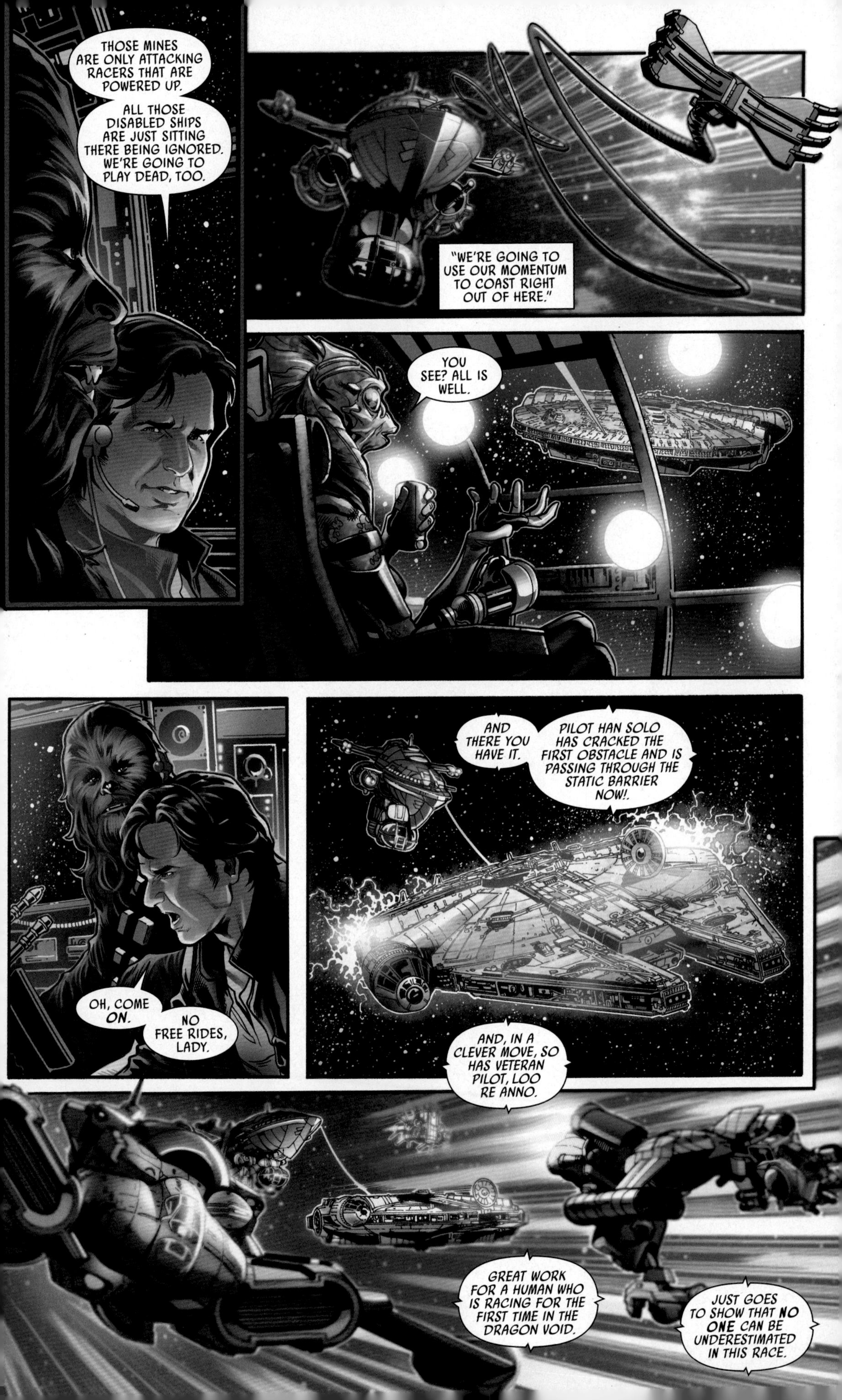
THOSE MINES ARE ONLY ATTACKING RACERS THAT ARE POWERED UP.
ALL THOSE DISABLED SHIPS ARE JUST SITTING THERE BEING IGNORED. WE'RE GOING TO PLAY DEAD, TOO.
"WE'RE GOING TO USE OUR MOMENTUM TO COAST RIGHT OUT OF HERE."
YOU SEE? ALL IS WELL.
OH, COME ON.
NO FREE RIDES, LADY.
AND THERE YOU HAVE IT.
PILOT HAN SOLO HAS CRACKED THE FIRST OBSTACLE AND IS PASSING THROUGH THE STATIC BARRIER NOW!.
AND, IN A CLEVER MOVE, SO HAS VETERAN PILOT, LOO RE ANNO.
GREAT WORK FOR A HUMAN WHO IS RACING FOR THE FIRST TIME IN THE DRAGON VOID.
JUST GOES TO SHOW THAT NO ONE CAN BE UNDERESTIMATED IN THIS RACE.

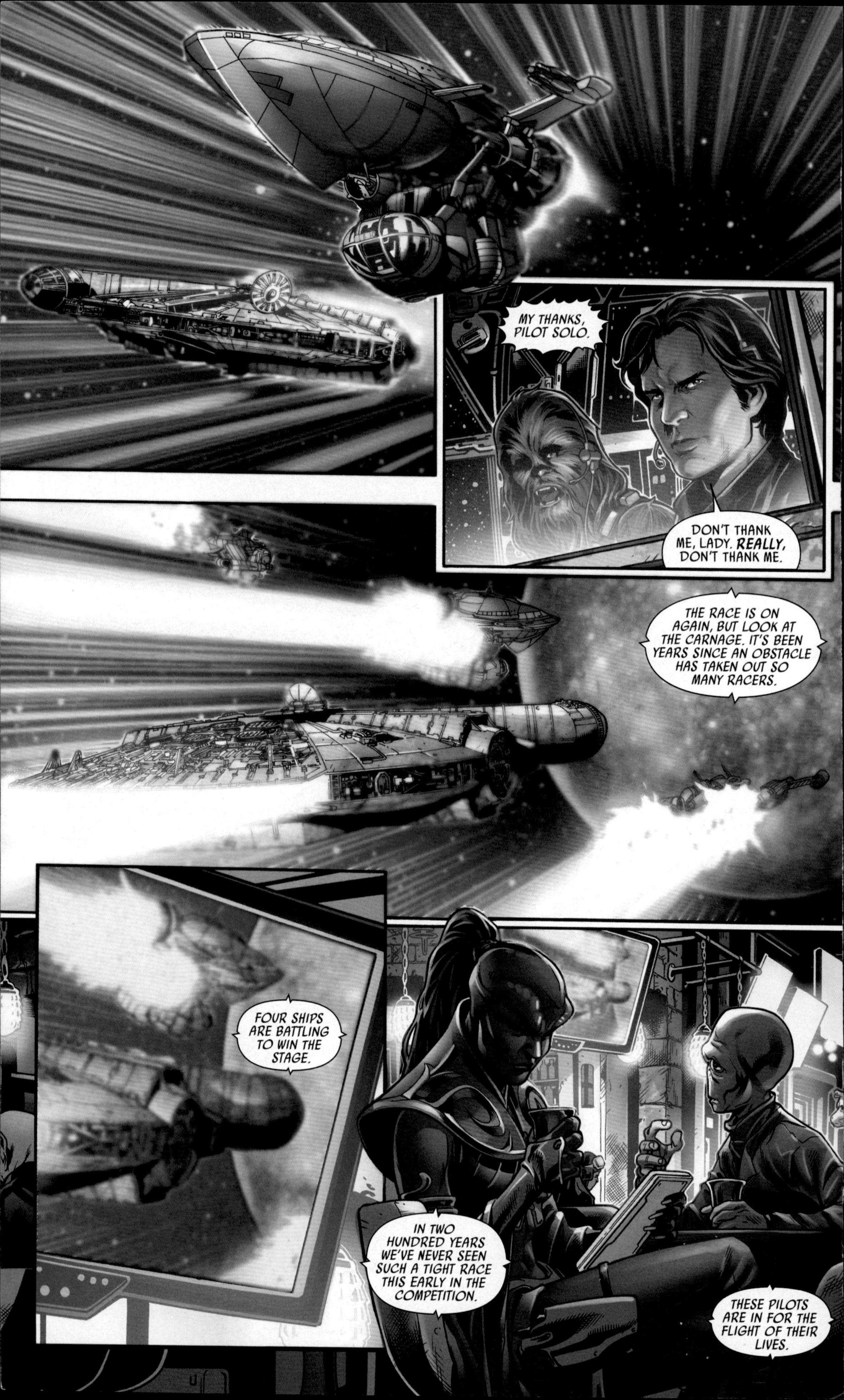
MY THANKS, PILOT SOLO.
DON'T THANK ME, LADY. **REALLY,** DON'T THANK ME.
THE RACE IS ON AGAIN, BUT LOOK AT THE CARNAGE. IT'S BEEN YEARS SINCE AN OBSTACLE HAS TAKEN OUT SO MANY RACERS.
FOUR SHIPS ARE BATTLING TO WIN THE STAGE.
IN TWO HUNDRED YEARS WE'VE NEVER SEEN SUCH A TIGHT RACE THIS EARLY IN THE COMPETITION.
THESE PILOTS ARE IN FOR THE FLIGHT OF THEIR LIVES.

THAT LOUSY, NO GOOD...

ARRRGGGH! NNNAARGH CCAAAARRRGH!

I KNOW, CHEWIE. I HAVEN'T FORGOTTEN WHY WE'RE HERE. BUT I'M NOT GOING TO LET THAT...*PANTORAN PLAYBOY*...GET AWAY WITH SHOOTING AT *MY* SHIP.

I HAVE A *REPUTATION*, YOU KNOW.

GO AHEAD. I'LL CATCH UP.

THIS ISN'T GOING TO TAKE LONG.

HEY! YOU!

SNNNAAARGH.

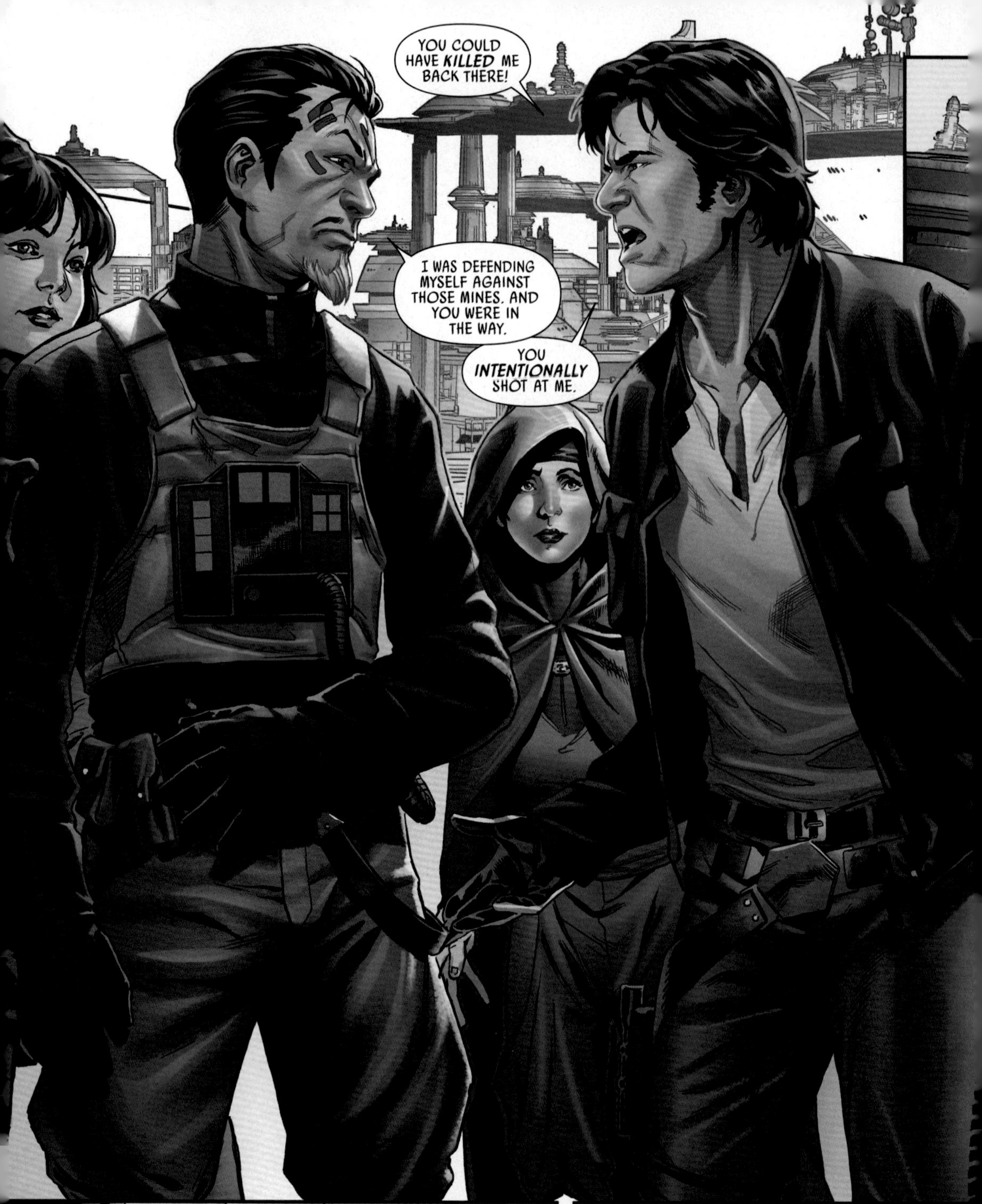
YOU COULD HAVE KILLED ME BACK THERE!
I WAS DEFENDING MYSELF AGAINST THOSE MINES. AND YOU WERE IN THE WAY.
YOU INTENTIONALLY SHOT AT ME.

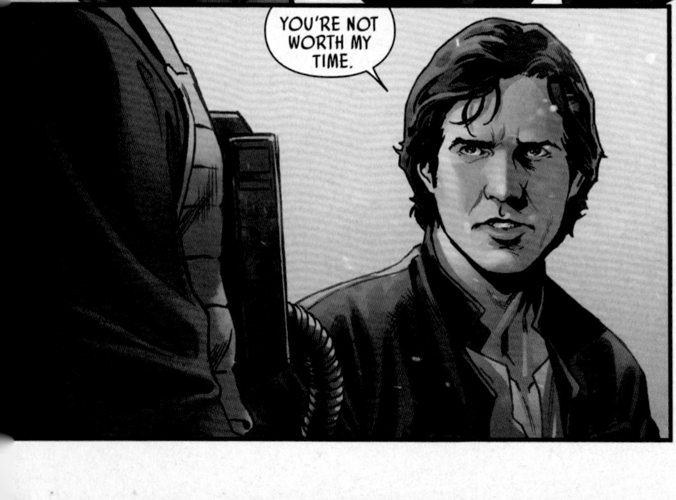
YOU'RE NOT WORTH MY TIME.

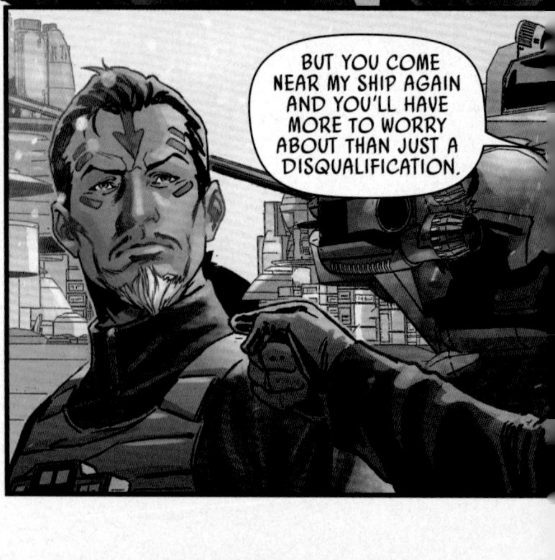
BUT YOU COME NEAR MY SHIP AGAIN AND YOU'LL HAVE MORE TO WORRY ABOUT THAN JUST A DISQUALIFICATION.

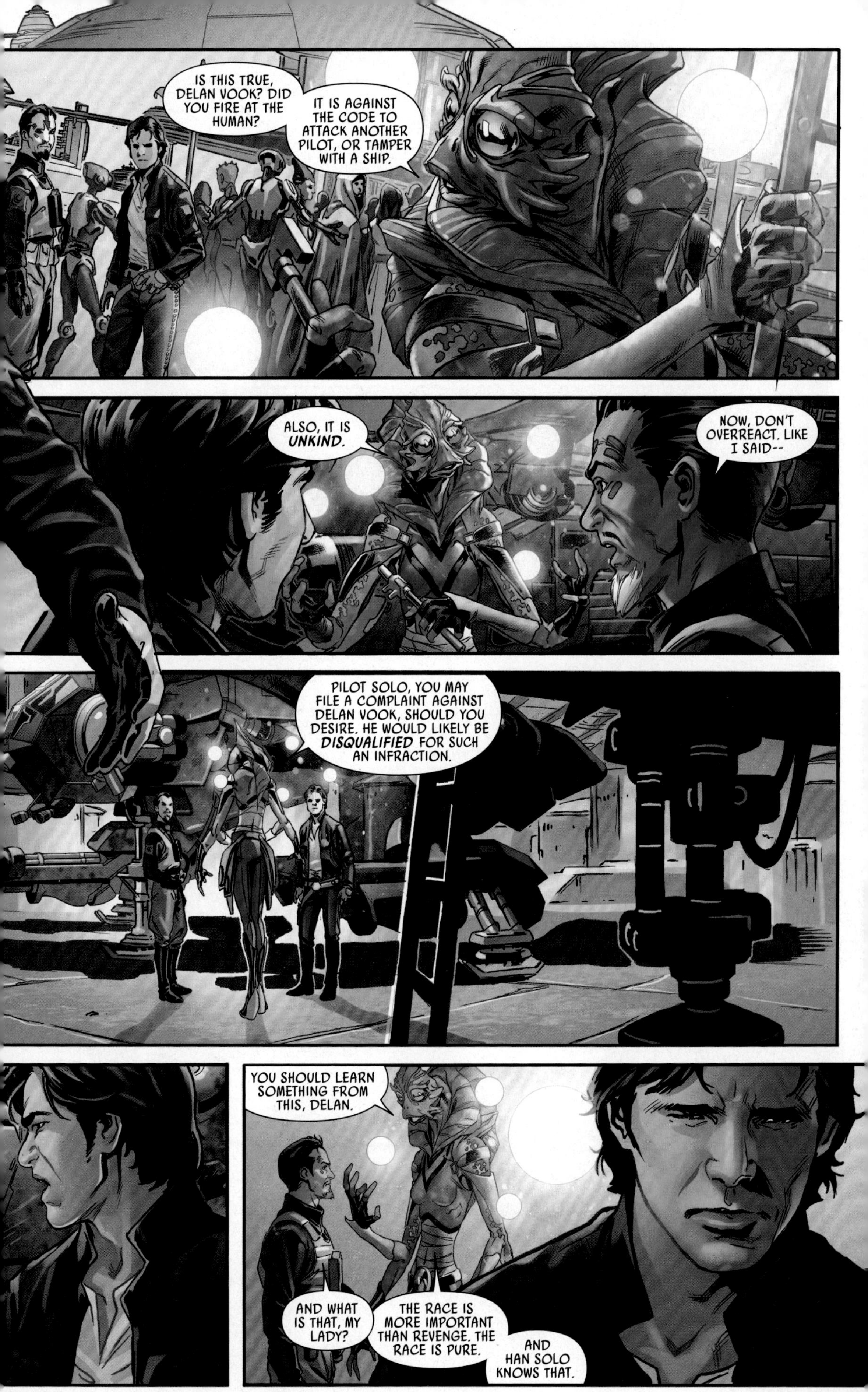
IS THIS TRUE, DELAN VOOK? DID YOU FIRE AT THE HUMAN?
IT IS AGAINST THE CODE TO ATTACK ANOTHER PILOT, OR TAMPER WITH A SHIP.
ALSO, IT IS UNKIND.
NOW, DON'T OVERREACT. LIKE I SAID--
PILOT SOLO, YOU MAY FILE A COMPLAINT AGAINST DELAN VOOK, SHOULD YOU DESIRE. HE WOULD LIKELY BE DISQUALIFIED FOR SUCH AN INFRACTION.
YOU SHOULD LEARN SOMETHING FROM THIS, DELAN.
AND WHAT IS THAT, MY LADY?
THE RACE IS MORE IMPORTANT THAN REVENGE. THE RACE IS PURE.
AND HAN SOLO KNOWS THAT.

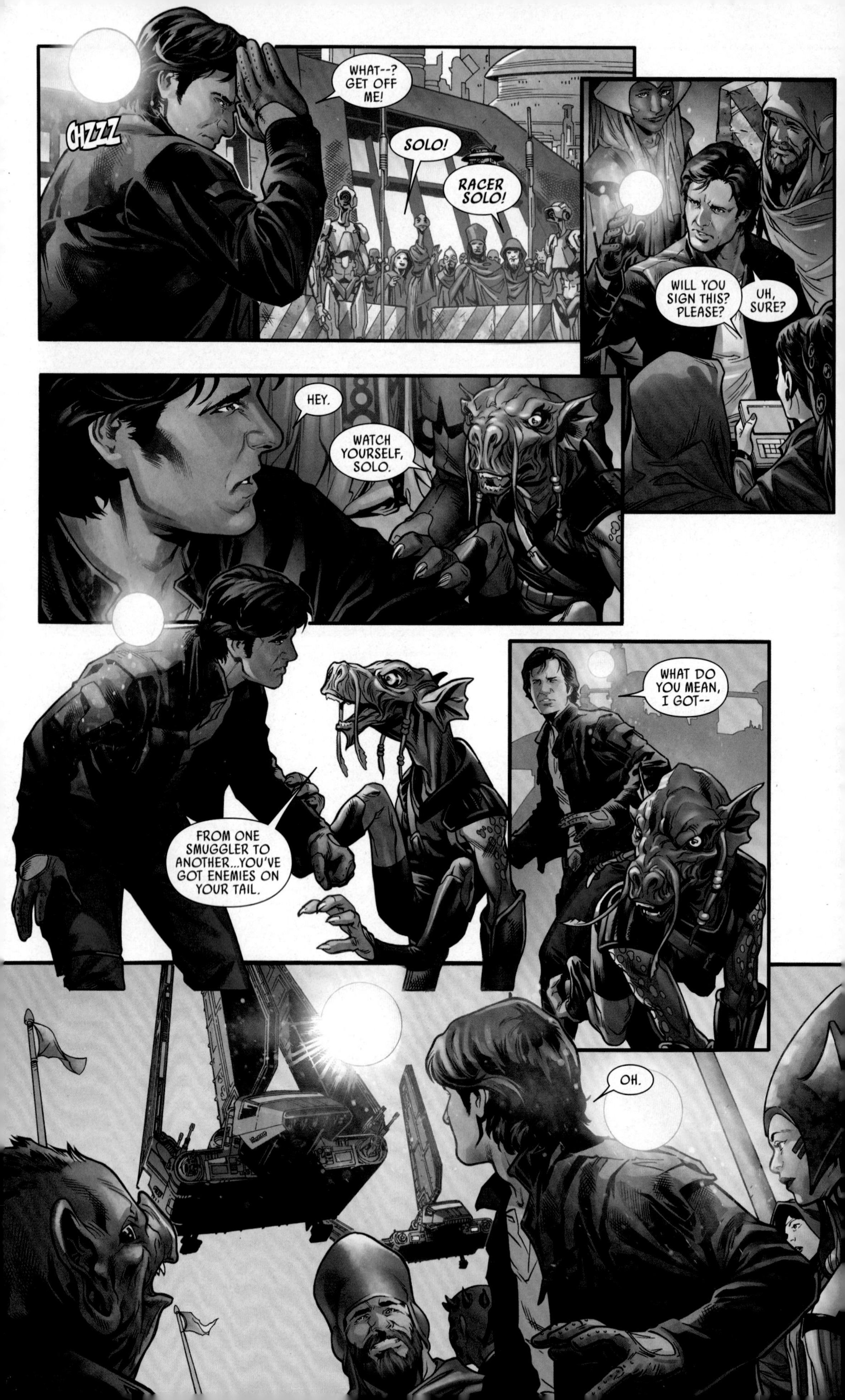
CHZZZ
WHAT--? GET OFF ME!
SOLO!
RACER SOLO!
WILL YOU SIGN THIS? PLEASE?
UH, SURE?
HEY.
WATCH YOURSELF, SOLO.
FROM ONE SMUGGLER TO ANOTHER...YOU'VE GOT ENEMIES ON YOUR TAIL.
WHAT DO YOU MEAN, I GOT--
OH.

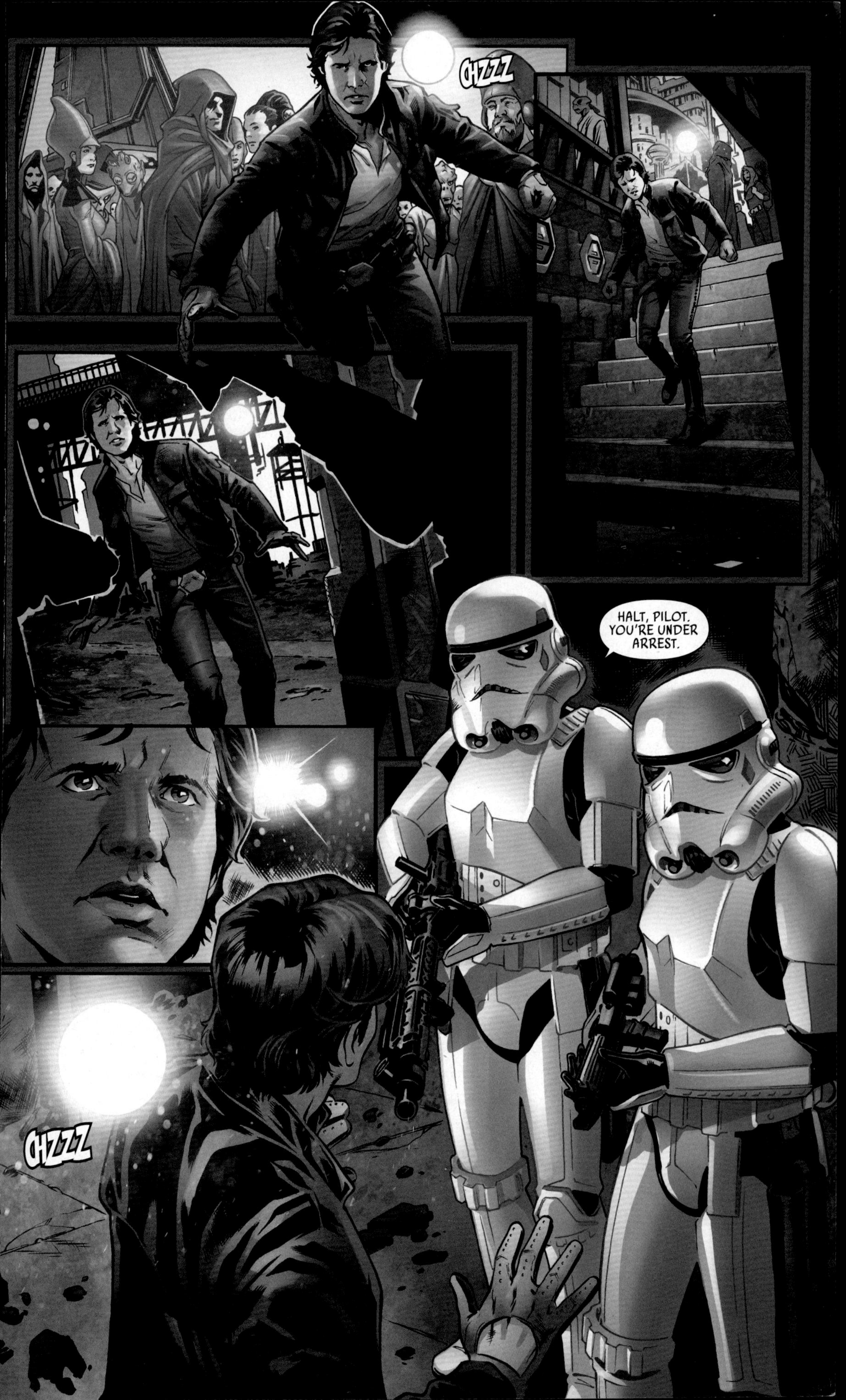
CHZZZ
HALT, PILOT. YOU'RE UNDER ARREST.
CHZZZ

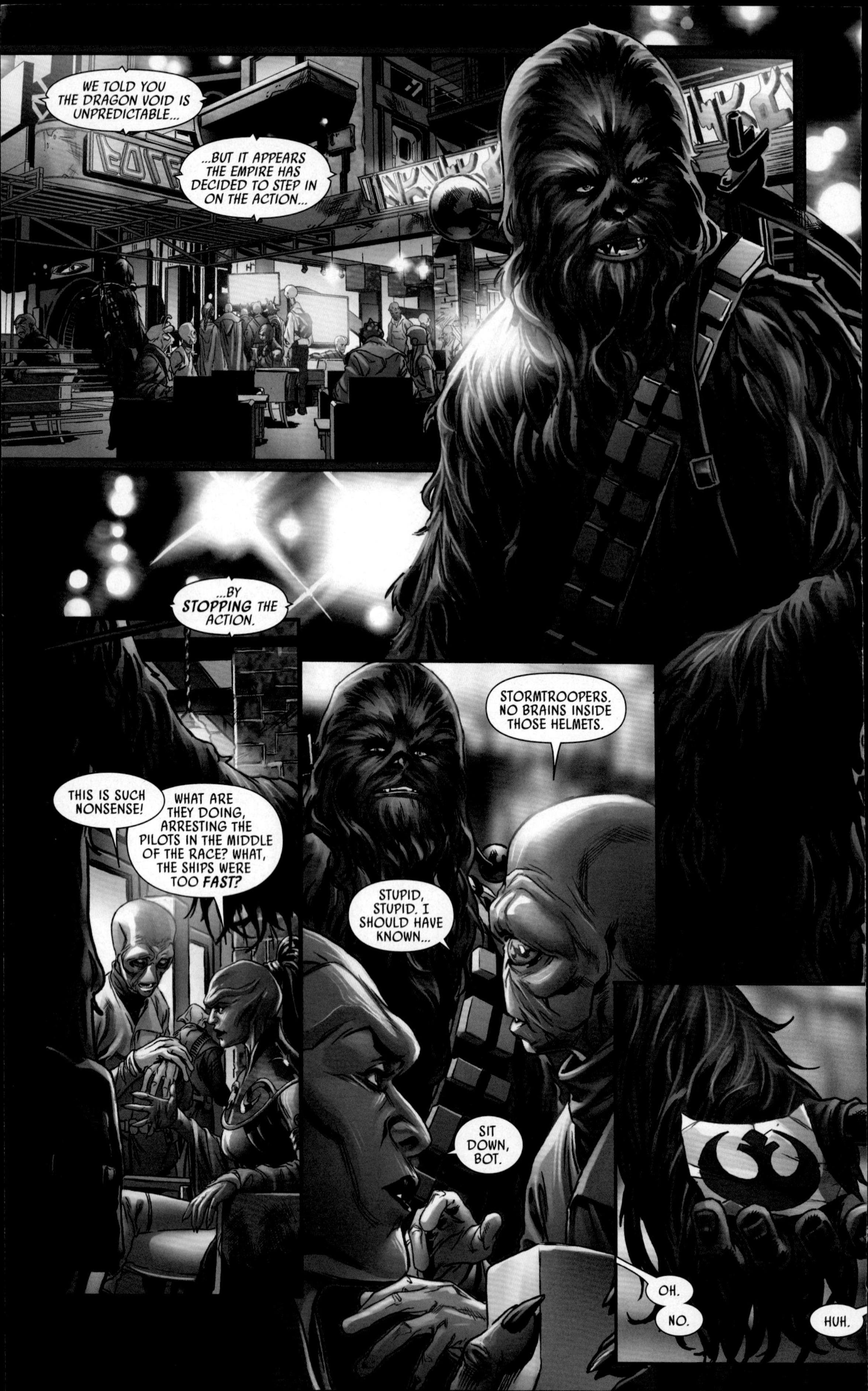
WE TOLD YOU THE DRAGON VOID IS UNPREDICTABLE...
...BUT IT APPEARS THE EMPIRE HAS DECIDED TO STEP IN ON THE ACTION...
...BY STOPPING THE ACTION.
THIS IS SUCH NONSENSE!
WHAT ARE THEY DOING, ARRESTING THE PILOTS IN THE MIDDLE OF THE RACE? WHAT, THE SHIPS WERE TOO FAST?
STORMTROOPERS. NO BRAINS INSIDE THOSE HELMETS.
STUPID, STUPID. I SHOULD HAVE KNOWN...
SIT DOWN, BOT.
OH.
NO.
HUH.

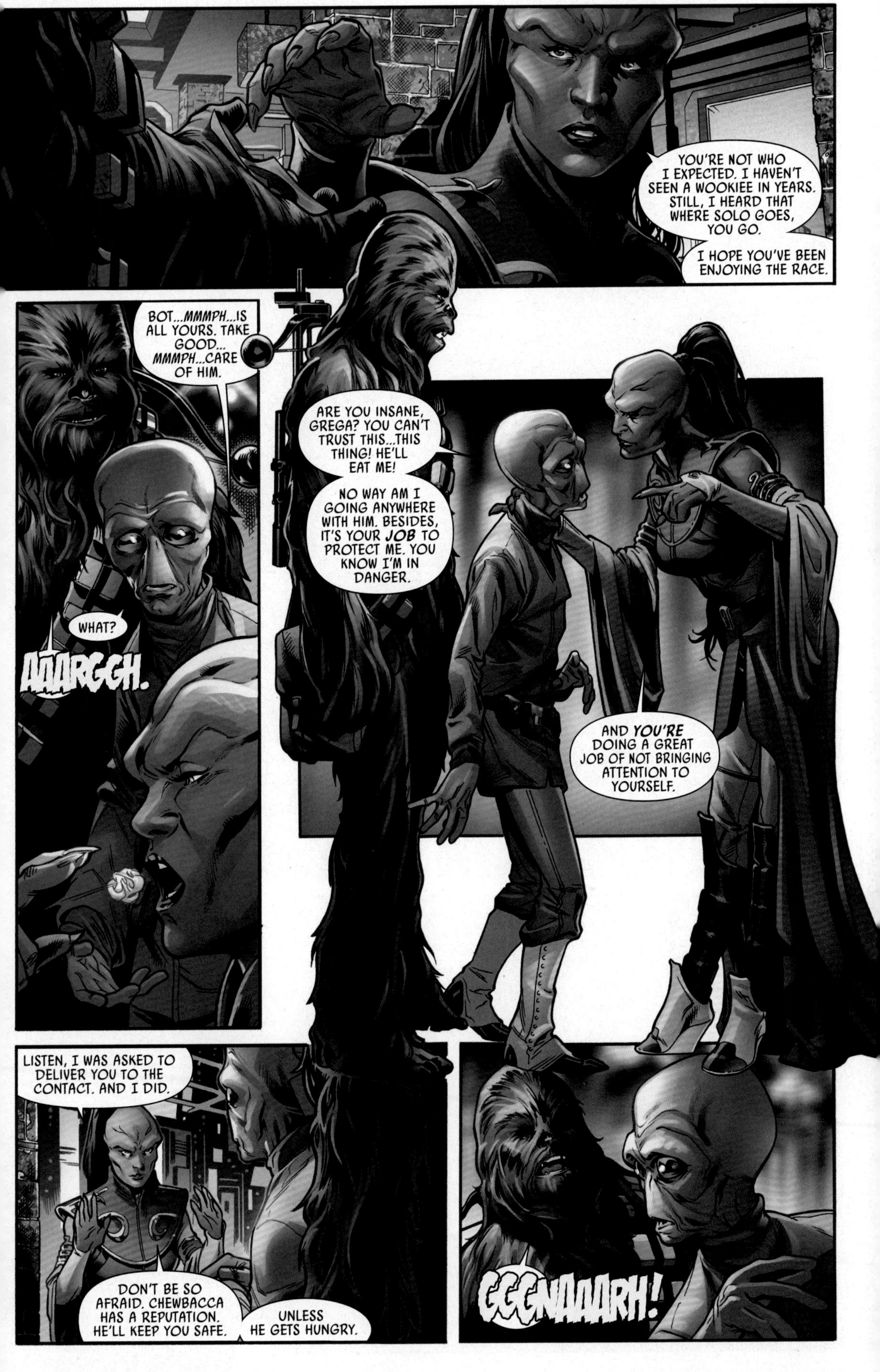

YOU'RE NOT WHO I EXPECTED. I HAVEN'T SEEN A WOOKIEE IN YEARS. STILL, I HEARD THAT WHERE SOLO GOES, YOU GO.
I HOPE YOU'VE BEEN ENJOYING THE RACE.
BOT...MMMPH...IS ALL YOURS. TAKE GOOD... MMMPH...CARE OF HIM.
WHAT?
AAARGGH.
ARE YOU INSANE, GREGA? YOU CAN'T TRUST THIS...THIS THING! HE'LL EAT ME!
NO WAY AM I GOING ANYWHERE WITH HIM. BESIDES, IT'S YOUR *JOB* TO PROTECT ME. YOU KNOW I'M IN DANGER.
AND *YOU'RE* DOING A GREAT JOB OF NOT BRINGING ATTENTION TO YOURSELF.
LISTEN, I WAS ASKED TO DELIVER YOU TO THE CONTACT. AND I DID.
DON'T BE SO AFRAID. CHEWBACCA HAS A REPUTATION. HE'LL KEEP YOU SAFE.
UNLESS HE GETS HUNGRY.
GGGNAAARH!

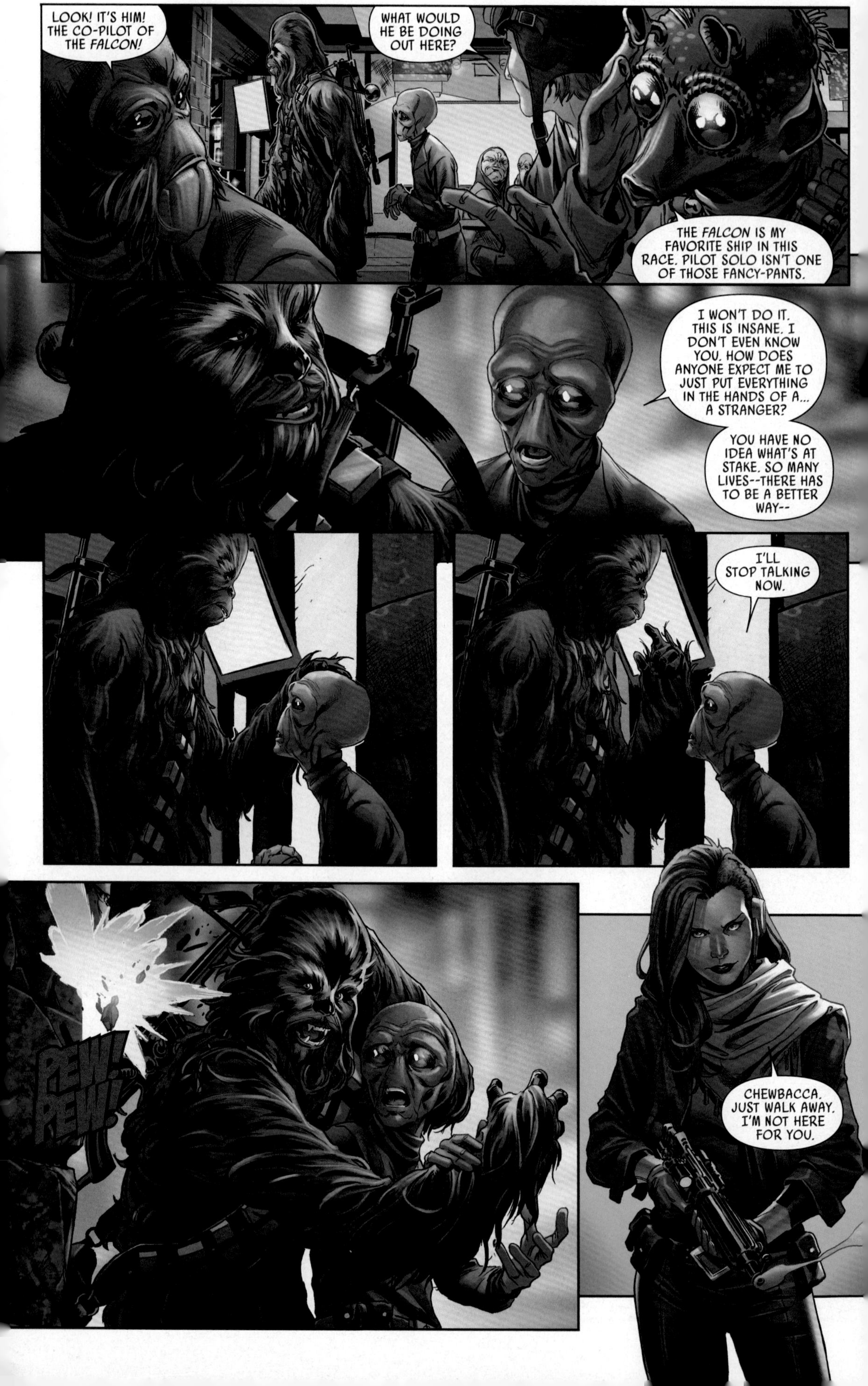
LOOK! IT'S HIM! THE CO-PILOT OF THE *FALCON*!
WHAT WOULD HE BE DOING OUT HERE?
THE *FALCON* IS MY FAVORITE SHIP IN THIS RACE. PILOT SOLO ISN'T ONE OF THOSE FANCY-PANTS.
I WON'T DO IT. THIS IS INSANE. I DON'T EVEN KNOW YOU. HOW DOES ANYONE EXPECT ME TO JUST PUT EVERYTHING IN THE HANDS OF A... A STRANGER?
YOU HAVE NO IDEA WHAT'S AT STAKE. SO MANY LIVES--THERE HAS TO BE A BETTER WAY--
I'LL STOP TALKING NOW.
PEW! PEW!
CHEWBACCA. JUST WALK AWAY. I'M NOT HERE FOR YOU.

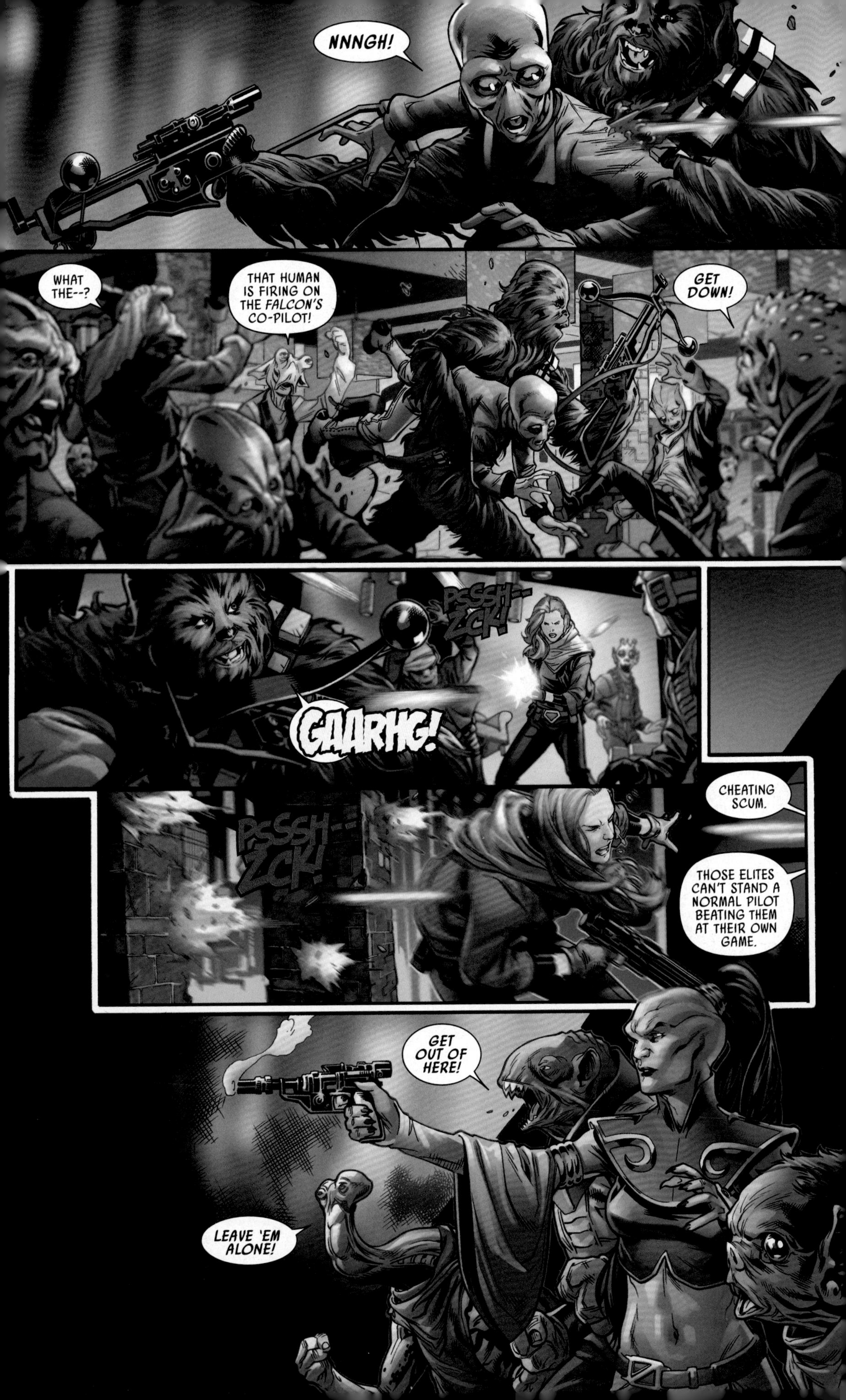
NNNGH!
WHAT THE--?
THAT HUMAN IS FIRING ON THE *FALCON'S* CO-PILOT!
GET DOWN!
PSSSH-ZCK!
GAARHG!
PSSSH-ZCK!
CHEATING SCUM.
THOSE ELITES CAN'T STAND A NORMAL PILOT BEATING THEM AT THEIR OWN GAME.
GET OUT OF HERE!
LEAVE 'EM ALONE!

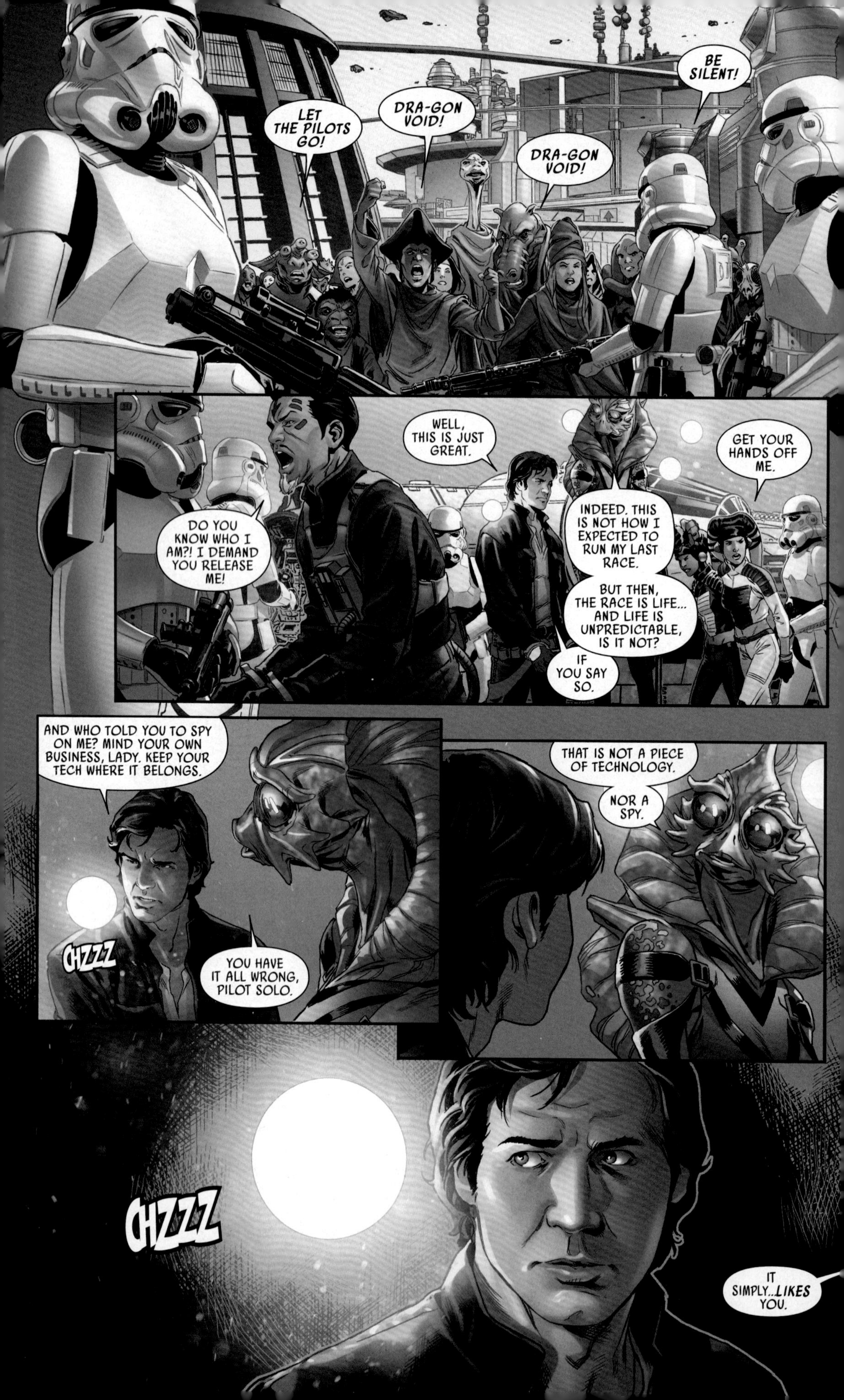
LET THE PILOTS GO!
DRA-GON VOID!
DRA-GON VOID!
BE SILENT!
DO YOU KNOW WHO I AM?! I DEMAND YOU RELEASE ME!
WELL, THIS IS JUST GREAT.
INDEED. THIS IS NOT HOW I EXPECTED TO RUN MY LAST RACE.
BUT THEN, THE RACE IS LIFE... AND LIFE IS UNPREDICTABLE, IS IT NOT?
IF YOU SAY SO.
GET YOUR HANDS OFF ME.
AND WHO TOLD YOU TO SPY ON ME? MIND YOUR OWN BUSINESS, LADY. KEEP YOUR TECH WHERE IT BELONGS.
CHZZZ
YOU HAVE IT ALL WRONG, PILOT SOLO.
THAT IS NOT A PIECE OF TECHNOLOGY.
NOR A SPY.
CHZZZ
IT SIMPLY...LIKES YOU.

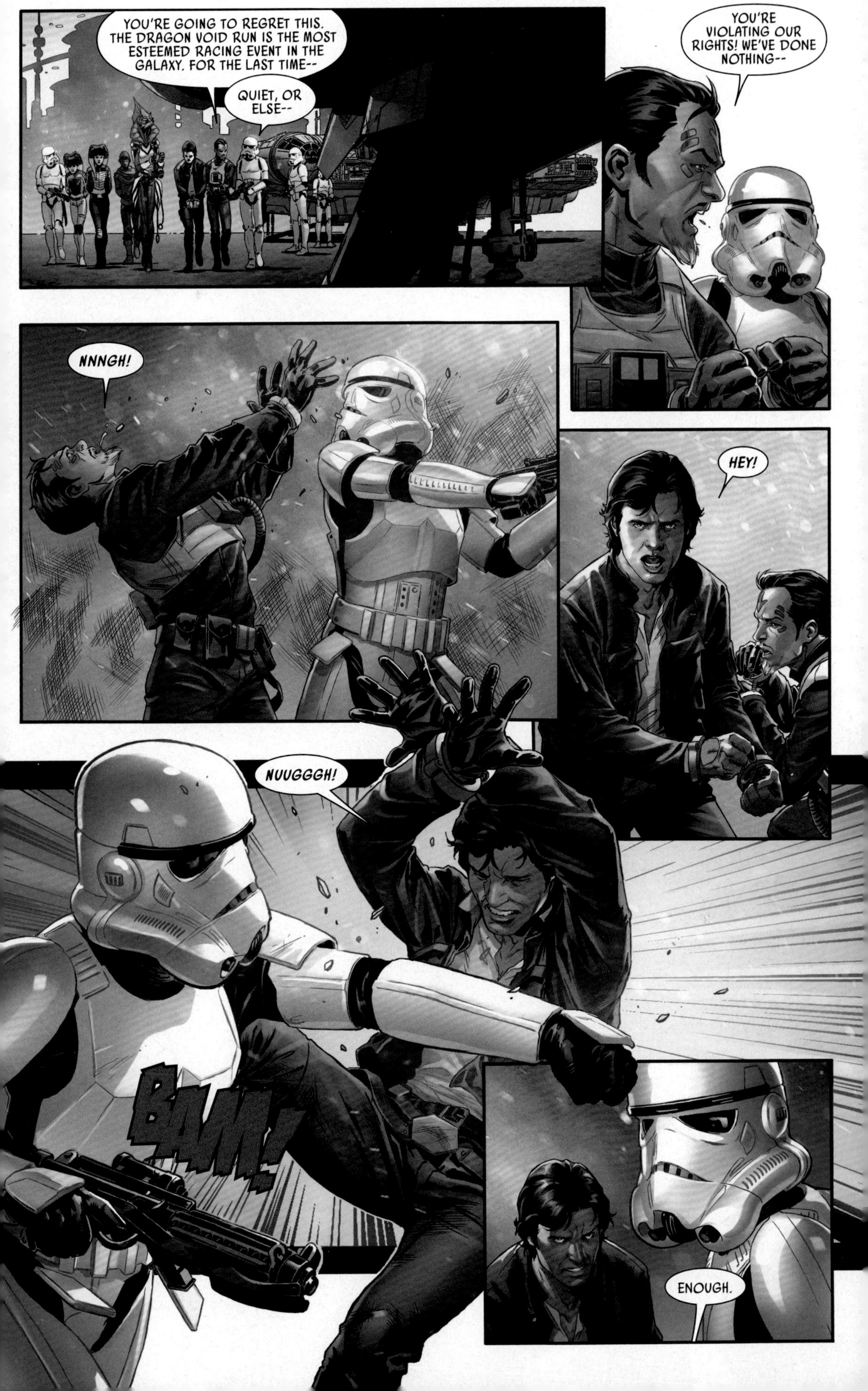

YOU'RE GOING TO REGRET THIS. THE DRAGON VOID RUN IS THE MOST ESTEEMED RACING EVENT IN THE GALAXY. FOR THE LAST TIME--
QUIET, OR ELSE--
YOU'RE VIOLATING OUR RIGHTS! WE'VE DONE NOTHING--
NNNGH!
HEY!
NUUGGGH!
BAM!
ENOUGH.

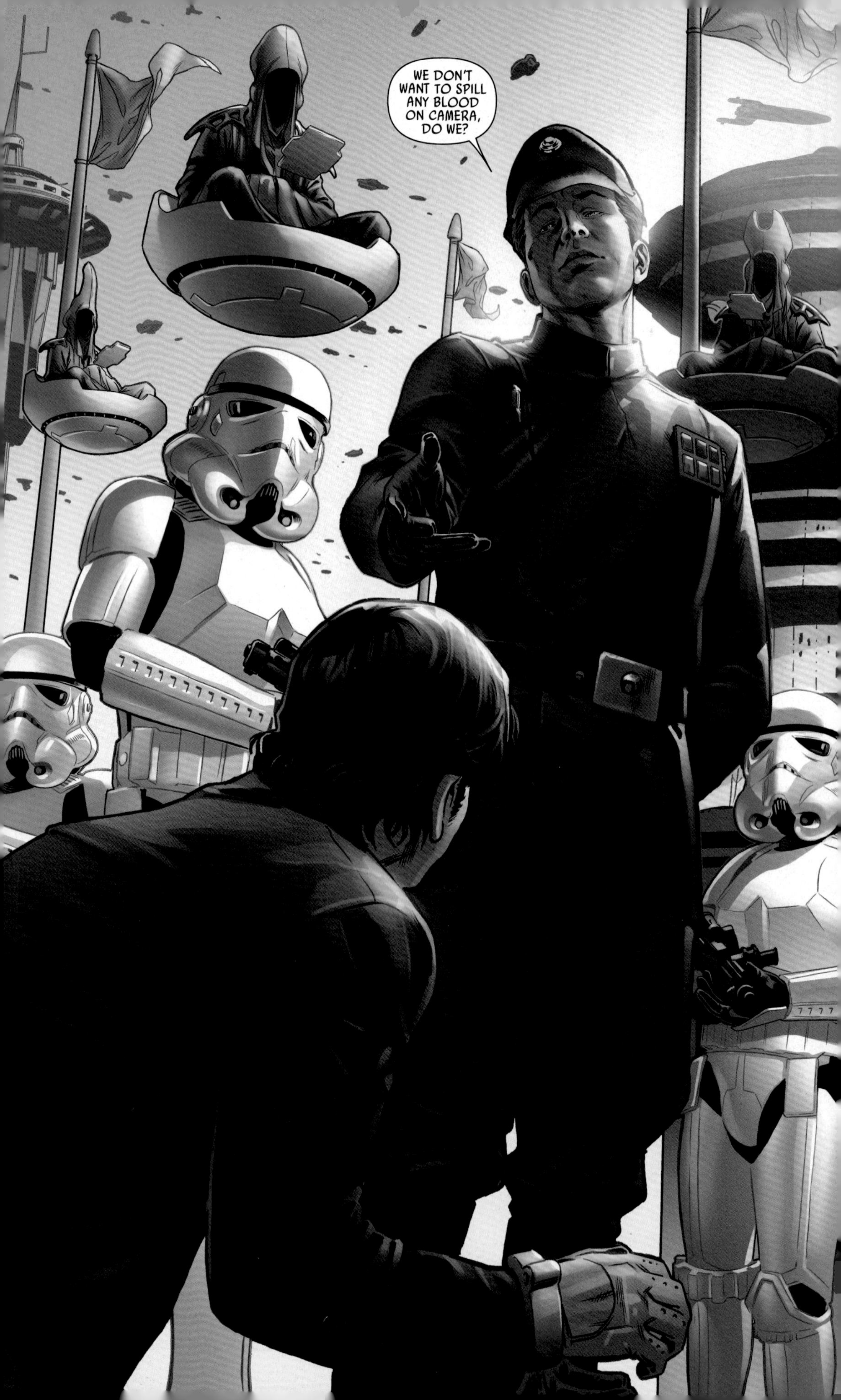
WE DON'T WANT TO SPILL ANY BLOOD ON CAMERA, DO WE?

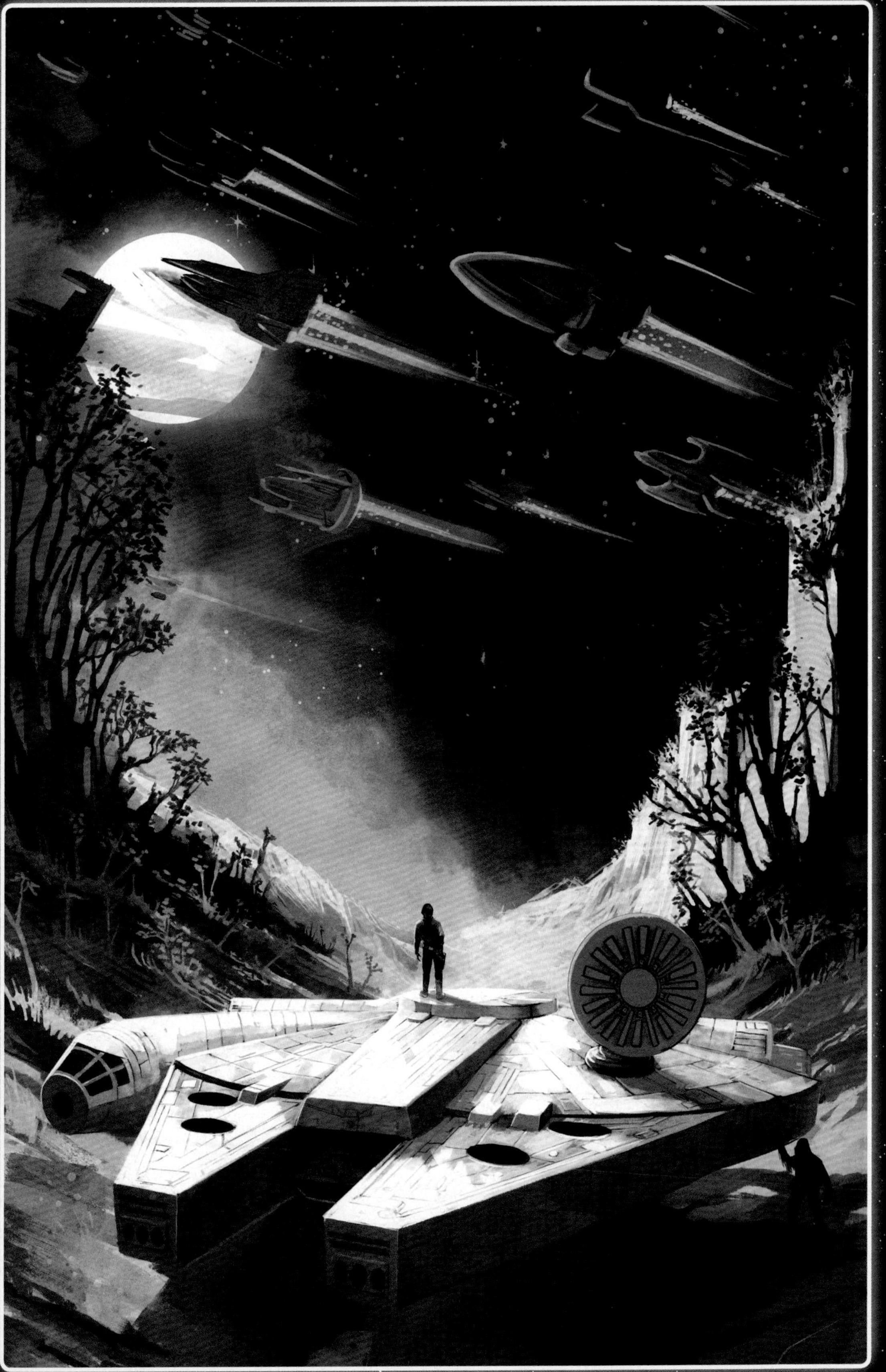

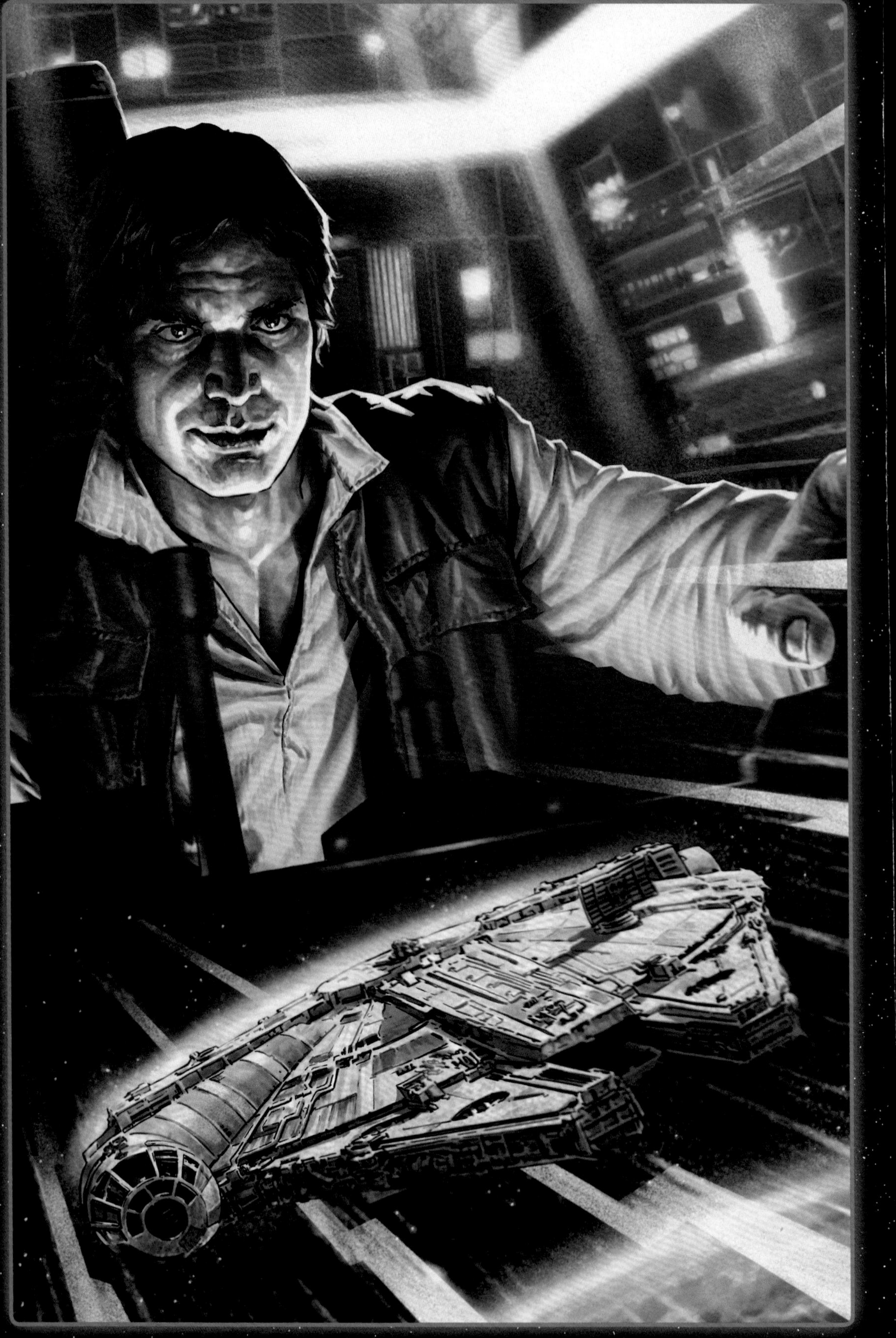

3

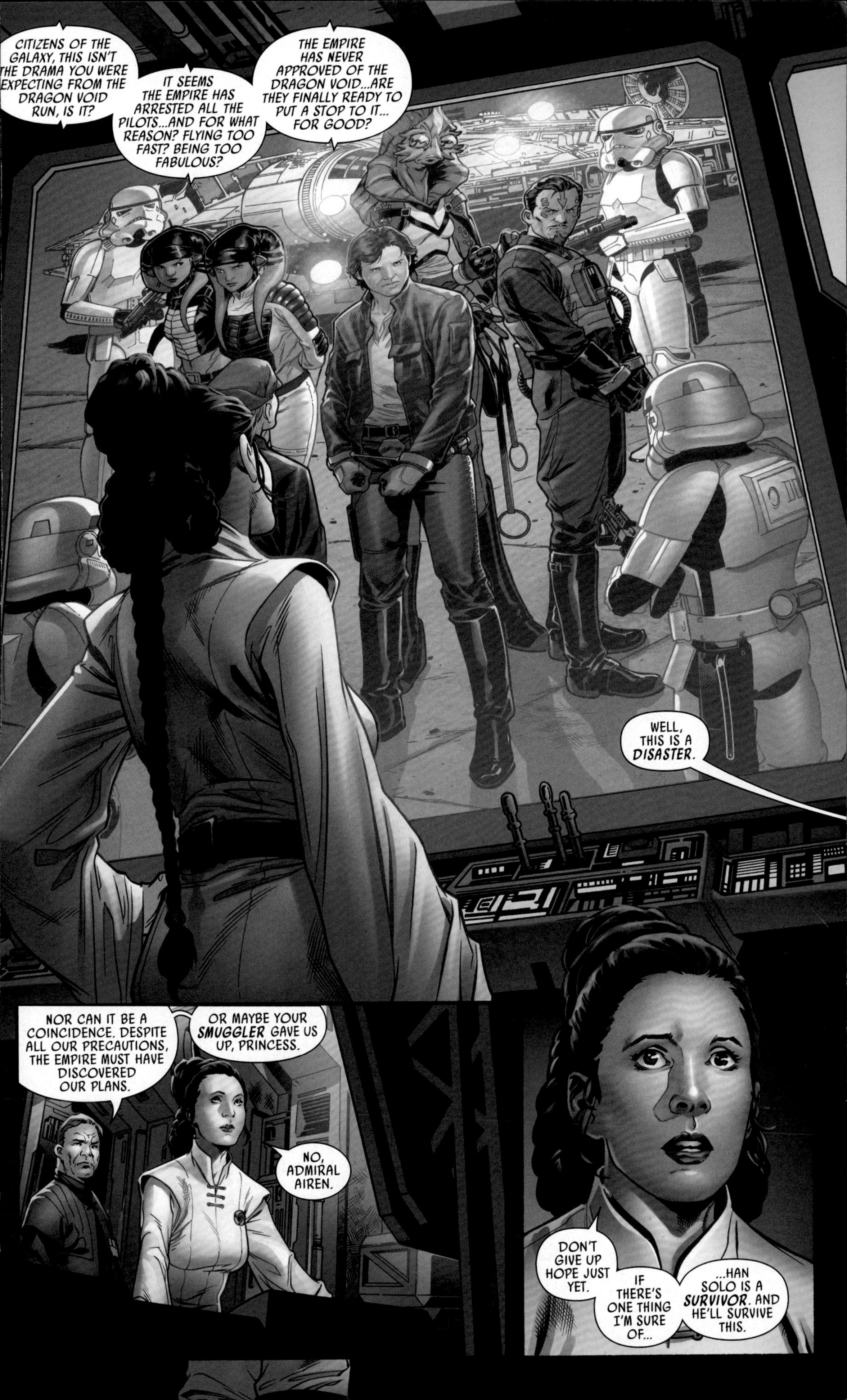
CITIZENS OF THE GALAXY, THIS ISN'T THE DRAMA YOU WERE EXPECTING FROM THE DRAGON VOID RUN, IS IT?
IT SEEMS THE EMPIRE HAS ARRESTED ALL THE PILOTS...AND FOR WHAT REASON? FLYING TOO FAST? BEING TOO FABULOUS?
THE EMPIRE HAS NEVER APPROVED OF THE DRAGON VOID...ARE THEY FINALLY READY TO PUT A STOP TO IT... FOR GOOD?
WELL, THIS IS A DISASTER.
NOR CAN IT BE A COINCIDENCE. DESPITE ALL OUR PRECAUTIONS, THE EMPIRE MUST HAVE DISCOVERED OUR PLANS.
OR MAYBE YOUR SMUGGLER GAVE US UP, PRINCESS.
NO, ADMIRAL AIREN.
DON'T GIVE UP HOPE JUST YET.
IF THERE'S ONE THING I'M SURE OF...
...HAN SOLO IS A SURVIVOR. AND HE'LL SURVIVE THIS.

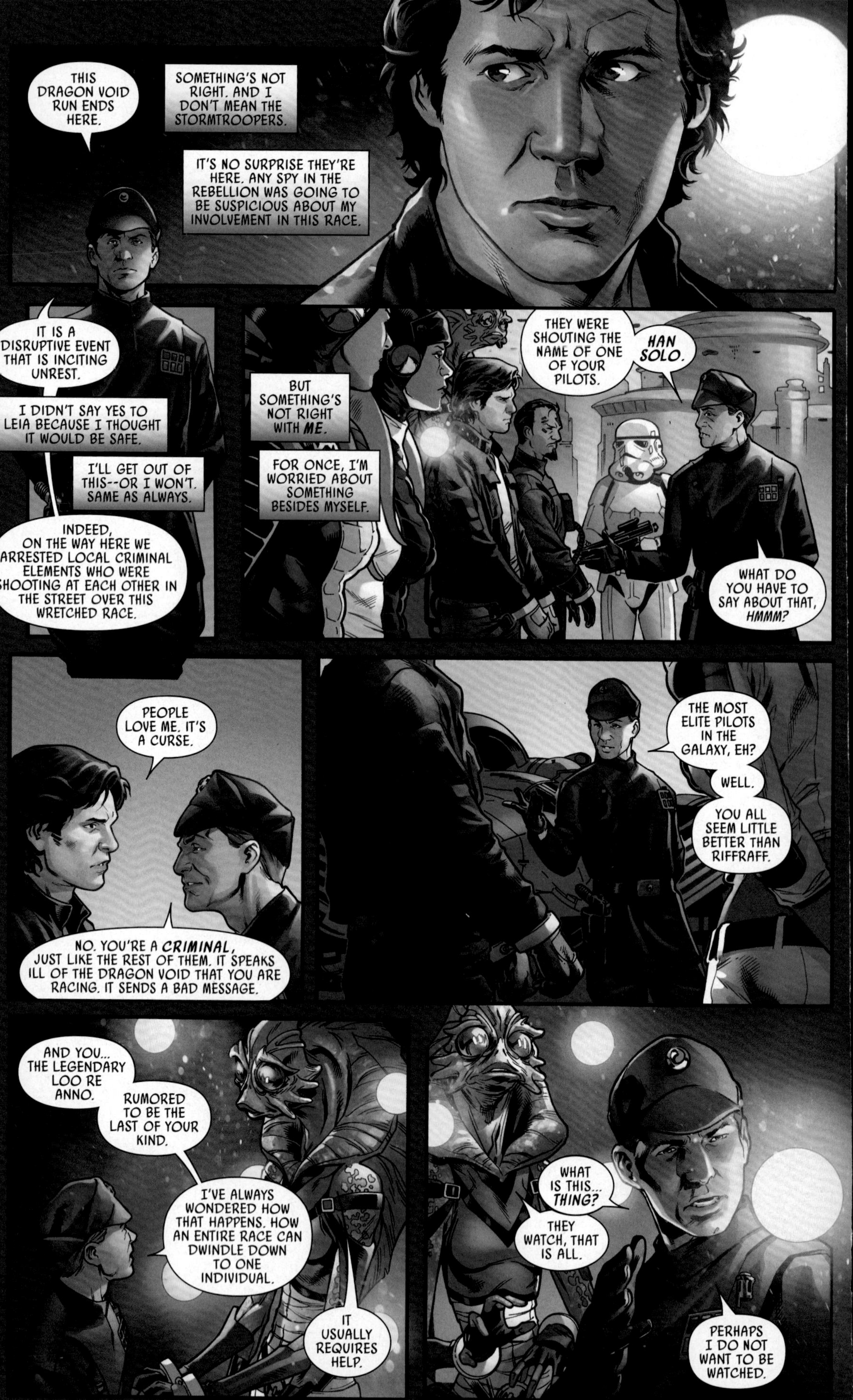

THIS DRAGON VOID RUN ENDS HERE.
SOMETHING'S NOT RIGHT. AND I DON'T MEAN THE STORMTROOPERS.
IT'S NO SURPRISE THEY'RE HERE. ANY SPY IN THE REBELLION WAS GOING TO BE SUSPICIOUS ABOUT MY INVOLVEMENT IN THIS RACE.
IT IS A DISRUPTIVE EVENT THAT IS INCITING UNREST.
I DIDN'T SAY YES TO LEIA BECAUSE I THOUGHT IT WOULD BE SAFE.
I'LL GET OUT OF THIS--OR I WON'T. SAME AS ALWAYS.
INDEED, ON THE WAY HERE WE ARRESTED LOCAL CRIMINAL ELEMENTS WHO WERE SHOOTING AT EACH OTHER IN THE STREET OVER THIS WRETCHED RACE.
BUT SOMETHING'S NOT RIGHT WITH *ME*.
FOR ONCE, I'M WORRIED ABOUT SOMETHING BESIDES MYSELF.
THEY WERE SHOUTING THE NAME OF ONE OF YOUR PILOTS. *HAN SOLO*.
WHAT DO YOU HAVE TO SAY ABOUT THAT, *HMMM?*
PEOPLE LOVE ME. IT'S A CURSE.
NO. YOU'RE A *CRIMINAL*, JUST LIKE THE REST OF THEM. IT SPEAKS ILL OF THE DRAGON VOID THAT YOU ARE RACING. IT SENDS A BAD MESSAGE.
THE MOST ELITE PILOTS IN THE GALAXY, EH?
WELL.
YOU ALL SEEM LITTLE BETTER THAN RIFFRAFF.
AND YOU... THE LEGENDARY LOO RE ANNO.
RUMORED TO BE THE LAST OF YOUR KIND.
I'VE ALWAYS WONDERED HOW THAT HAPPENS. HOW AN ENTIRE RACE CAN DWINDLE DOWN TO ONE INDIVIDUAL.
IT USUALLY REQUIRES HELP.
WHAT IS THIS... *THING?*
THEY WATCH, THAT IS ALL.
PERHAPS I DO NOT WANT TO BE WATCHED.

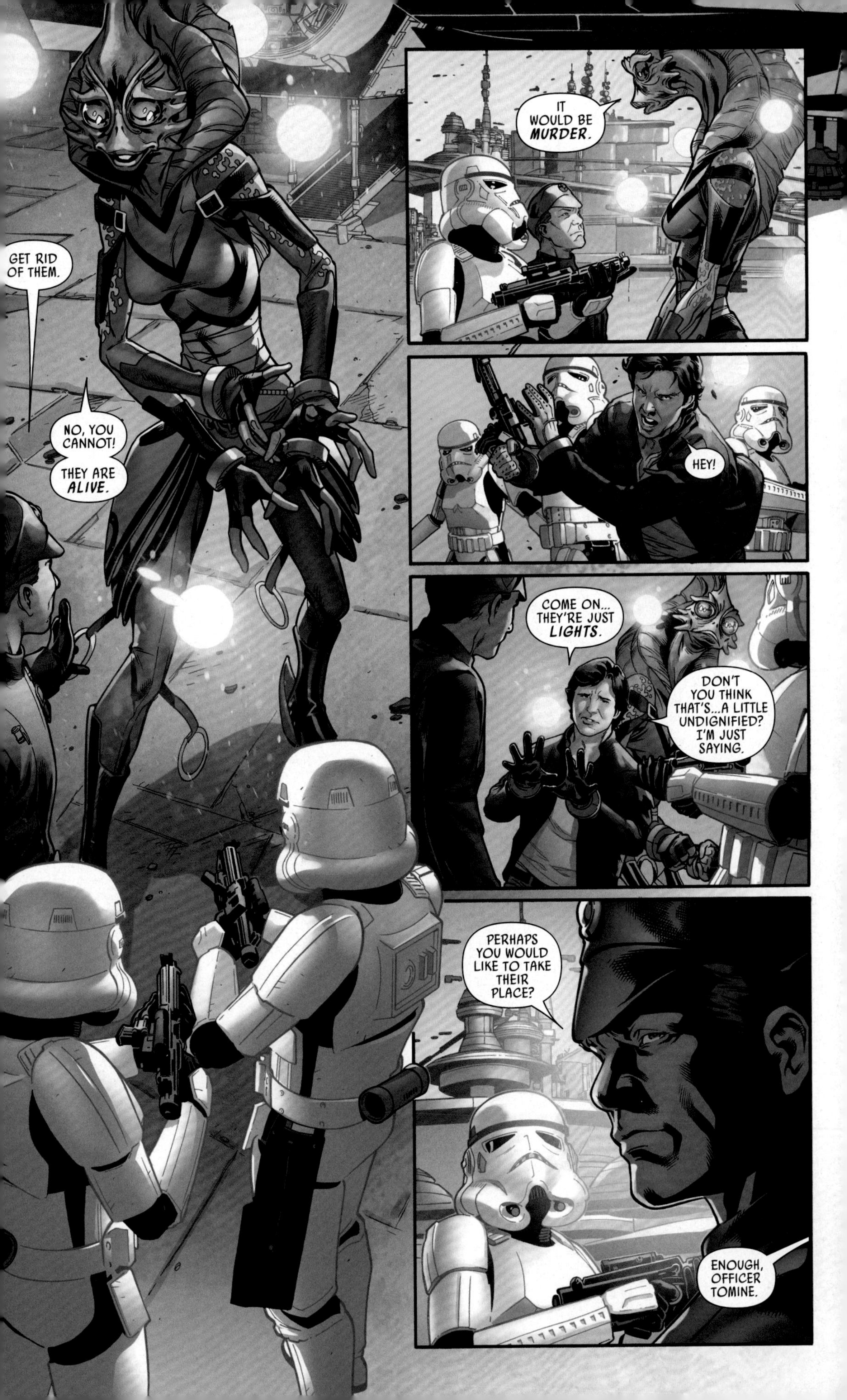
GET RID OF THEM.
NO, YOU CANNOT!
THEY ARE ALIVE.
IT WOULD BE MURDER.
HEY!
COME ON... THEY'RE JUST LIGHTS.
DON'T YOU THINK THAT'S...A LITTLE UNDIGNIFIED? I'M JUST SAYING.
PERHAPS YOU WOULD LIKE TO TAKE THEIR PLACE?
ENOUGH, OFFICER TOMINE.

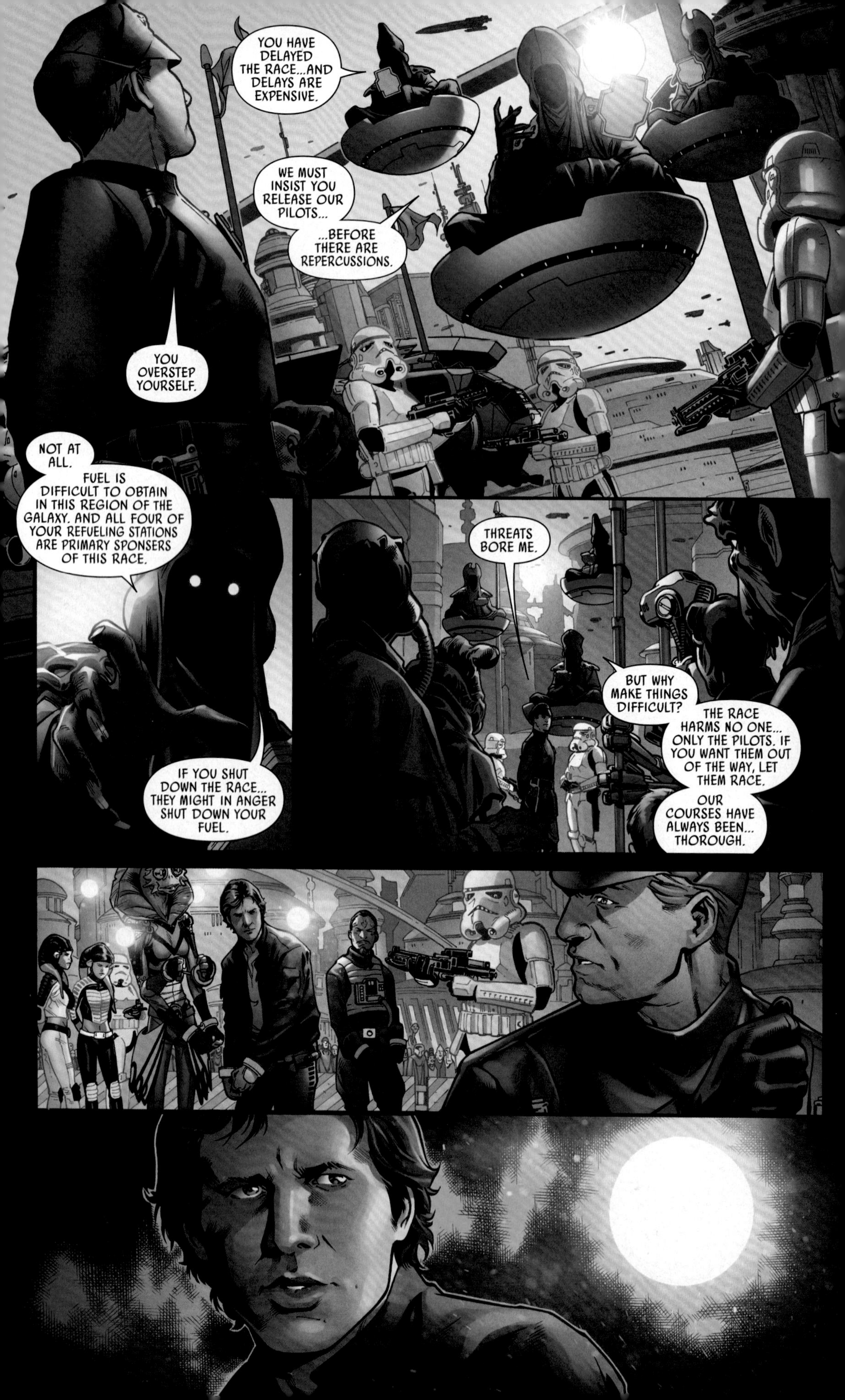

YOU HAVE DELAYED THE RACE...AND DELAYS ARE EXPENSIVE.
WE MUST INSIST YOU RELEASE OUR PILOTS...
...BEFORE THERE ARE REPERCUSSIONS.
YOU OVERSTEP YOURSELF.
NOT AT ALL.
FUEL IS DIFFICULT TO OBTAIN IN THIS REGION OF THE GALAXY. AND ALL FOUR OF YOUR REFUELING STATIONS ARE PRIMARY SPONSERS OF THIS RACE.
IF YOU SHUT DOWN THE RACE... THEY MIGHT IN ANGER SHUT DOWN YOUR FUEL.
THREATS BORE ME.
BUT WHY MAKE THINGS DIFFICULT?
THE RACE HARMS NO ONE... ONLY THE PILOTS. IF YOU WANT THEM OUT OF THE WAY, LET THEM RACE.
OUR COURSES HAVE ALWAYS BEEN... THOROUGH.

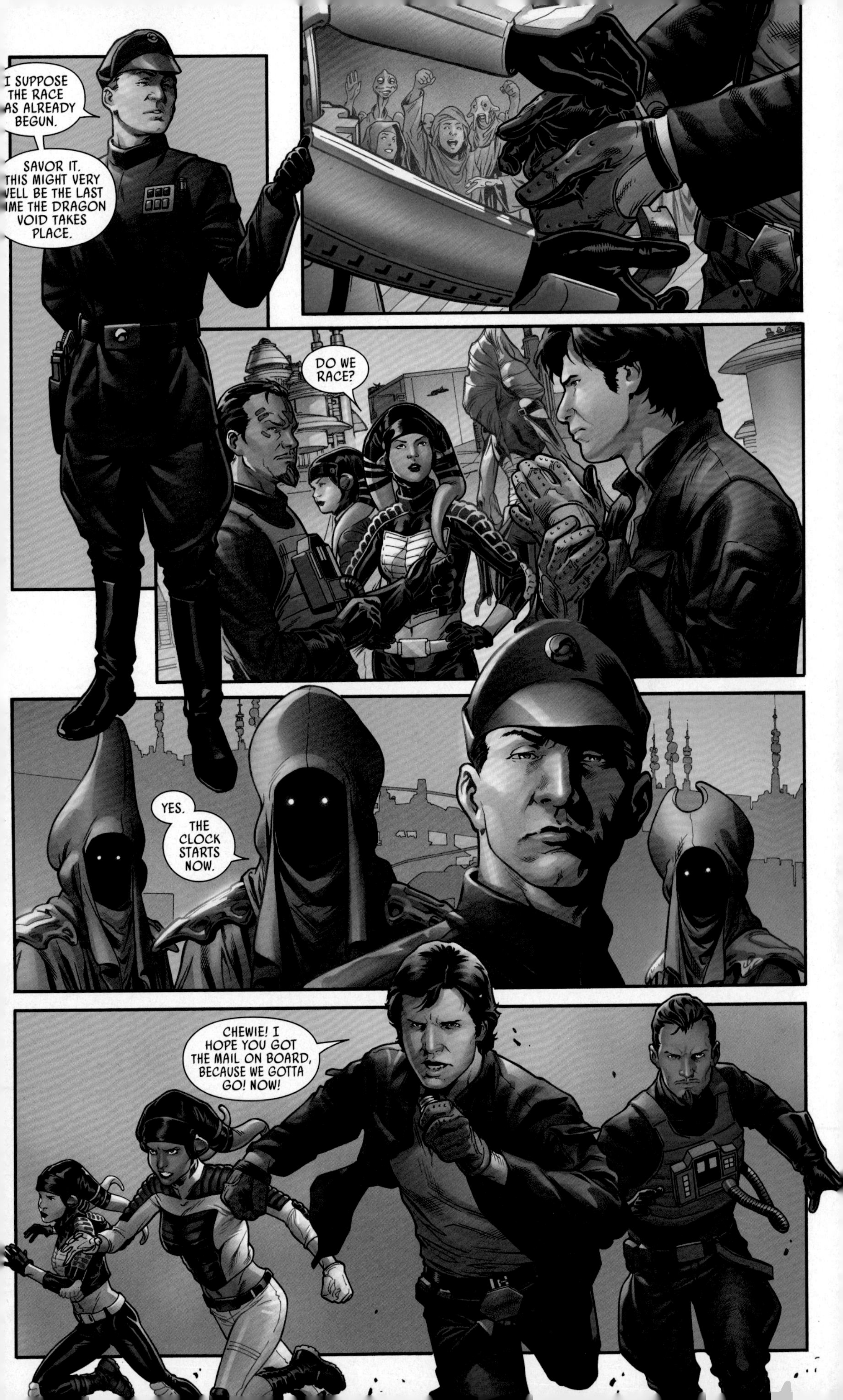
I SUPPOSE THE RACE AS ALREADY BEGUN.
SAVOR IT. THIS MIGHT VERY VELL BE THE LAST IME THE DRAGON VOID TAKES PLACE.
DO WE RACE?
YES.
THE CLOCK STARTS NOW.
CHEWIE! I HOPE YOU GOT THE MAIL ON BOARD, BECAUSE WE GOTTA GO! NOW!

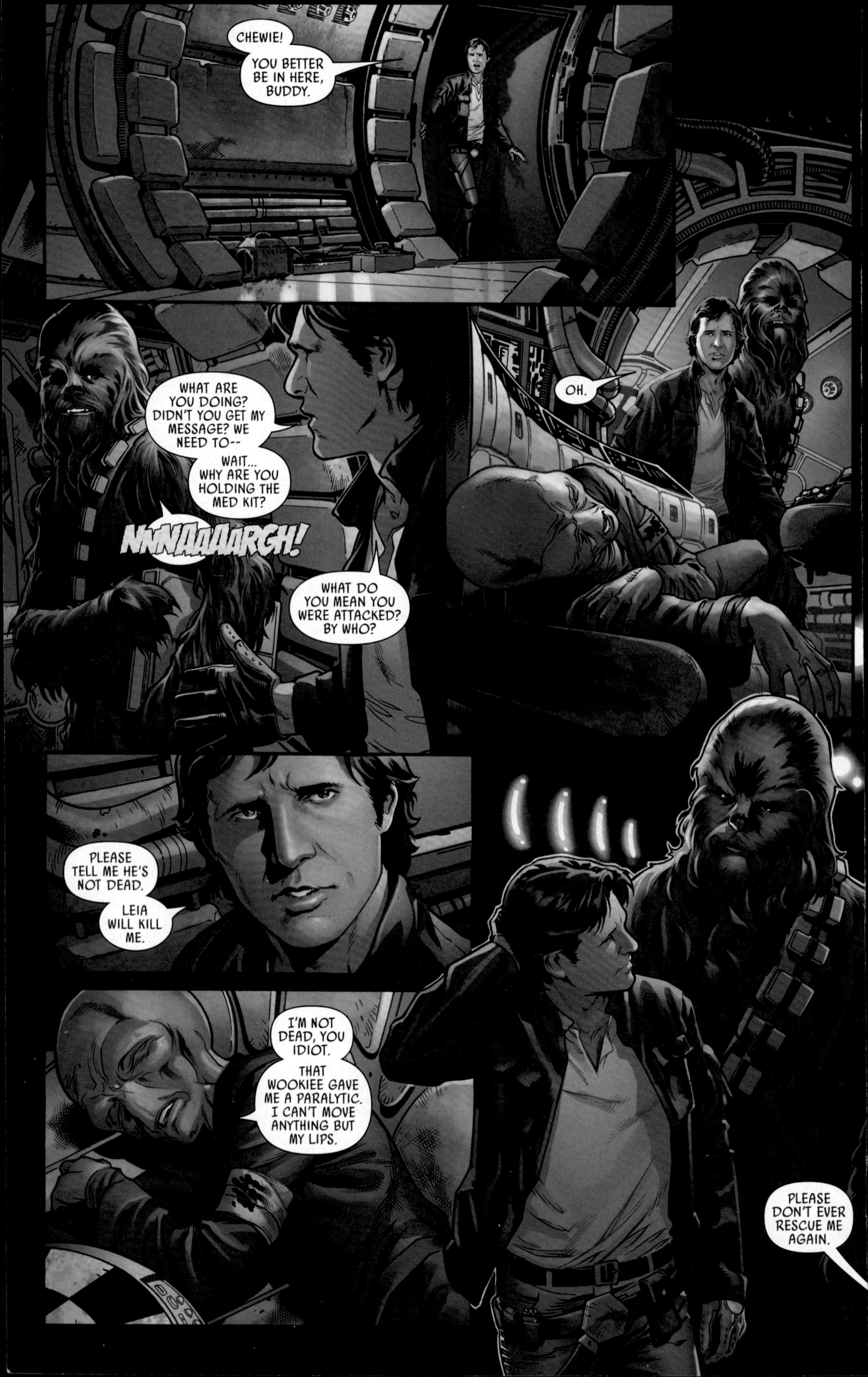
CHEWIE!
YOU BETTER BE IN HERE, BUDDY.
WHAT ARE YOU DOING? DIDN'T YOU GET MY MESSAGE? WE NEED TO--
WAIT... WHY ARE YOU HOLDING THE MED KIT?
NNNAAAARGH!
WHAT DO YOU MEAN YOU WERE ATTACKED? BY WHO?
OH.
PLEASE TELL ME HE'S NOT DEAD.
LEIA WILL KILL ME.
I'M NOT DEAD, YOU IDIOT.
THAT WOOKIEE GAVE ME A PARALYTIC. I CAN'T MOVE ANYTHING BUT MY LIPS.
PLEASE DON'T EVER RESCUE ME AGAIN.

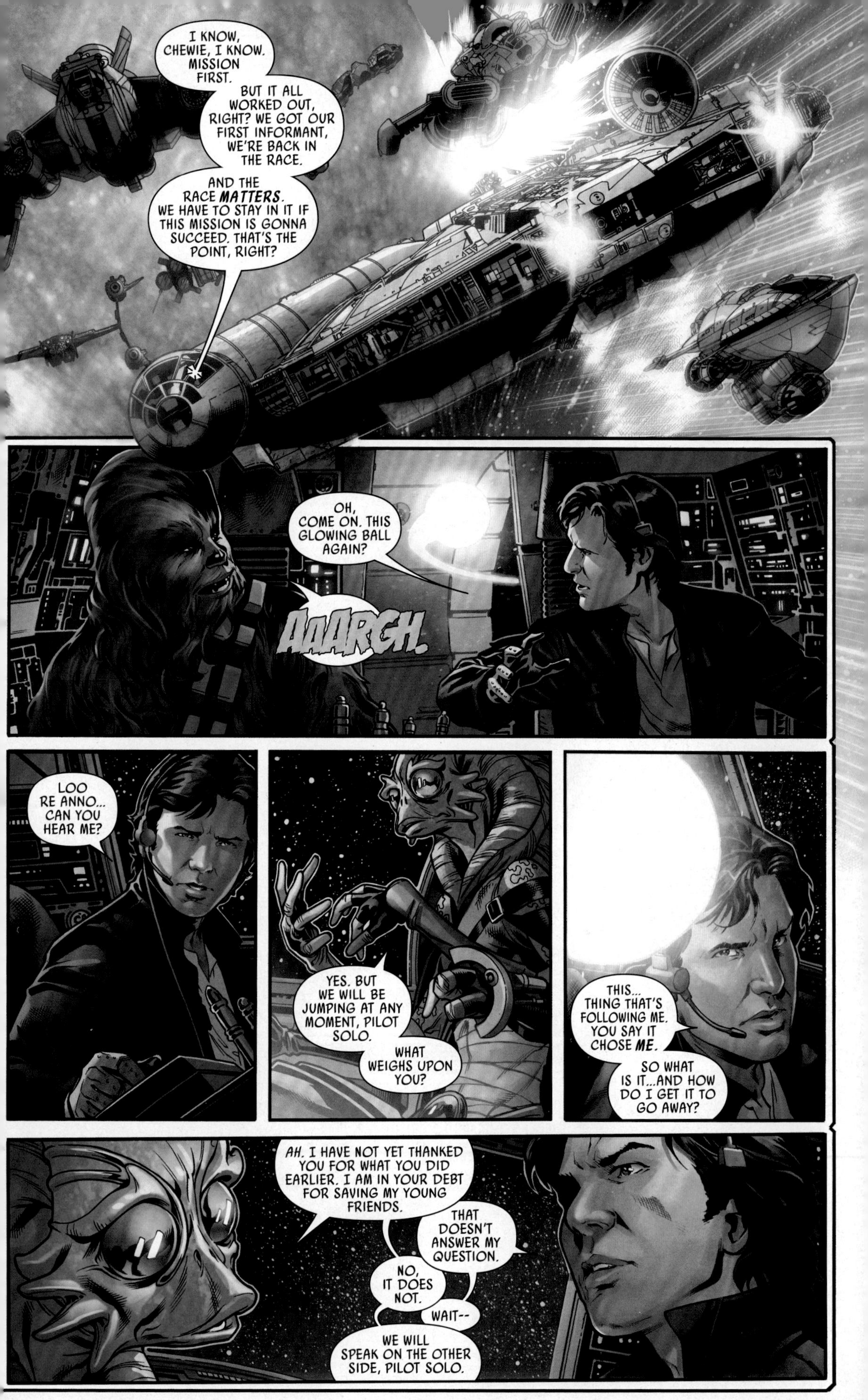
I KNOW, CHEWIE, I KNOW. MISSION FIRST.
BUT IT ALL WORKED OUT, RIGHT? WE GOT OUR FIRST INFORMANT, WE'RE BACK IN THE RACE.
AND THE RACE MATTERS. WE HAVE TO STAY IN IT IF THIS MISSION IS GONNA SUCCEED. THAT'S THE POINT, RIGHT?
OH, COME ON. THIS GLOWING BALL AGAIN?
AAARGH.
LOO RE ANNO... CAN YOU HEAR ME?
YES. BUT WE WILL BE JUMPING AT ANY MOMENT, PILOT SOLO.
WHAT WEIGHS UPON YOU?
THIS... THING THAT'S FOLLOWING ME. YOU SAY IT CHOSE ME.
SO WHAT IS IT...AND HOW DO I GET IT TO GO AWAY?
AH. I HAVE NOT YET THANKED YOU FOR WHAT YOU DID EARLIER. I AM IN YOUR DEBT FOR SAVING MY YOUNG FRIENDS.
THAT DOESN'T ANSWER MY QUESTION.
NO, IT DOES NOT.
WAIT--
WE WILL SPEAK ON THE OTHER SIDE, PILOT SOLO.

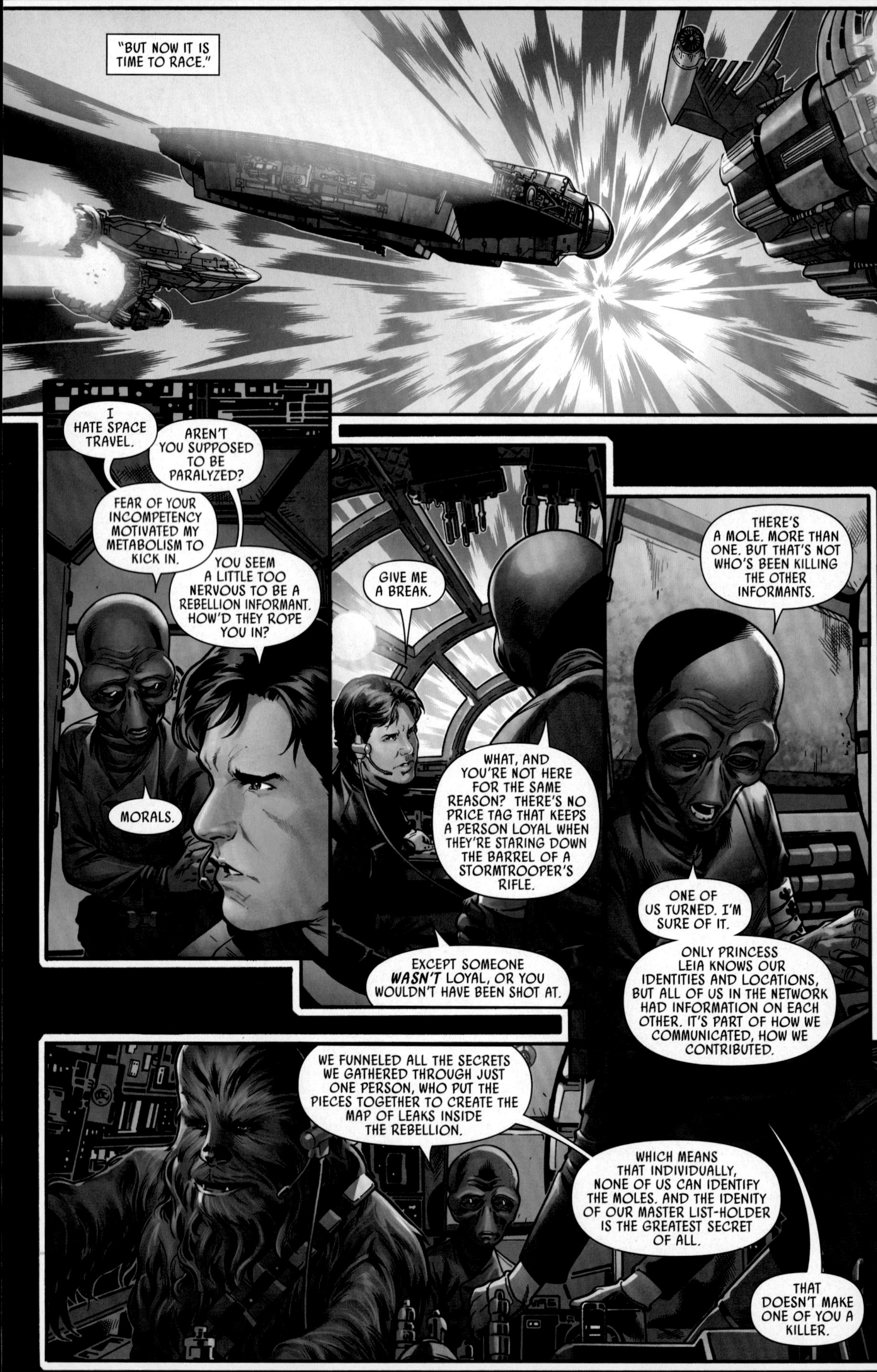

"BUT NOW IT IS TIME TO RACE."
I HATE SPACE TRAVEL.
AREN'T YOU SUPPOSED TO BE PARALYZED?
FEAR OF YOUR INCOMPETENCY MOTIVATED MY METABOLISM TO KICK IN.
YOU SEEM A LITTLE TOO NERVOUS TO BE A REBELLION INFORMANT. HOW'D THEY ROPE YOU IN?
MORALS.
GIVE ME A BREAK.
WHAT, AND YOU'RE NOT HERE FOR THE SAME REASON? THERE'S NO PRICE TAG THAT KEEPS A PERSON LOYAL WHEN THEY'RE STARING DOWN THE BARREL OF A STORMTROOPER'S RIFLE.
EXCEPT SOMEONE ***WASN'T*** LOYAL, OR YOU WOULDN'T HAVE BEEN SHOT AT.
THERE'S A MOLE. MORE THAN ONE. BUT THAT'S NOT WHO'S BEEN KILLING THE OTHER INFORMANTS.
ONE OF US TURNED. I'M SURE OF IT.
ONLY PRINCESS LEIA KNOWS OUR IDENTITIES AND LOCATIONS, BUT ALL OF US IN THE NETWORK HAD INFORMATION ON EACH OTHER. IT'S PART OF HOW WE COMMUNICATED, HOW WE CONTRIBUTED.
WE FUNNELED ALL THE SECRETS WE GATHERED THROUGH JUST ONE PERSON, WHO PUT THE PIECES TOGETHER TO CREATE THE MAP OF LEAKS INSIDE THE REBELLION.
WHICH MEANS THAT INDIVIDUALLY, NONE OF US CAN IDENTIFY THE MOLES. AND THE IDENITY OF OUR MASTER LIST-HOLDER IS THE GREATEST SECRET OF ALL.
THAT DOESN'T MAKE ONE OF YOU A KILLER.

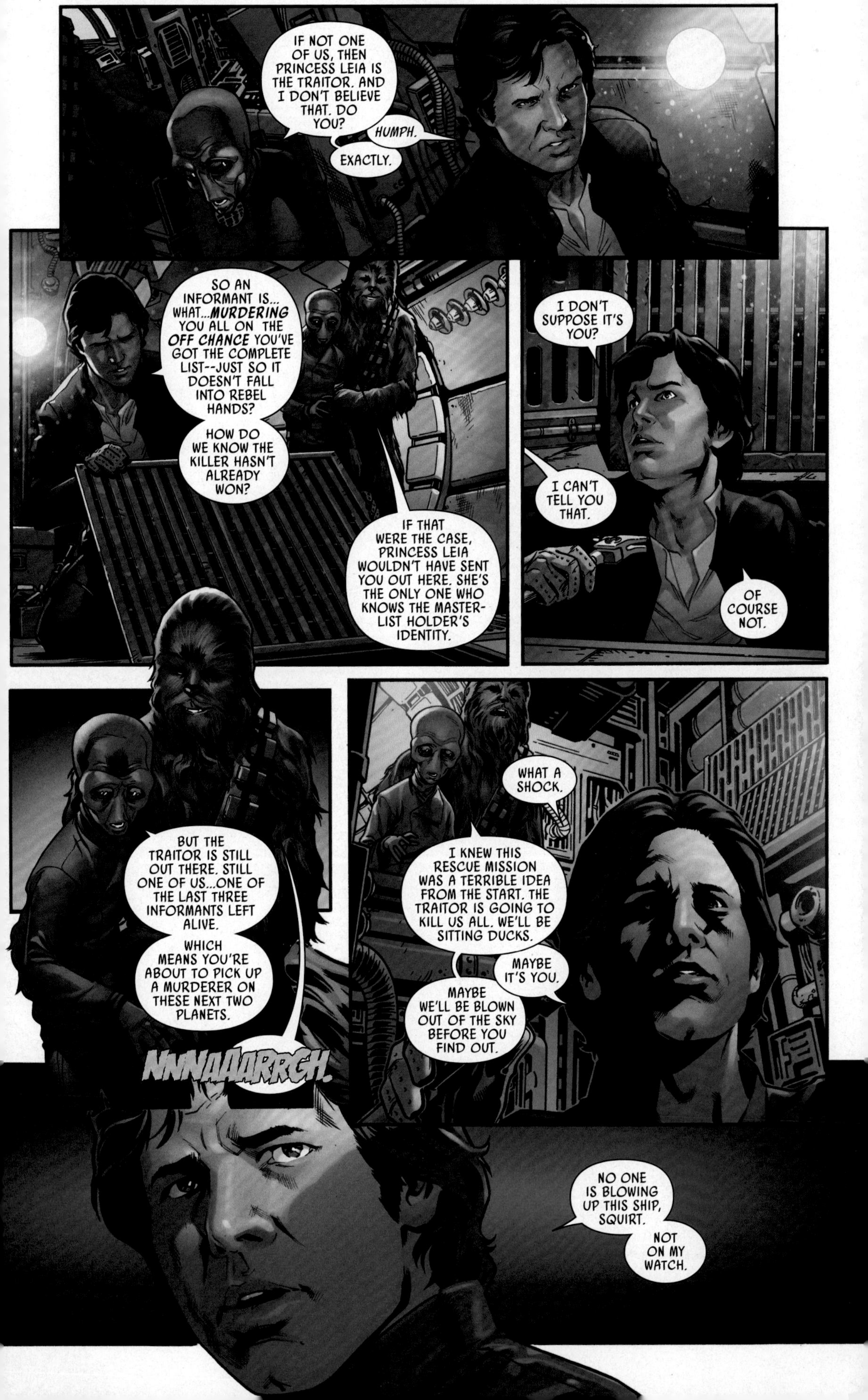
IF NOT ONE OF US, THEN PRINCESS LEIA IS THE TRAITOR. AND I DON'T BELIEVE THAT. DO YOU?
HUMPH.
EXACTLY.
SO AN INFORMANT IS... WHAT...MURDERING YOU ALL ON THE OFF CHANCE YOU'VE GOT THE COMPLETE LIST--JUST SO IT DOESN'T FALL INTO REBEL HANDS?
HOW DO WE KNOW THE KILLER HASN'T ALREADY WON?
IF THAT WERE THE CASE, PRINCESS LEIA WOULDN'T HAVE SENT YOU OUT HERE. SHE'S THE ONLY ONE WHO KNOWS THE MASTER-LIST HOLDER'S IDENTITY.
I DON'T SUPPOSE IT'S YOU?
I CAN'T TELL YOU THAT.
OF COURSE NOT.
BUT THE TRAITOR IS STILL OUT THERE. STILL ONE OF US...ONE OF THE LAST THREE INFORMANTS LEFT ALIVE.
WHICH MEANS YOU'RE ABOUT TO PICK UP A MURDERER ON THESE NEXT TWO PLANETS.
NNNAAARRRGH.
WHAT A SHOCK.
I KNEW THIS RESCUE MISSION WAS A TERRIBLE IDEA FROM THE START. THE TRAITOR IS GOING TO KILL US ALL. WE'LL BE SITTING DUCKS.
MAYBE IT'S YOU.
MAYBE WE'LL BE BLOWN OUT OF THE SKY BEFORE YOU FIND OUT.
NO ONE IS BLOWING UP THIS SHIP, SQUIRT.
NOT ON MY WATCH.

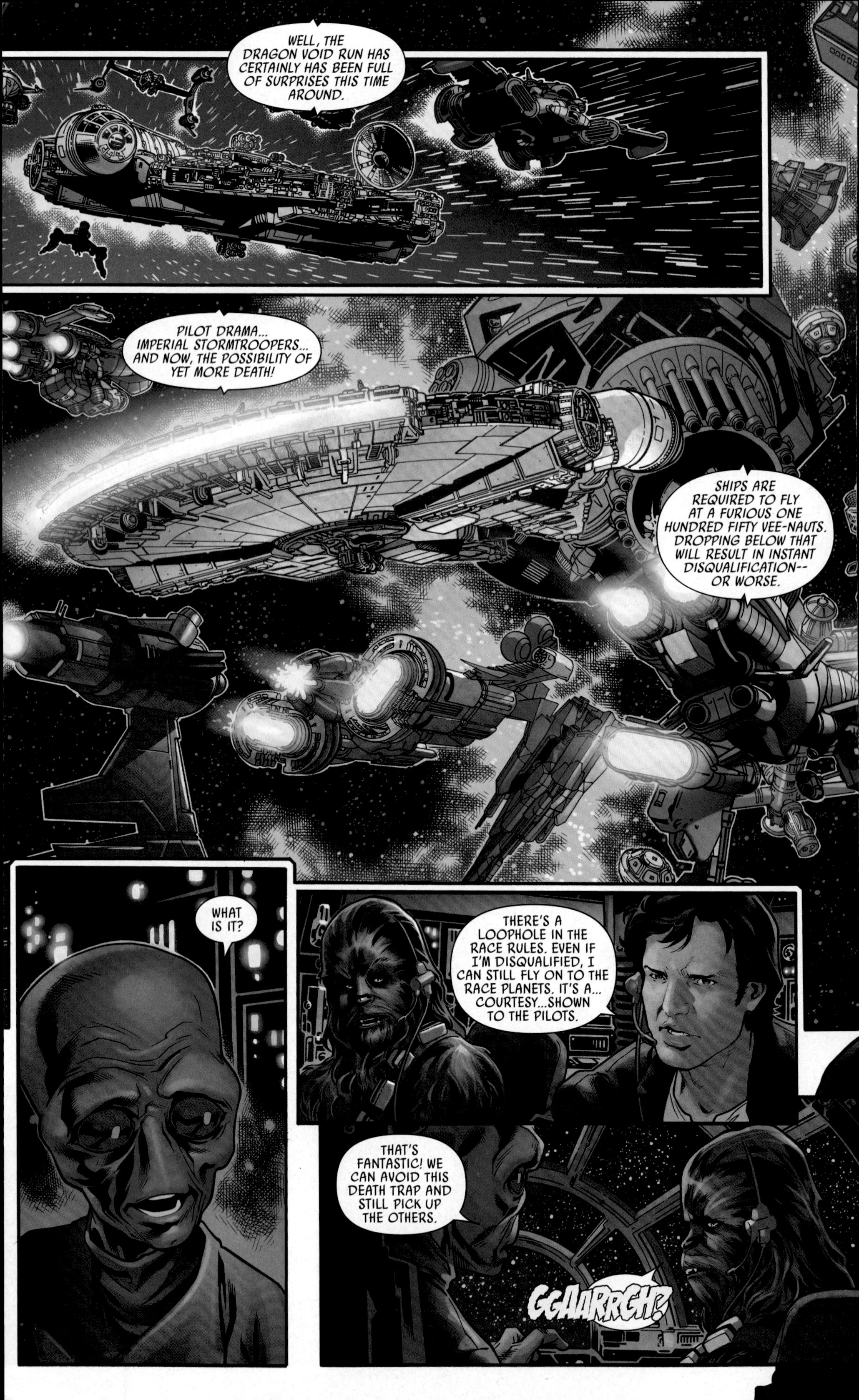
WELL, THE DRAGON VOID RUN HAS CERTAINLY HAS BEEN FULL OF SURPRISES THIS TIME AROUND.
PILOT DRAMA... IMPERIAL STORMTROOPERS... AND NOW, THE POSSIBILITY OF YET MORE DEATH!
SHIPS ARE REQUIRED TO FLY AT A FURIOUS ONE HUNDRED FIFTY VEE-NAUTS. DROPPING BELOW THAT WILL RESULT IN INSTANT DISQUALIFICATION-- OR WORSE.
WHAT IS IT?
THERE'S A LOOPHOLE IN THE RACE RULES. EVEN IF I'M DISQUALIFIED, I CAN STILL FLY ON TO THE RACE PLANETS. IT'S A... COURTESY...SHOWN TO THE PILOTS.
THAT'S FANTASTIC! WE CAN AVOID THIS DEATH TRAP AND STILL PICK UP THE OTHERS.
GGAARRGH?

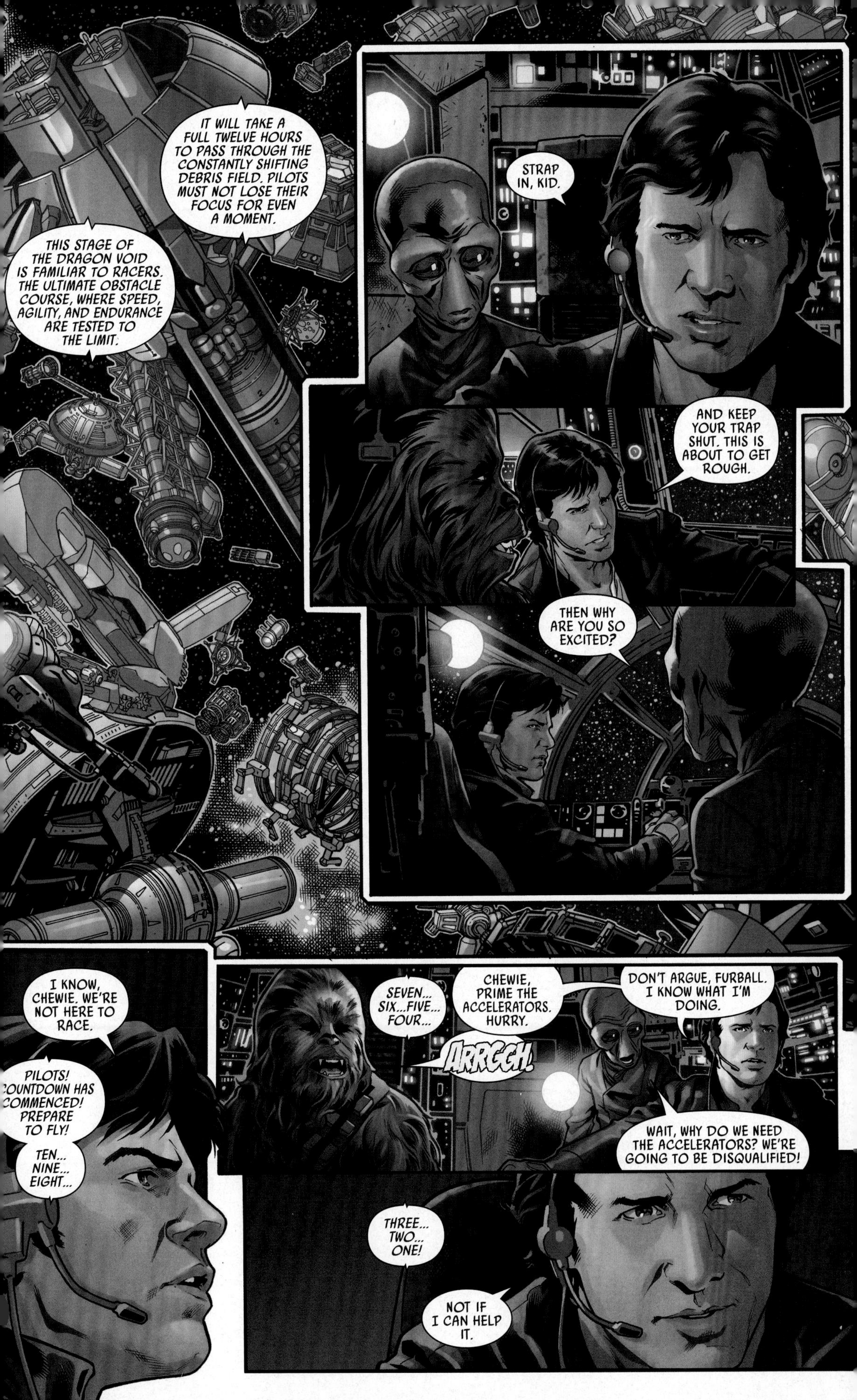
THIS STAGE OF THE DRAGON VOID IS FAMILIAR TO RACERS. THE ULTIMATE OBSTACLE COURSE, WHERE SPEED, AGILITY, AND ENDURANCE ARE TESTED TO THE LIMIT.
IT WILL TAKE A FULL TWELVE HOURS TO PASS THROUGH THE CONSTANTLY SHIFTING DEBRIS FIELD. PILOTS MUST NOT LOSE THEIR FOCUS FOR EVEN A MOMENT.
STRAP IN, KID.
AND KEEP YOUR TRAP SHUT. THIS IS ABOUT TO GET ROUGH.
THEN WHY ARE YOU SO EXCITED?
I KNOW, CHEWIE. WE'RE NOT HERE TO RACE.
PILOTS! COUNTDOWN HAS COMMENCED! PREPARE TO FLY!
TEN... NINE... EIGHT...
SEVEN... SIX...FIVE... FOUR...
ARRGGH!
CHEWIE, PRIME THE ACCELERATORS. HURRY.
DON'T ARGUE, FURBALL. I KNOW WHAT I'M DOING.
WAIT, WHY DO WE NEED THE ACCELERATORS? WE'RE GOING TO BE DISQUALIFIED!
THREE... TWO... ONE!
NOT IF I CAN HELP IT.

AND THEY'RE OFF!

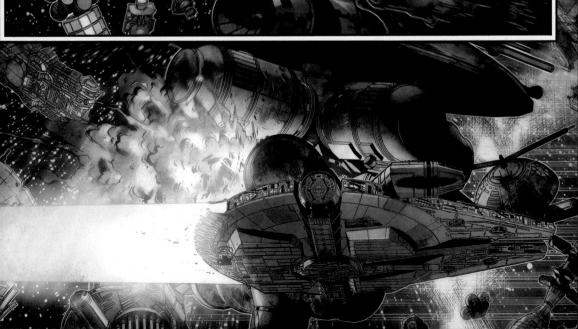

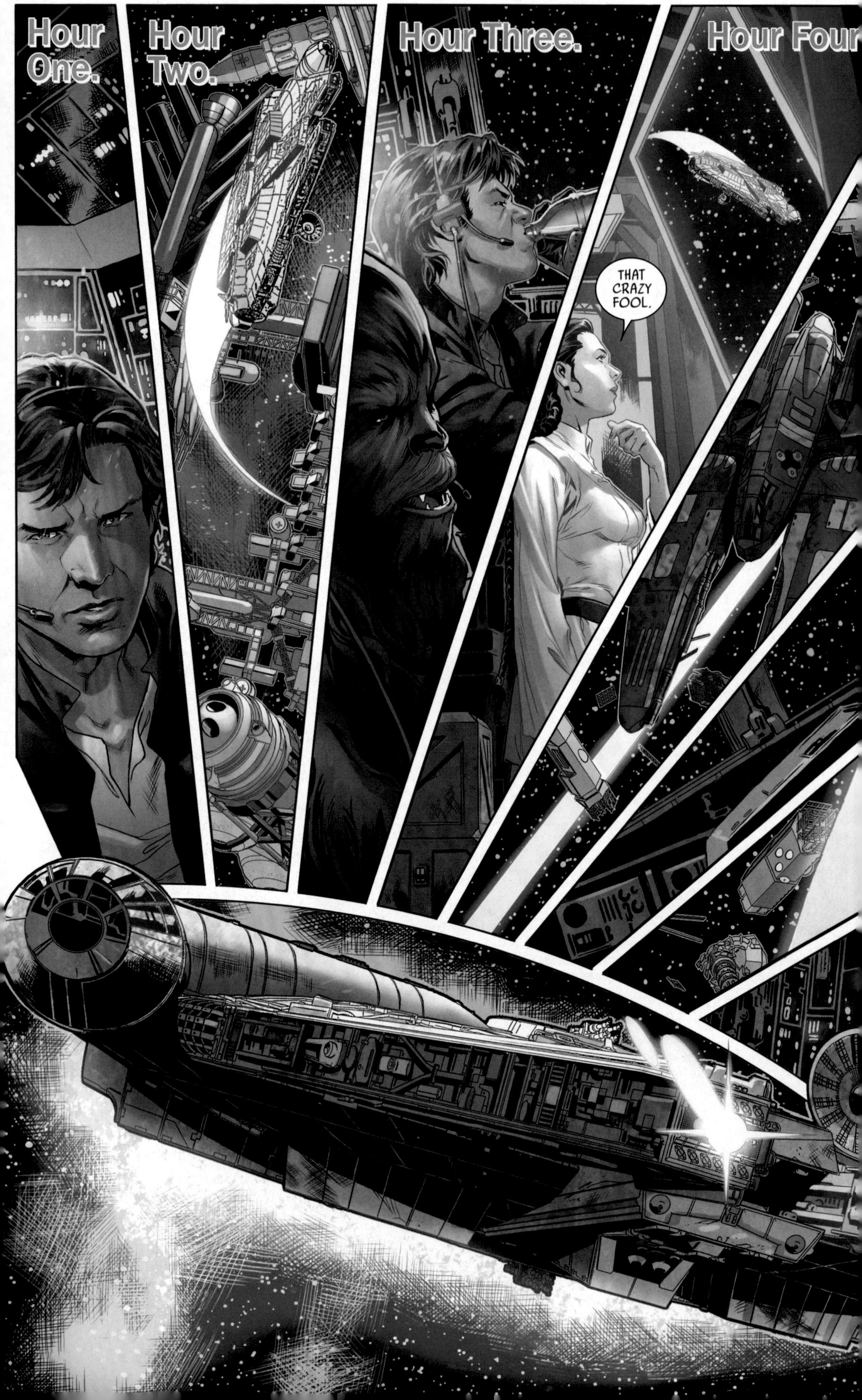

Hour One.
Hour Two.
Hour Three.
THAT CRAZY FOOL.
Hour Four

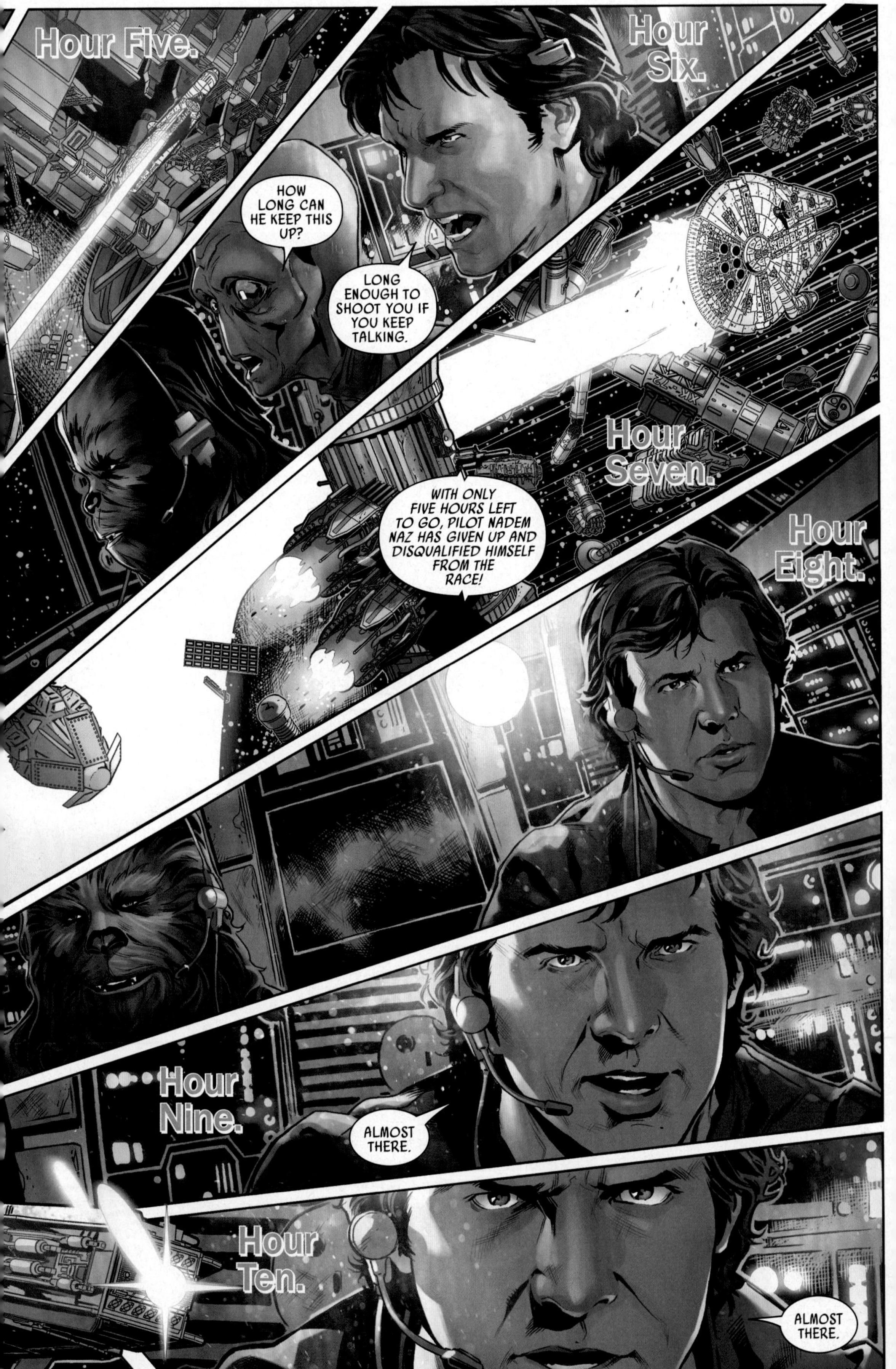
Hour Five.
Hour Six.
HOW LONG CAN HE KEEP THIS UP?
LONG ENOUGH TO SHOOT YOU IF YOU KEEP TALKING.
Hour Seven.
WITH ONLY FIVE HOURS LEFT TO GO, PILOT NADEM NAZ HAS GIVEN UP AND DISQUALIFIED HIMSELF FROM THE RACE!
Hour Eight.
Hour Nine.
ALMOST THERE.
Hour Ten.
ALMOST THERE.

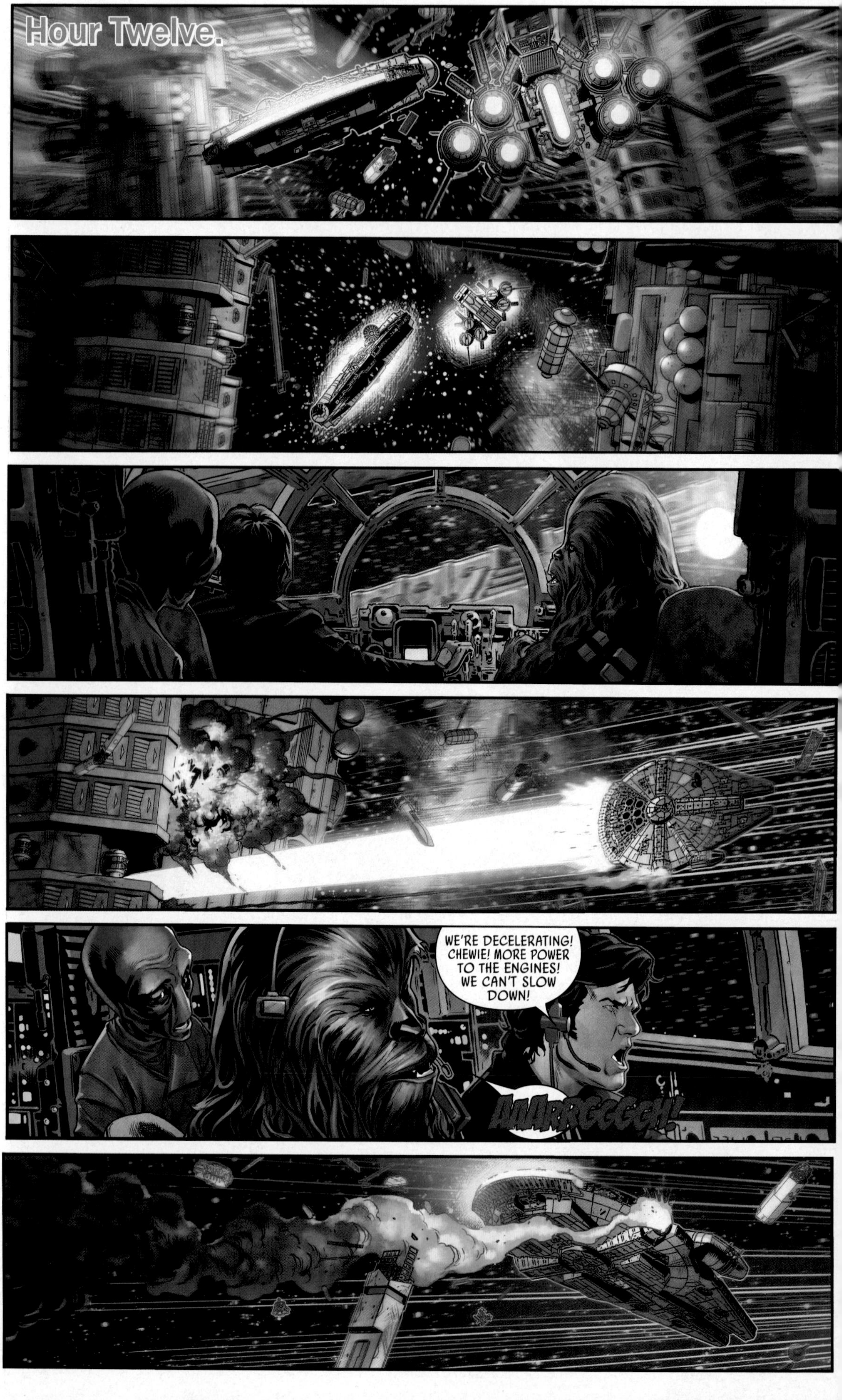

Hour Twelve.
WE'RE DECELERATING! CHEWIE! MORE POWER TO THE ENGINES! WE CAN'T SLOW DOWN!
AAARRGGGGH!

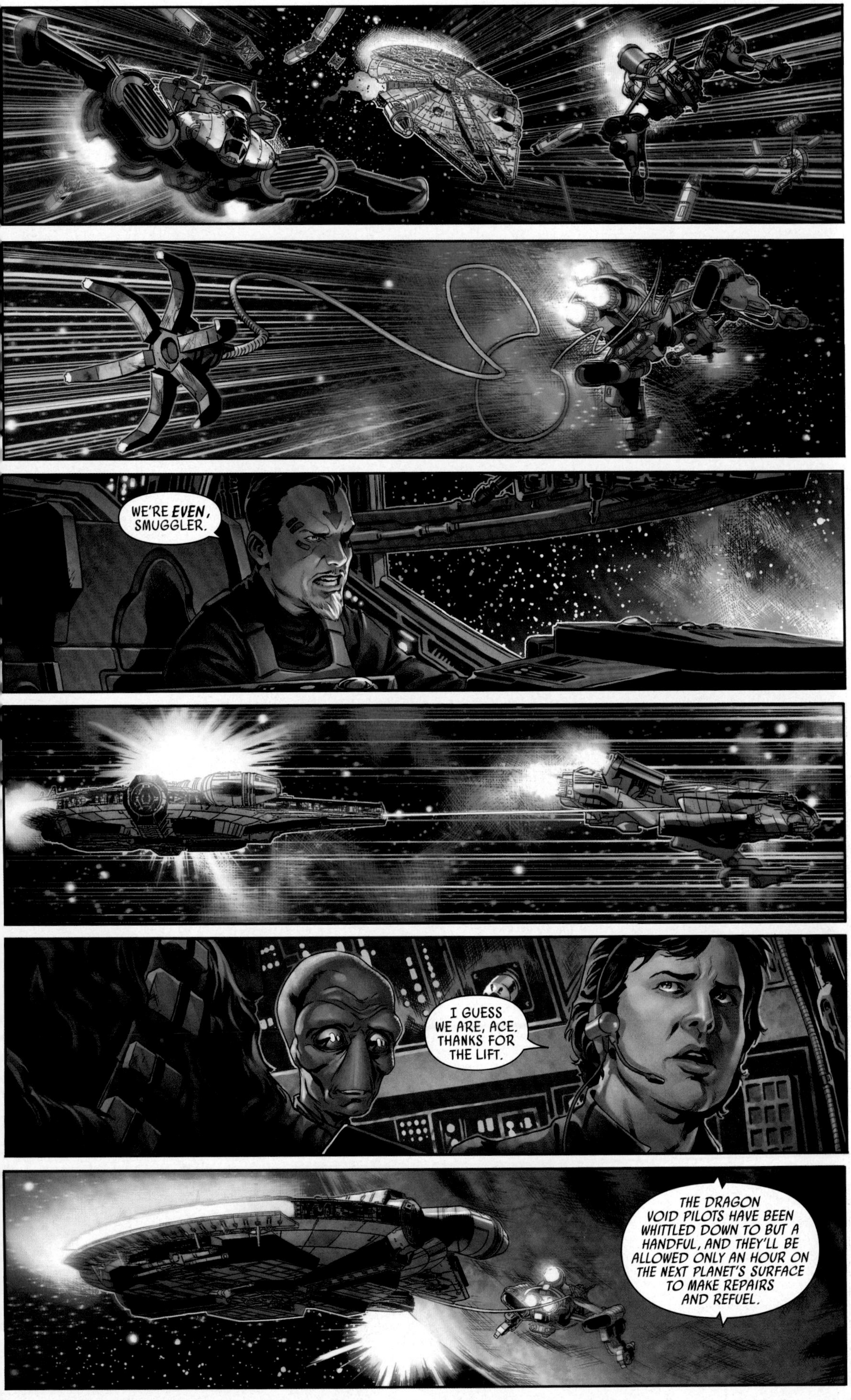
WE'RE EVEN, SMUGGLER.
I GUESS WE ARE, ACE. THANKS FOR THE LIFT.
THE DRAGON VOID PILOTS HAVE BEEN WHITTLED DOWN TO BUT A HANDFUL, AND THEY'LL BE ALLOWED ONLY AN HOUR ON THE NEXT PLANET'S SURFACE TO MAKE REPAIRS AND REFUEL.

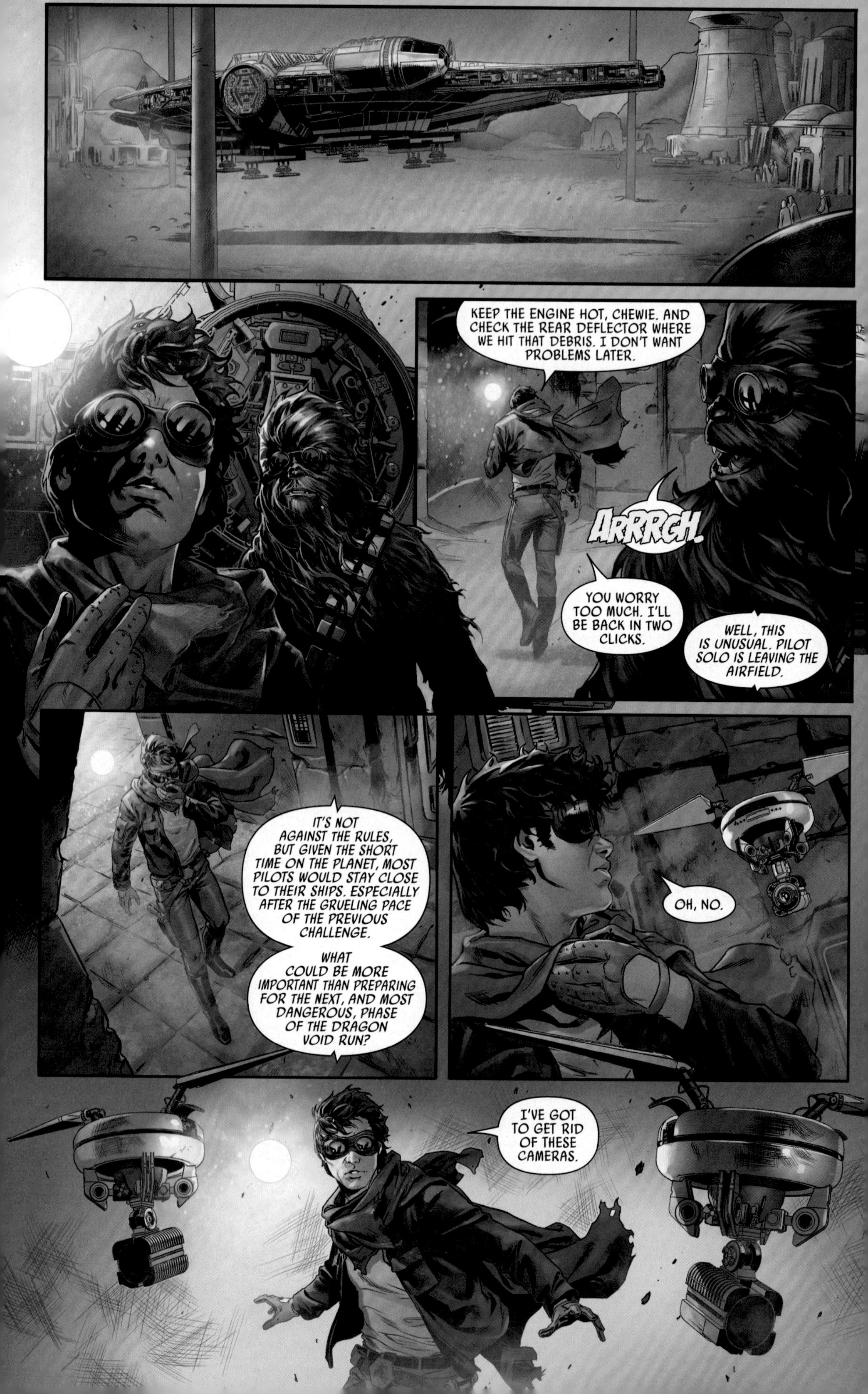
KEEP THE ENGINE HOT, CHEWIE. AND CHECK THE REAR DEFLECTOR WHERE WE HIT THAT DEBRIS. I DON'T WANT PROBLEMS LATER.
ARRRGH.
YOU WORRY TOO MUCH. I'LL BE BACK IN TWO CLICKS.
WELL, THIS IS UNUSUAL. PILOT SOLO IS LEAVING THE AIRFIELD.
IT'S NOT AGAINST THE RULES, BUT GIVEN THE SHORT TIME ON THE PLANET, MOST PILOTS WOULD STAY CLOSE TO THEIR SHIPS. ESPECIALLY AFTER THE GRUELING PACE OF THE PREVIOUS CHALLENGE.
WHAT COULD BE MORE IMPORTANT THAN PREPARING FOR THE NEXT, AND MOST DANGEROUS, PHASE OF THE DRAGON VOID RUN?
OH, NO.
I'VE GOT TO GET RID OF THESE CAMERAS.

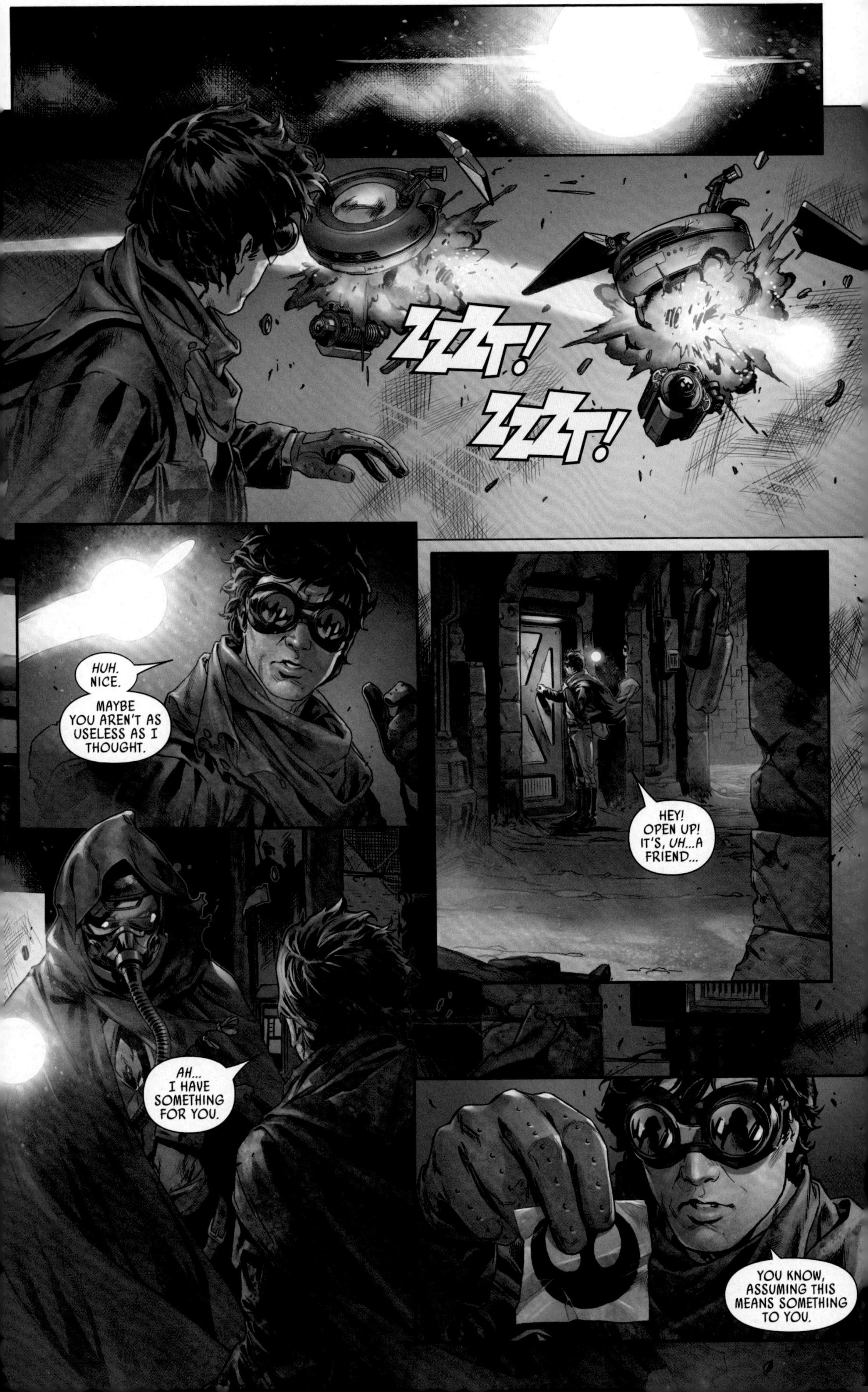
ZZZT!
ZZZT!
HUH. NICE.
MAYBE YOU AREN'T AS USELESS AS I THOUGHT.
HEY! OPEN UP! IT'S, UH...A FRIEND...
AH... I HAVE SOMETHING FOR YOU.
YOU KNOW, ASSUMING THIS MEANS SOMETHING TO YOU.

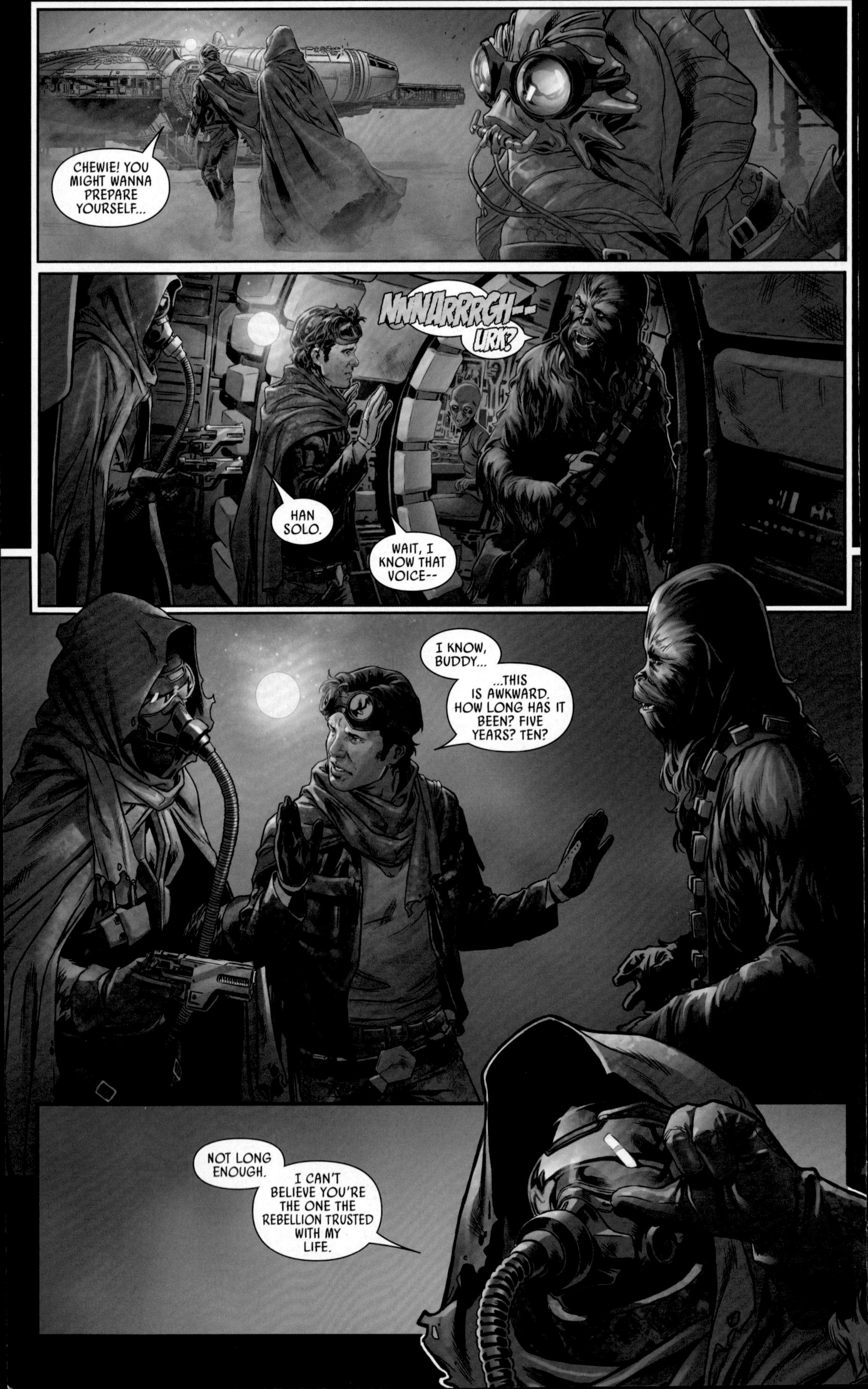
CHEWIE! YOU MIGHT WANNA PREPARE YOURSELF...
NNNARRRGH--
URK?
HAN SOLO.
WAIT, I KNOW THAT VOICE--
I KNOW, BUDDY...
...THIS IS AWKWARD. HOW LONG HAS IT BEEN? FIVE YEARS? TEN?
NOT LONG ENOUGH.
I CAN'T BELIEVE YOU'RE THE ONE THE REBELLION TRUSTED WITH MY LIFE.

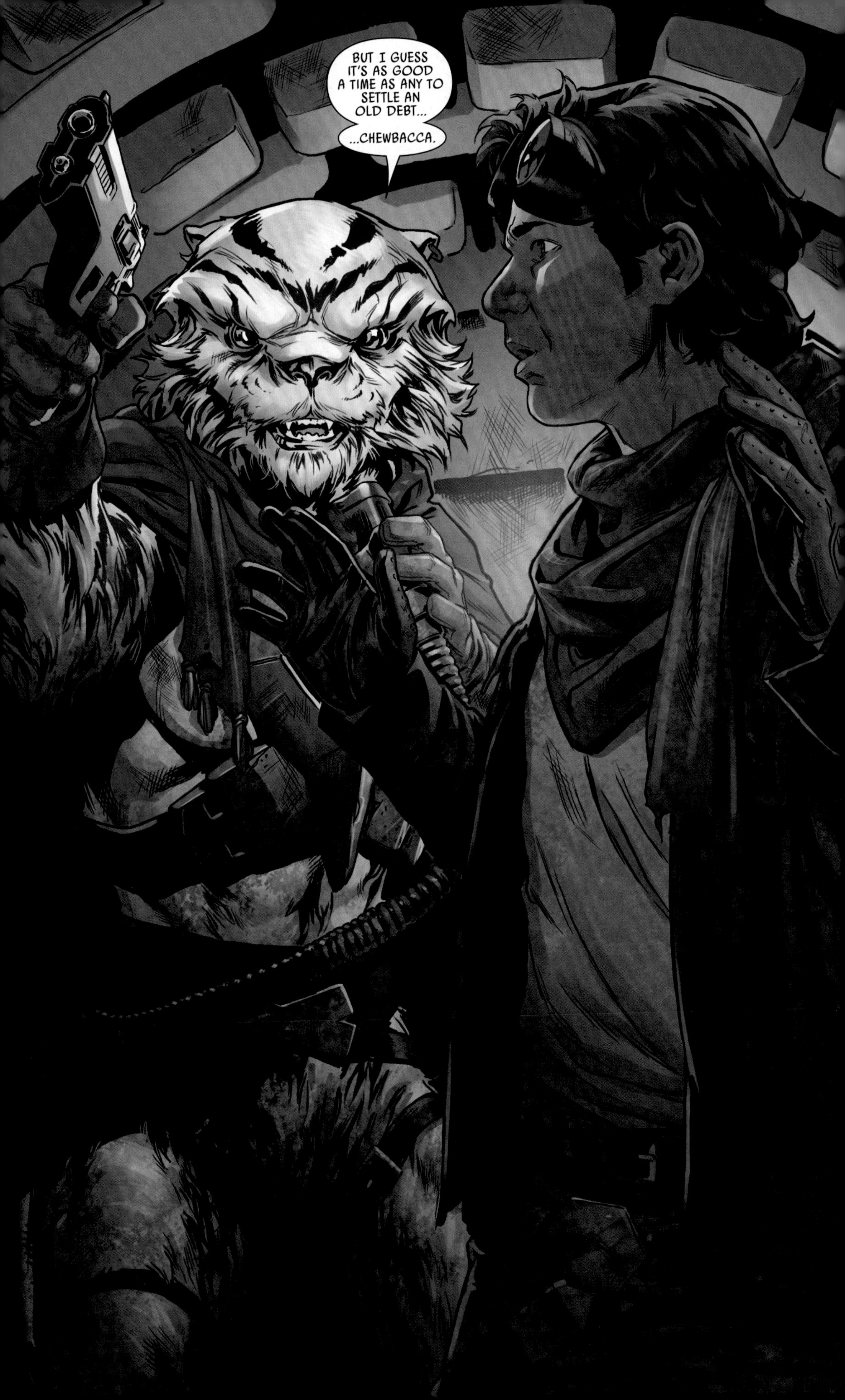
BUT I GUESS IT'S AS GOOD A TIME AS ANY TO SETTLE AN OLD DEBT...
...CHEWBACCA.

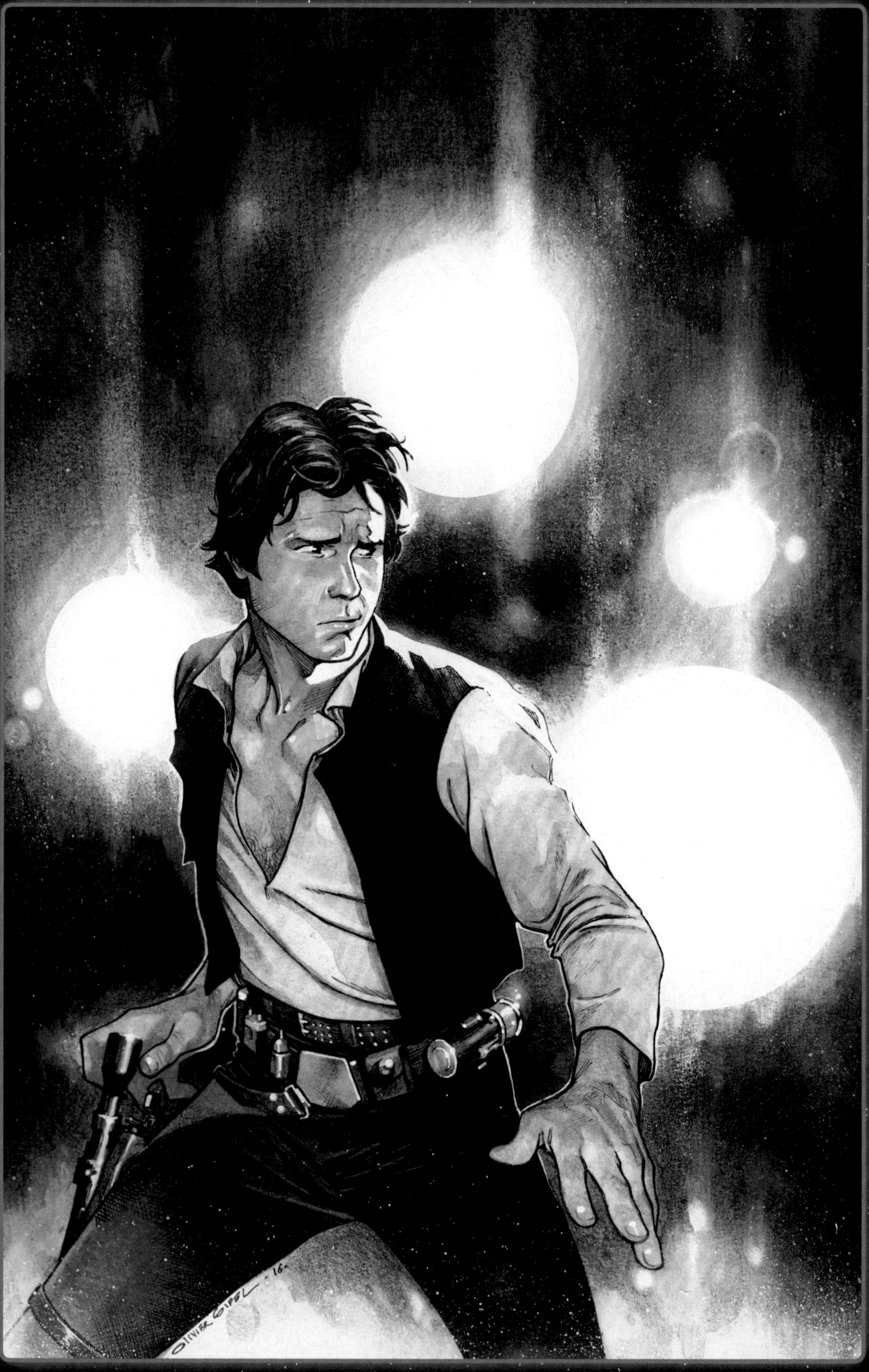

4

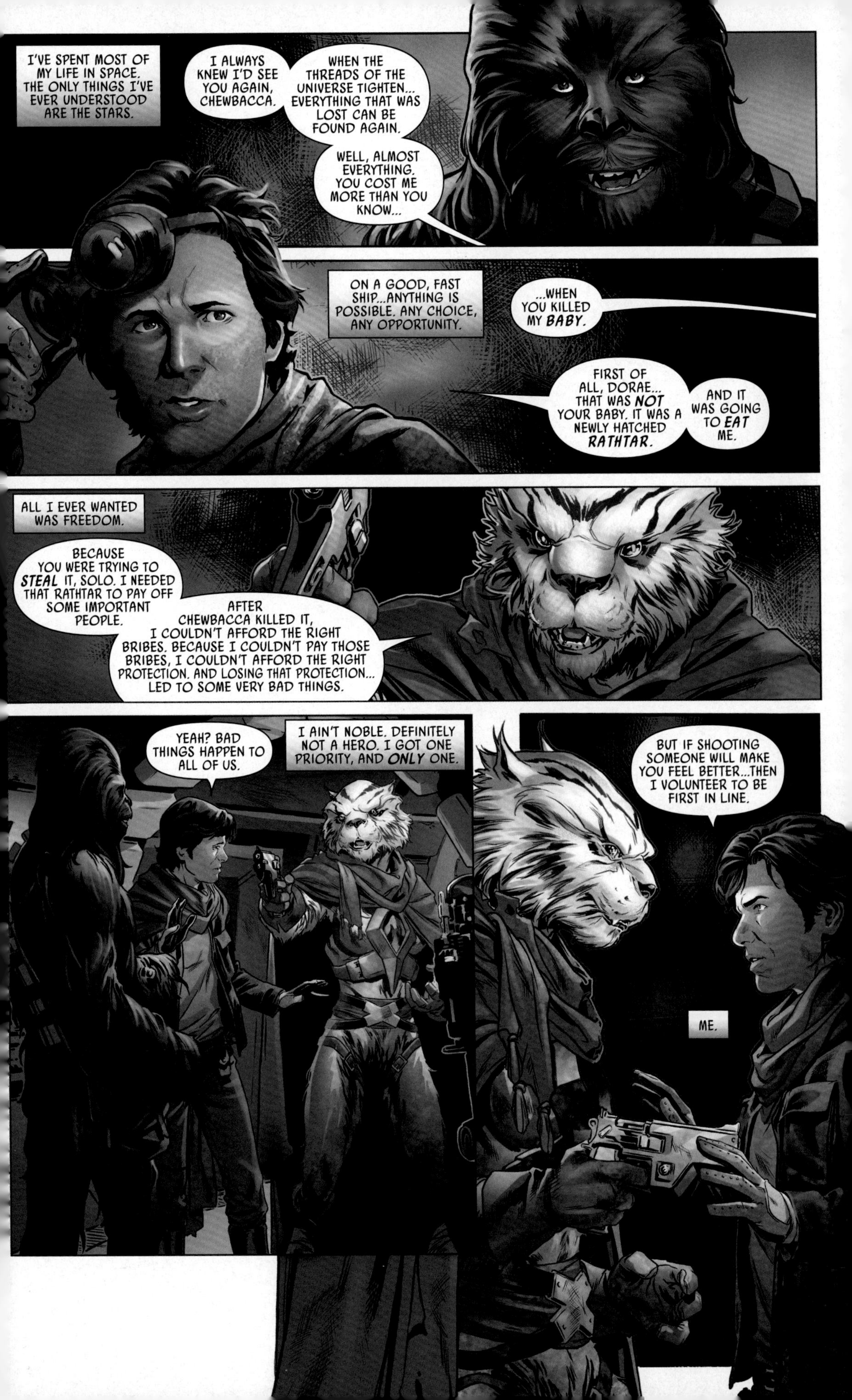

I'VE SPENT MOST OF MY LIFE IN SPACE. THE ONLY THINGS I'VE EVER UNDERSTOOD ARE THE STARS.
I ALWAYS KNEW I'D SEE YOU AGAIN, CHEWBACCA.
WHEN THE THREADS OF THE UNIVERSE TIGHTEN... EVERYTHING THAT WAS LOST CAN BE FOUND AGAIN.
WELL, ALMOST EVERYTHING. YOU COST ME MORE THAN YOU KNOW...
ON A GOOD, FAST SHIP...ANYTHING IS POSSIBLE. ANY CHOICE, ANY OPPORTUNITY.
...WHEN YOU KILLED MY BABY.
FIRST OF ALL, DORAE... THAT WAS NOT YOUR BABY. IT WAS A NEWLY HATCHED RATHTAR.
AND IT WAS GOING TO EAT ME.
ALL I EVER WANTED WAS FREEDOM.
BECAUSE YOU WERE TRYING TO STEAL IT, SOLO. I NEEDED THAT RATHTAR TO PAY OFF SOME IMPORTANT PEOPLE.
AFTER CHEWBACCA KILLED IT, I COULDN'T AFFORD THE RIGHT BRIBES. BECAUSE I COULDN'T PAY THOSE BRIBES, I COULDN'T AFFORD THE RIGHT PROTECTION. AND LOSING THAT PROTECTION... LED TO SOME VERY BAD THINGS.
YEAH? BAD THINGS HAPPEN TO ALL OF US.
I AIN'T NOBLE. DEFINITELY NOT A HERO. I GOT ONE PRIORITY, AND ONLY ONE.
BUT IF SHOOTING SOMEONE WILL MAKE YOU FEEL BETTER...THEN I VOLUNTEER TO BE FIRST IN LINE.
ME.

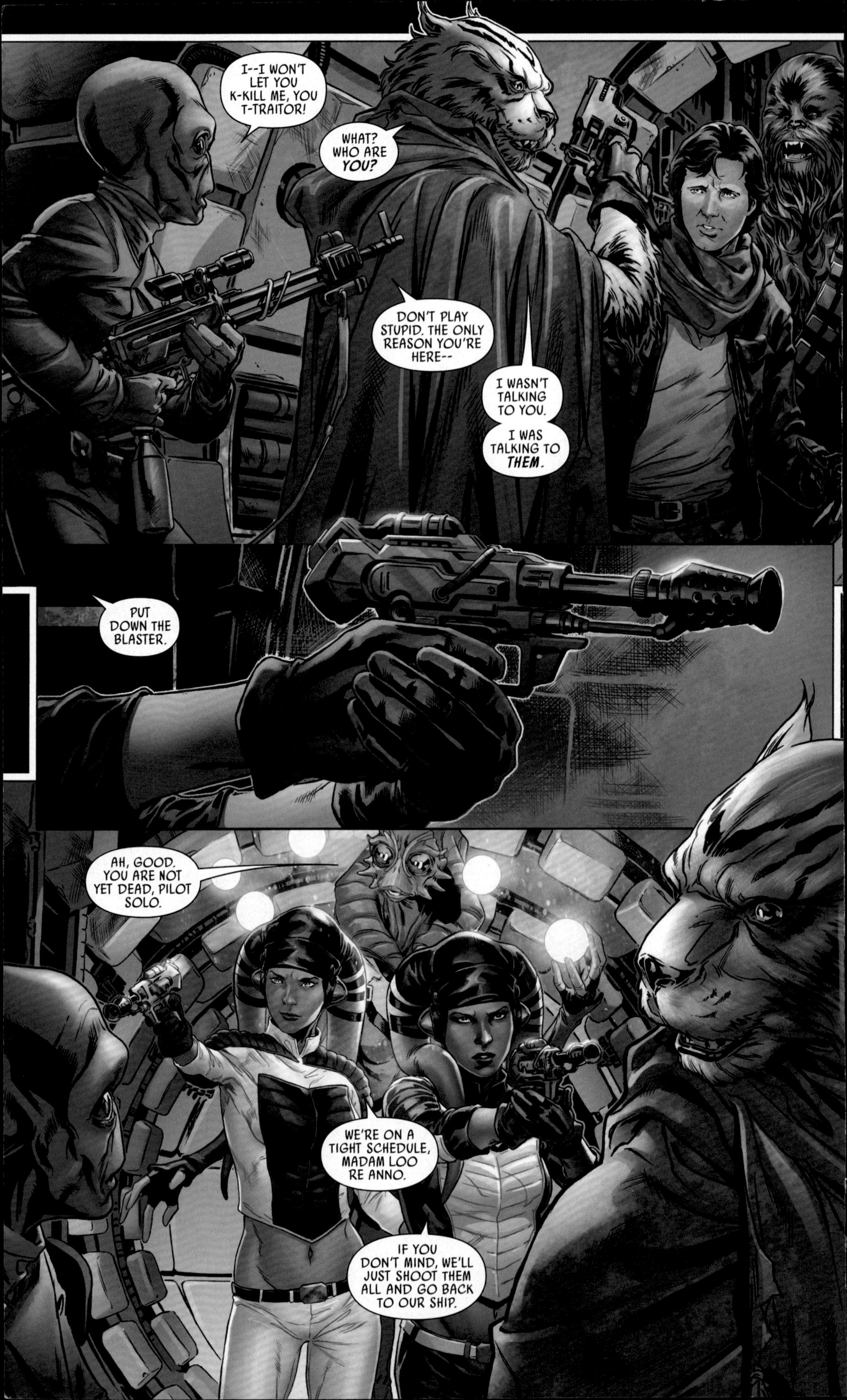
I--I WON'T LET YOU K-KILL ME, YOU T-TRAITOR!
WHAT? WHO ARE YOU?
DON'T PLAY STUPID. THE ONLY REASON YOU'RE HERE--
I WASN'T TALKING TO YOU.
I WAS TALKING TO THEM.
PUT DOWN THE BLASTER.
AH, GOOD. YOU ARE NOT YET DEAD, PILOT SOLO.
WE'RE ON A TIGHT SCHEDULE, MADAM LOO RE ANNO.
IF YOU DON'T MIND, WE'LL JUST SHOOT THEM ALL AND GO BACK TO OUR SHIP.

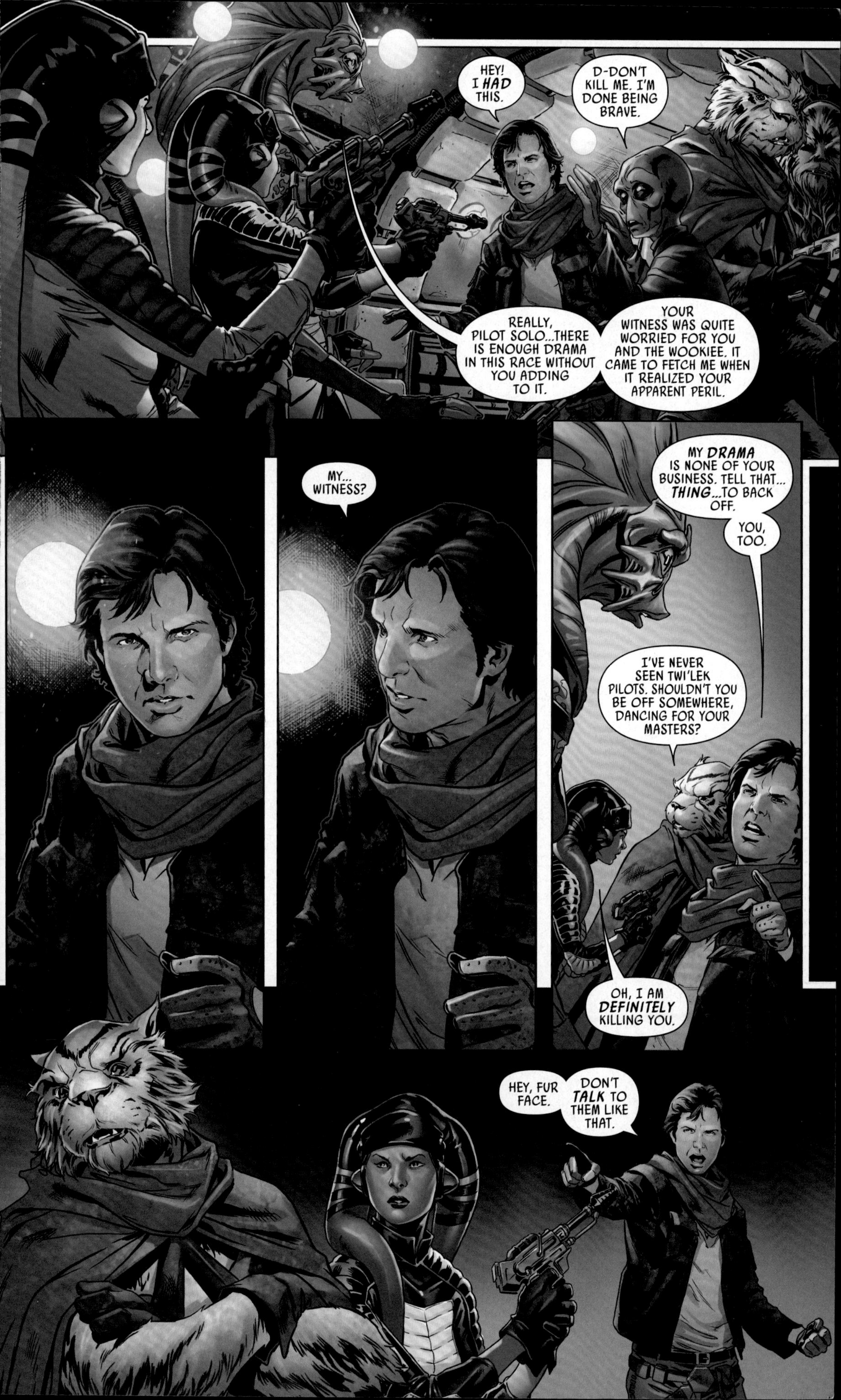
HEY! I HAD THIS.
D-DON'T KILL ME. I'M DONE BEING BRAVE.
REALLY, PILOT SOLO...THERE IS ENOUGH DRAMA IN THIS RACE WITHOUT YOU ADDING TO IT.
YOUR WITNESS WAS QUITE WORRIED FOR YOU AND THE WOOKIEE. IT CAME TO FETCH ME WHEN IT REALIZED YOUR APPARENT PERIL.
MY... WITNESS?
MY DRAMA IS NONE OF YOUR BUSINESS. TELL THAT... THING...TO BACK OFF.
YOU, TOO.
I'VE NEVER SEEN TWI'LEK PILOTS. SHOULDN'T YOU BE OFF SOMEWHERE, DANCING FOR YOUR MASTERS?
OH, I AM DEFINITELY KILLING YOU.
HEY, FUR FACE.
DON'T TALK TO THEM LIKE THAT.

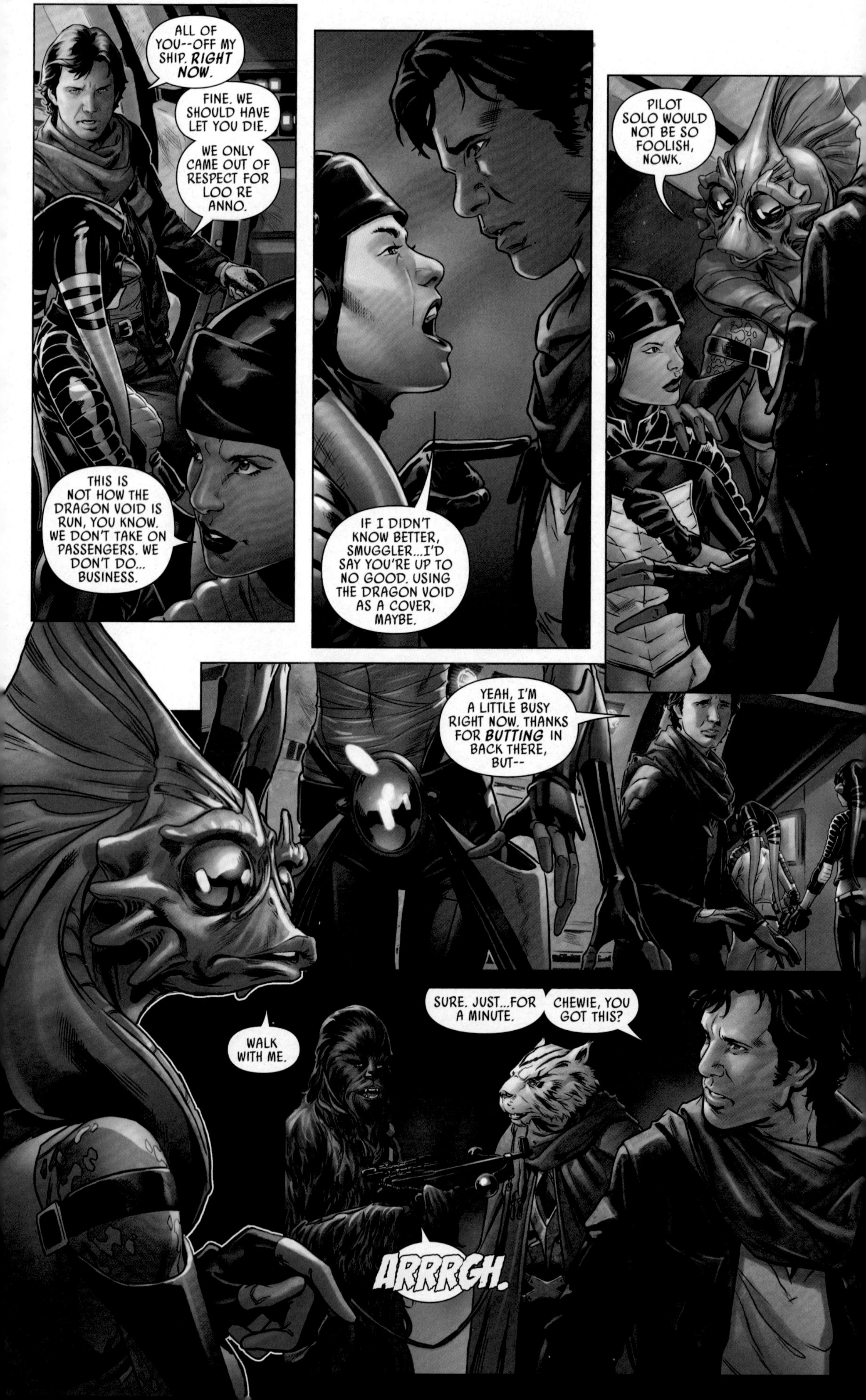
ALL OF YOU--OFF MY SHIP. RIGHT NOW.
FINE. WE SHOULD HAVE LET YOU DIE.
WE ONLY CAME OUT OF RESPECT FOR LOO RE ANNO.
THIS IS NOT HOW THE DRAGON VOID IS RUN, YOU KNOW. WE DON'T TAKE ON PASSENGERS. WE DON'T DO... BUSINESS.
IF I DIDN'T KNOW BETTER, SMUGGLER...I'D SAY YOU'RE UP TO NO GOOD. USING THE DRAGON VOID AS A COVER, MAYBE.
PILOT SOLO WOULD NOT BE SO FOOLISH, NOWK.
YEAH, I'M A LITTLE BUSY RIGHT NOW. THANKS FOR BUTTING IN BACK THERE, BUT--
WALK WITH ME.
SURE. JUST...FOR A MINUTE.
CHEWIE, YOU GOT THIS?
ARRRGH.

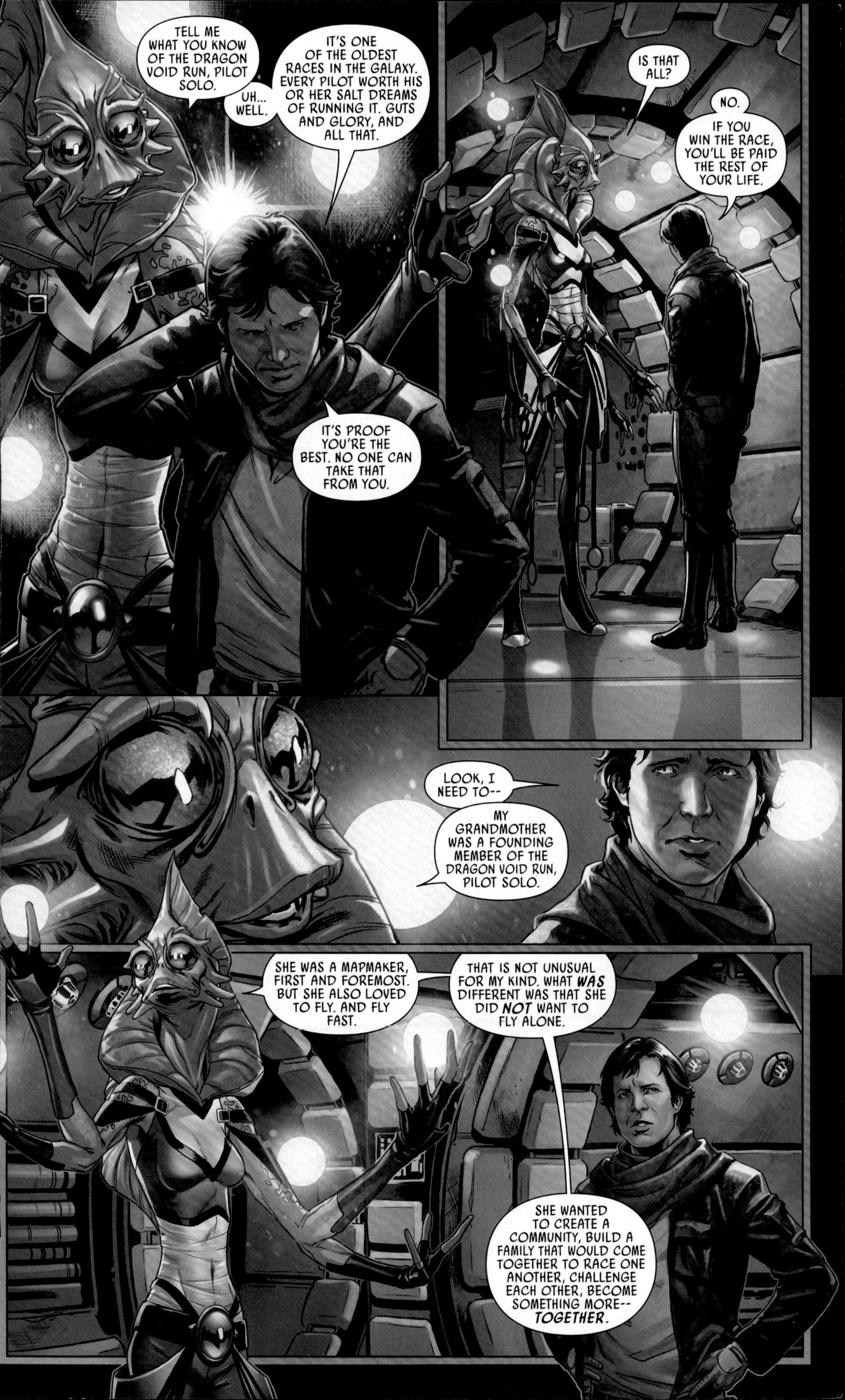
TELL ME WHAT YOU KNOW OF THE DRAGON VOID RUN, PILOT SOLO.
UH... WELL.
IT'S ONE OF THE OLDEST RACES IN THE GALAXY. EVERY PILOT WORTH HIS OR HER SALT DREAMS OF RUNNING IT. GUTS AND GLORY, AND ALL THAT.
IT'S PROOF YOU'RE THE BEST. NO ONE CAN TAKE THAT FROM YOU.
IS THAT ALL?
NO.
IF YOU WIN THE RACE, YOU'LL BE PAID THE REST OF YOUR LIFE.
LOOK, I NEED TO--
MY GRANDMOTHER WAS A FOUNDING MEMBER OF THE DRAGON VOID RUN, PILOT SOLO.
SHE WAS A MAPMAKER, FIRST AND FOREMOST. BUT SHE ALSO LOVED TO FLY. AND FLY FAST.
THAT IS NOT UNUSUAL FOR MY KIND. WHAT ***WAS*** DIFFERENT WAS THAT SHE DID ***NOT*** WANT TO FLY ALONE.
SHE WANTED TO CREATE A COMMUNITY, BUILD A FAMILY THAT WOULD COME TOGETHER TO RACE ONE ANOTHER, CHALLENGE EACH OTHER, BECOME SOMETHING MORE-- ***TOGETHER.***

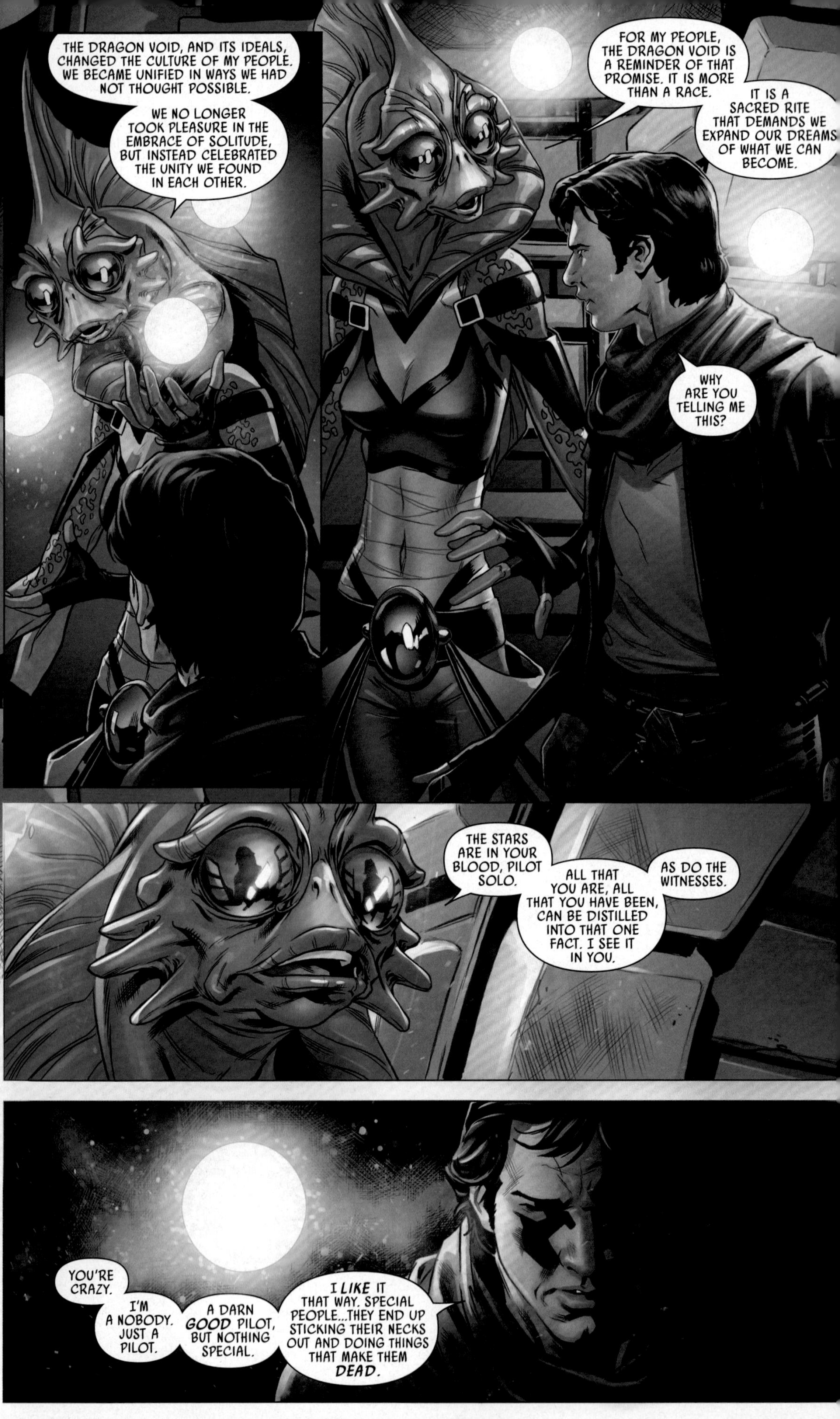
THE DRAGON VOID, AND ITS IDEALS, CHANGED THE CULTURE OF MY PEOPLE. WE BECAME UNIFIED IN WAYS WE HAD NOT THOUGHT POSSIBLE.
WE NO LONGER TOOK PLEASURE IN THE EMBRACE OF SOLITUDE, BUT INSTEAD CELEBRATED THE UNITY WE FOUND IN EACH OTHER.
FOR MY PEOPLE, THE DRAGON VOID IS A REMINDER OF THAT PROMISE. IT IS MORE THAN A RACE.
IT IS A SACRED RITE THAT DEMANDS WE EXPAND OUR DREAMS OF WHAT WE CAN BECOME.
WHY ARE YOU TELLING ME THIS?
THE STARS ARE IN YOUR BLOOD, PILOT SOLO.
ALL THAT YOU ARE, ALL THAT YOU HAVE BEEN, CAN BE DISTILLED INTO THAT ONE FACT. I SEE IT IN YOU.
AS DO THE WITNESSES.
YOU'RE CRAZY.
I'M A NOBODY. JUST A PILOT.
A DARN *GOOD* PILOT, BUT NOTHING SPECIAL.
I *LIKE* IT THAT WAY. SPECIAL PEOPLE...THEY END UP STICKING THEIR NECKS OUT AND DOING THINGS THAT MAKE THEM *DEAD*.

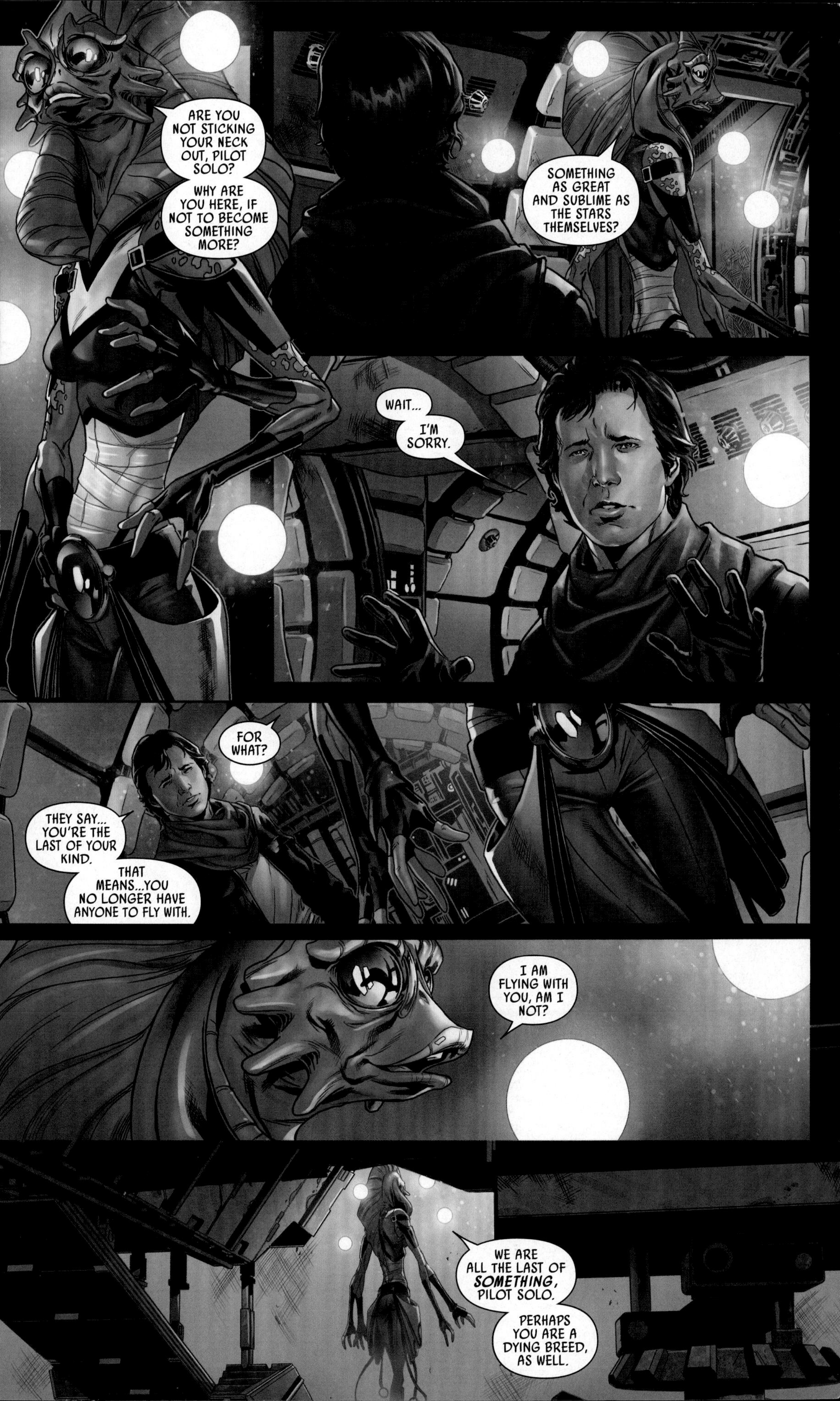
ARE YOU NOT STICKING YOUR NECK OUT, PILOT SOLO?
WHY ARE YOU HERE, IF NOT TO BECOME SOMETHING MORE?
SOMETHING AS GREAT AND SUBLIME AS THE STARS THEMSELVES?
WAIT...
I'M SORRY.
FOR WHAT?
THEY SAY... YOU'RE THE LAST OF YOUR KIND.
THAT MEANS...YOU NO LONGER HAVE ANYONE TO FLY WITH.
I AM FLYING WITH YOU, AM I NOT?
WE ARE ALL THE LAST OF *SOMETHING*, PILOT SOLO.
PERHAPS YOU ARE A DYING BREED, AS WELL.

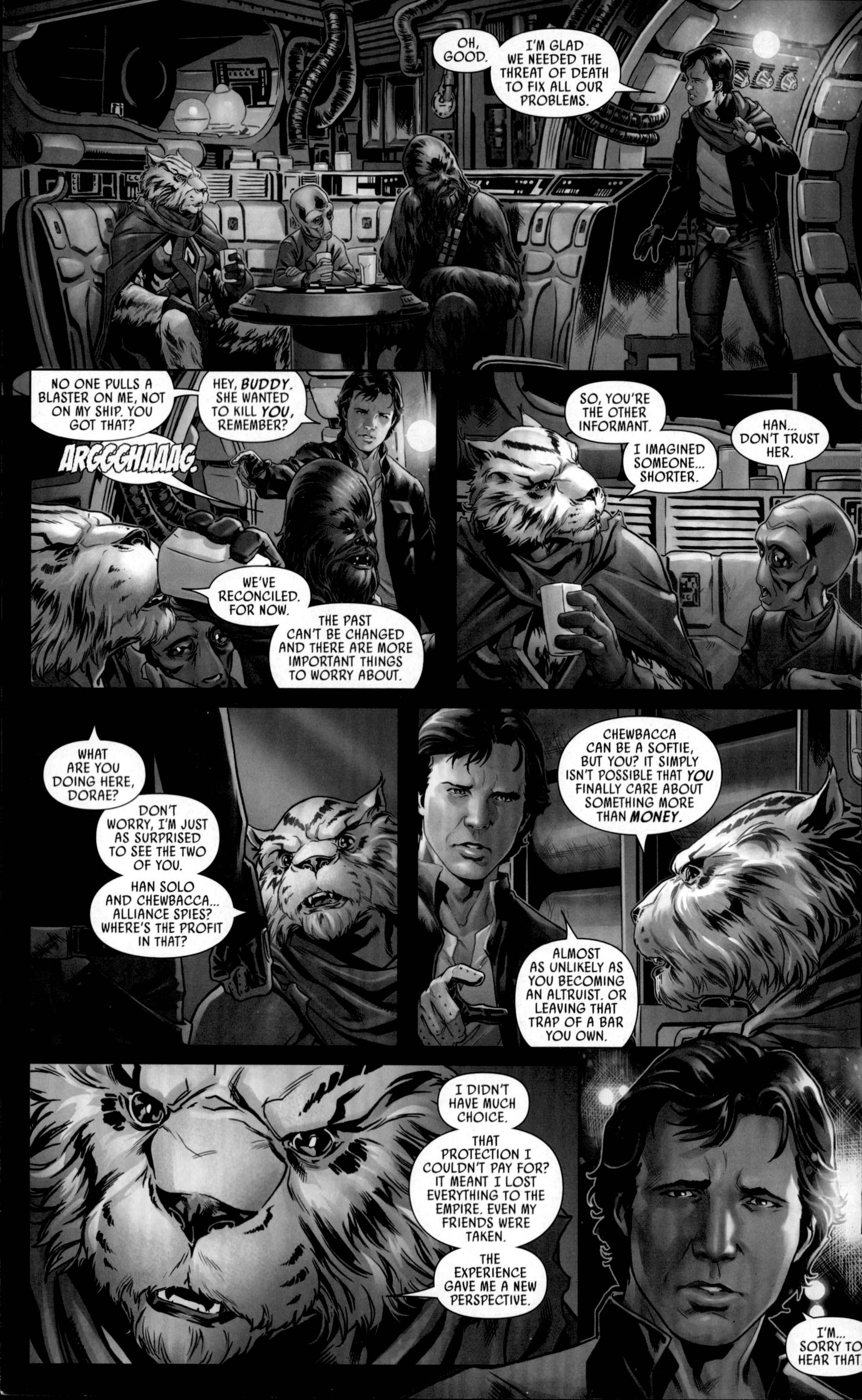
OH, GOOD.
I'M GLAD WE NEEDED THE THREAT OF DEATH TO FIX ALL OUR PROBLEMS.
NO ONE PULLS A BLASTER ON ME, NOT ON MY SHIP. YOU GOT THAT?
HEY, BUDDY. SHE WANTED TO KILL YOU, REMEMBER?
ARGGGHAAAG.
WE'VE RECONCILED. FOR NOW.
THE PAST CAN'T BE CHANGED AND THERE ARE MORE IMPORTANT THINGS TO WORRY ABOUT.
SO, YOU'RE THE OTHER INFORMANT.
I IMAGINED SOMEONE... SHORTER.
HAN... DON'T TRUST HER.
WHAT ARE YOU DOING HERE, DORAE?
DON'T WORRY, I'M JUST AS SURPRISED TO SEE THE TWO OF YOU.
HAN SOLO AND CHEWBACCA... ALLIANCE SPIES? WHERE'S THE PROFIT IN THAT?
CHEWBACCA CAN BE A SOFTIE, BUT YOU? IT SIMPLY ISN'T POSSIBLE THAT YOU FINALLY CARE ABOUT SOMETHING MORE THAN MONEY.
ALMOST AS UNLIKELY AS YOU BECOMING AN ALTRUIST. OR LEAVING THAT TRAP OF A BAR YOU OWN.
I DIDN'T HAVE MUCH CHOICE.
THAT PROTECTION I COULDN'T PAY FOR? IT MEANT I LOST EVERYTHING TO THE EMPIRE. EVEN MY FRIENDS WERE TAKEN.
THE EXPERIENCE GAVE ME A NEW PERSPECTIVE.
I'M... SORRY TO HEAR THAT

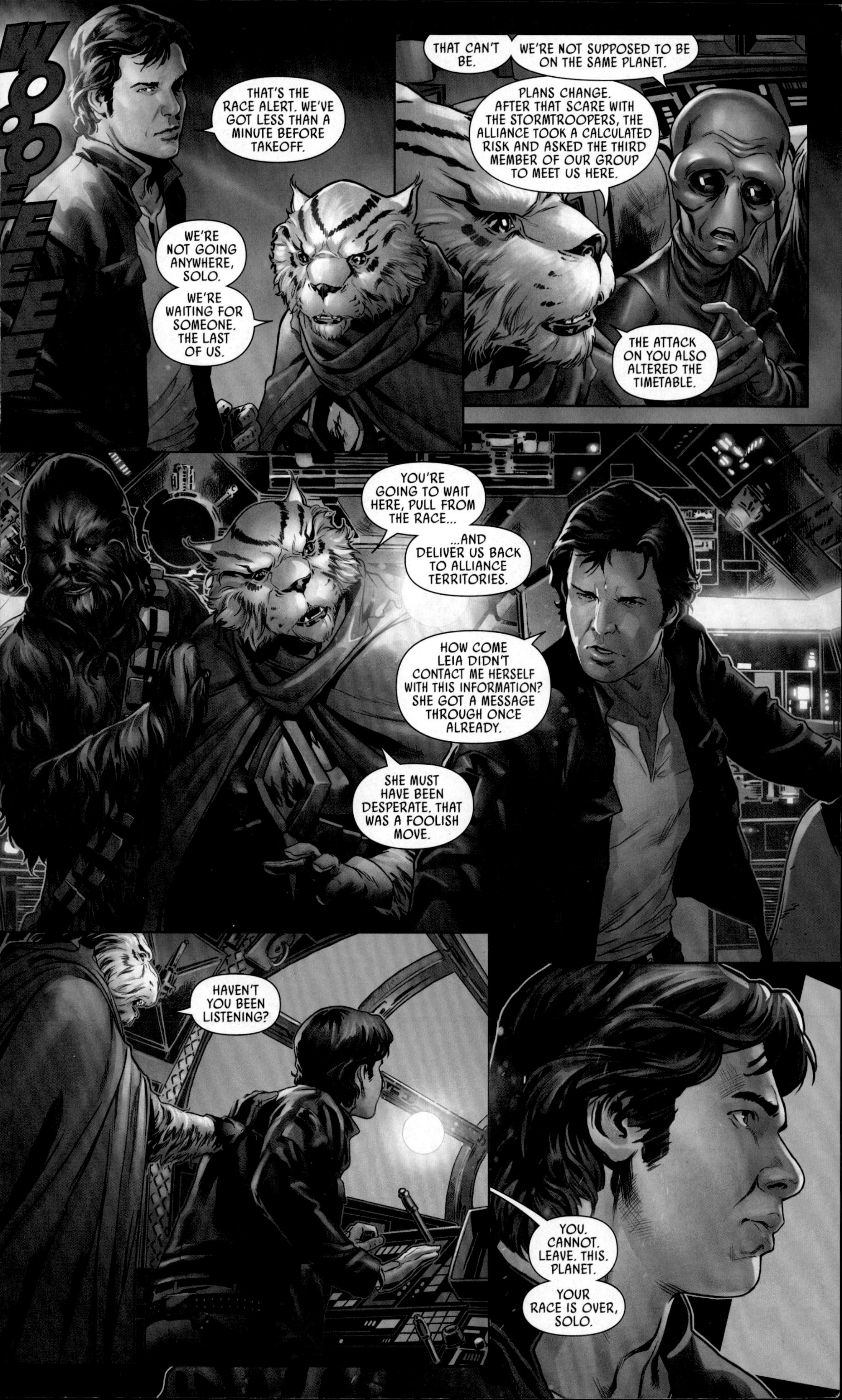
WOOOEEEEEE
THAT'S THE RACE ALERT. WE'VE GOT LESS THAN A MINUTE BEFORE TAKEOFF.
WE'RE NOT GOING ANYWHERE, SOLO.
WE'RE WAITING FOR SOMEONE. THE LAST OF US.
THAT CAN'T BE.
WE'RE NOT SUPPOSED TO BE ON THE SAME PLANET.
PLANS CHANGE. AFTER THAT SCARE WITH THE STORMTROOPERS, THE ALLIANCE TOOK A CALCULATED RISK AND ASKED THE THIRD MEMBER OF OUR GROUP TO MEET US HERE.
THE ATTACK ON YOU ALSO ALTERED THE TIMETABLE.
YOU'RE GOING TO WAIT HERE, PULL FROM THE RACE...
...AND DELIVER US BACK TO ALLIANCE TERRITORIES.
HOW COME LEIA DIDN'T CONTACT ME HERSELF WITH THIS INFORMATION? SHE GOT A MESSAGE THROUGH ONCE ALREADY.
SHE MUST HAVE BEEN DESPERATE. THAT WAS A FOOLISH MOVE.
HAVEN'T YOU BEEN LISTENING?
YOU. CANNOT. LEAVE. THIS. PLANET.
YOUR RACE IS OVER, SOLO.

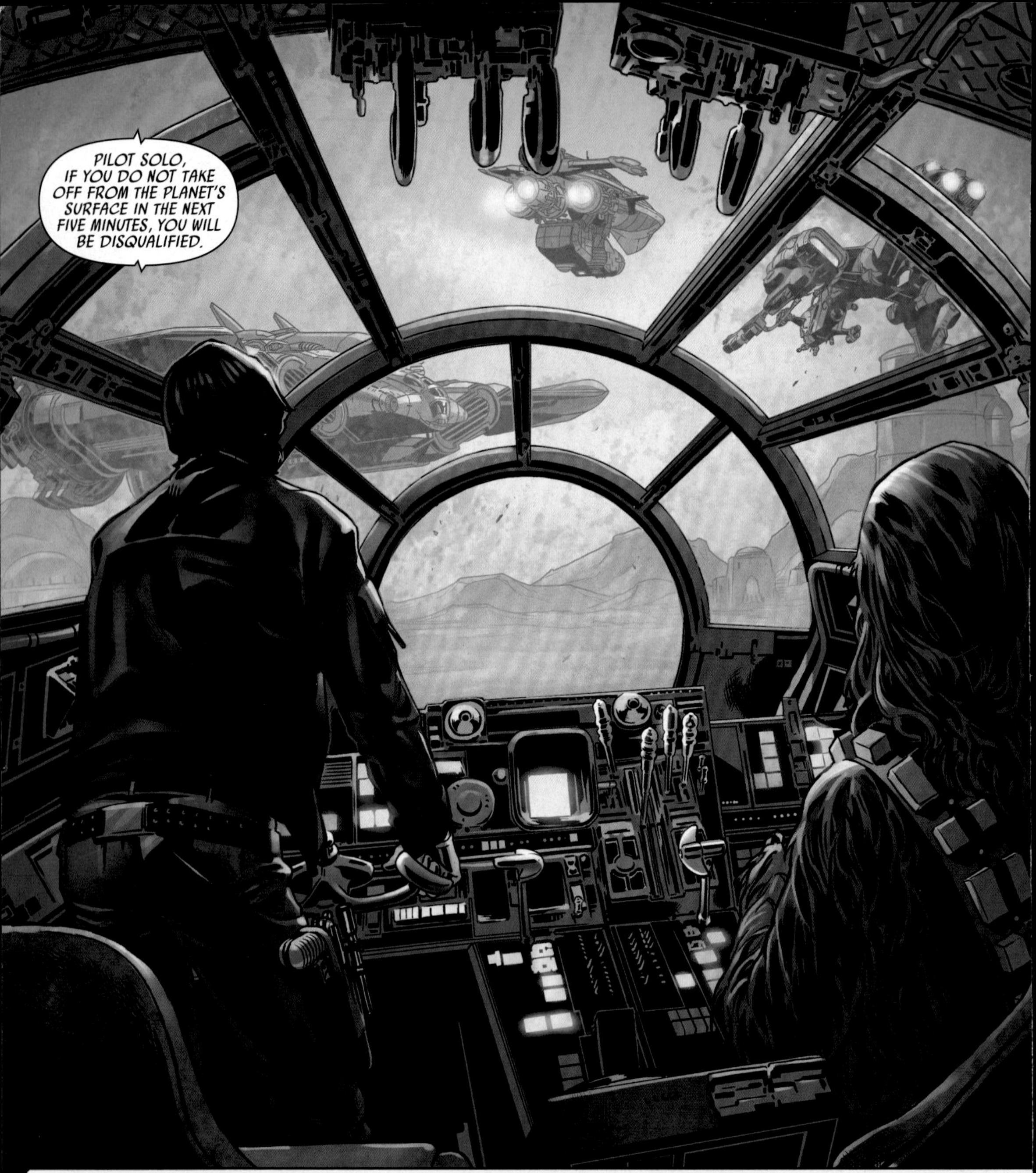
PILOT SOLO, IF YOU DO NOT TAKE OFF FROM THE PLANET'S SURFACE IN THE NEXT FIVE MINUTES, YOU WILL BE DISQUALIFIED.

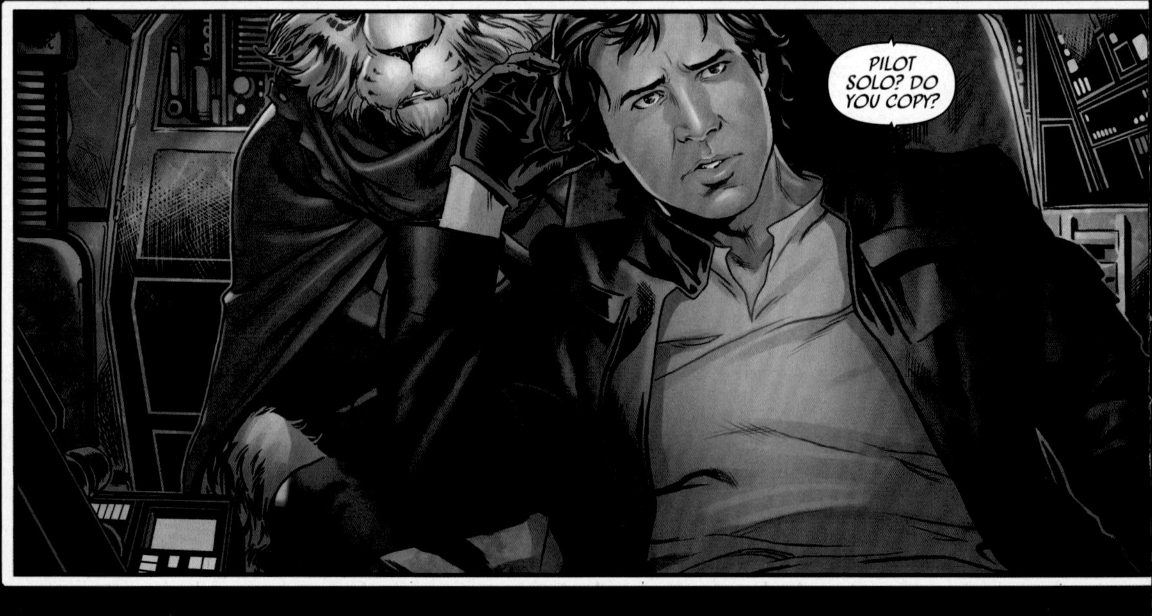
PILOT SOLO? DO YOU COPY?

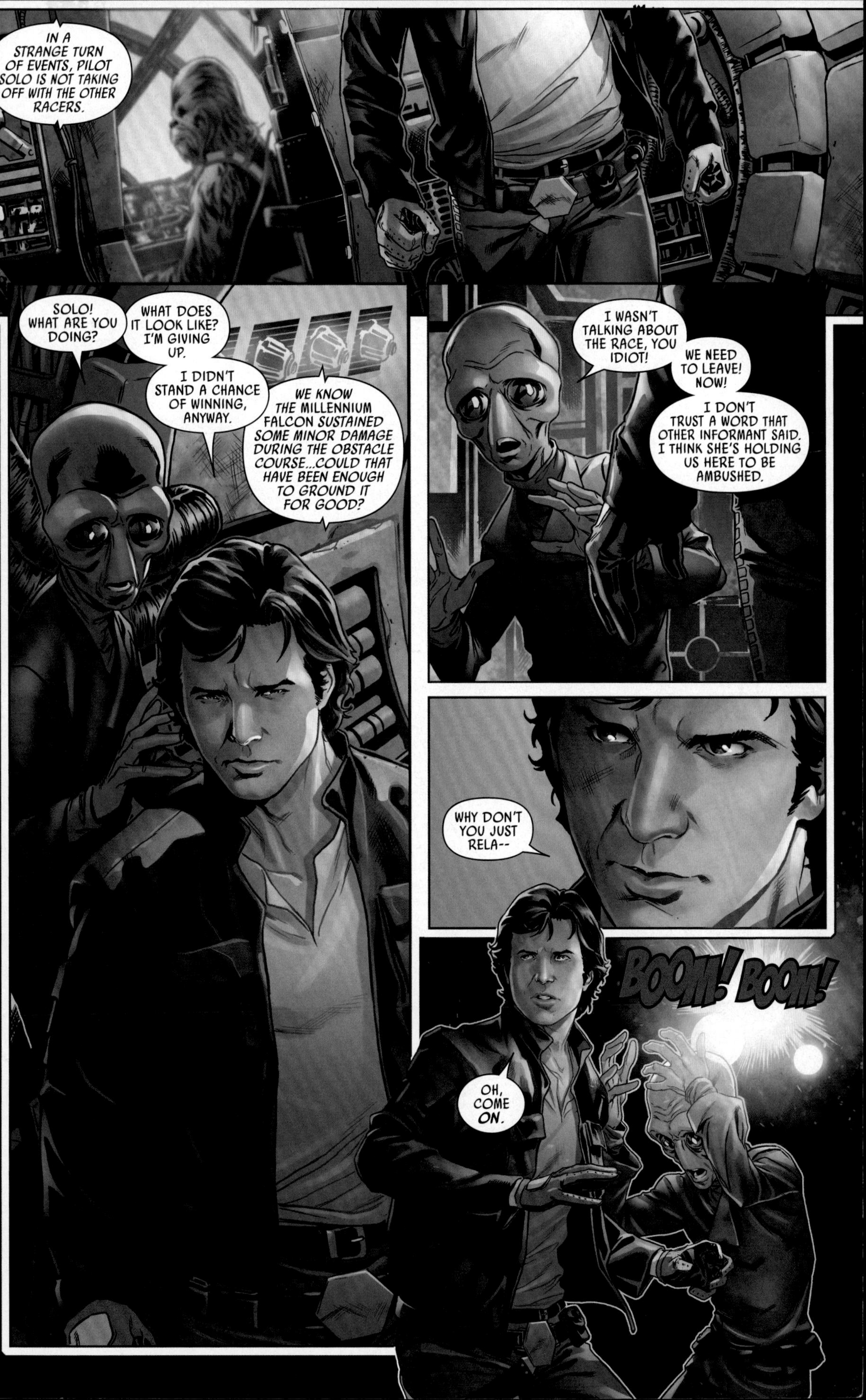
IN A STRANGE TURN OF EVENTS, PILOT SOLO IS NOT TAKING OFF WITH THE OTHER RACERS.
SOLO! WHAT ARE YOU DOING?
WHAT DOES IT LOOK LIKE? I'M GIVING UP.
I DIDN'T STAND A CHANCE OF WINNING, ANYWAY.
WE KNOW THE MILLENNIUM FALCON SUSTAINED SOME MINOR DAMAGE DURING THE OBSTACLE COURSE...COULD THAT HAVE BEEN ENOUGH TO GROUND IT FOR GOOD?
I WASN'T TALKING ABOUT THE RACE, YOU IDIOT!
WE NEED TO LEAVE! NOW!
I DON'T TRUST A WORD THAT OTHER INFORMANT SAID. I THINK SHE'S HOLDING US HERE TO BE AMBUSHED.
WHY DON'T YOU JUST RELA--
BOOM! BOOM!
OH, COME ON.

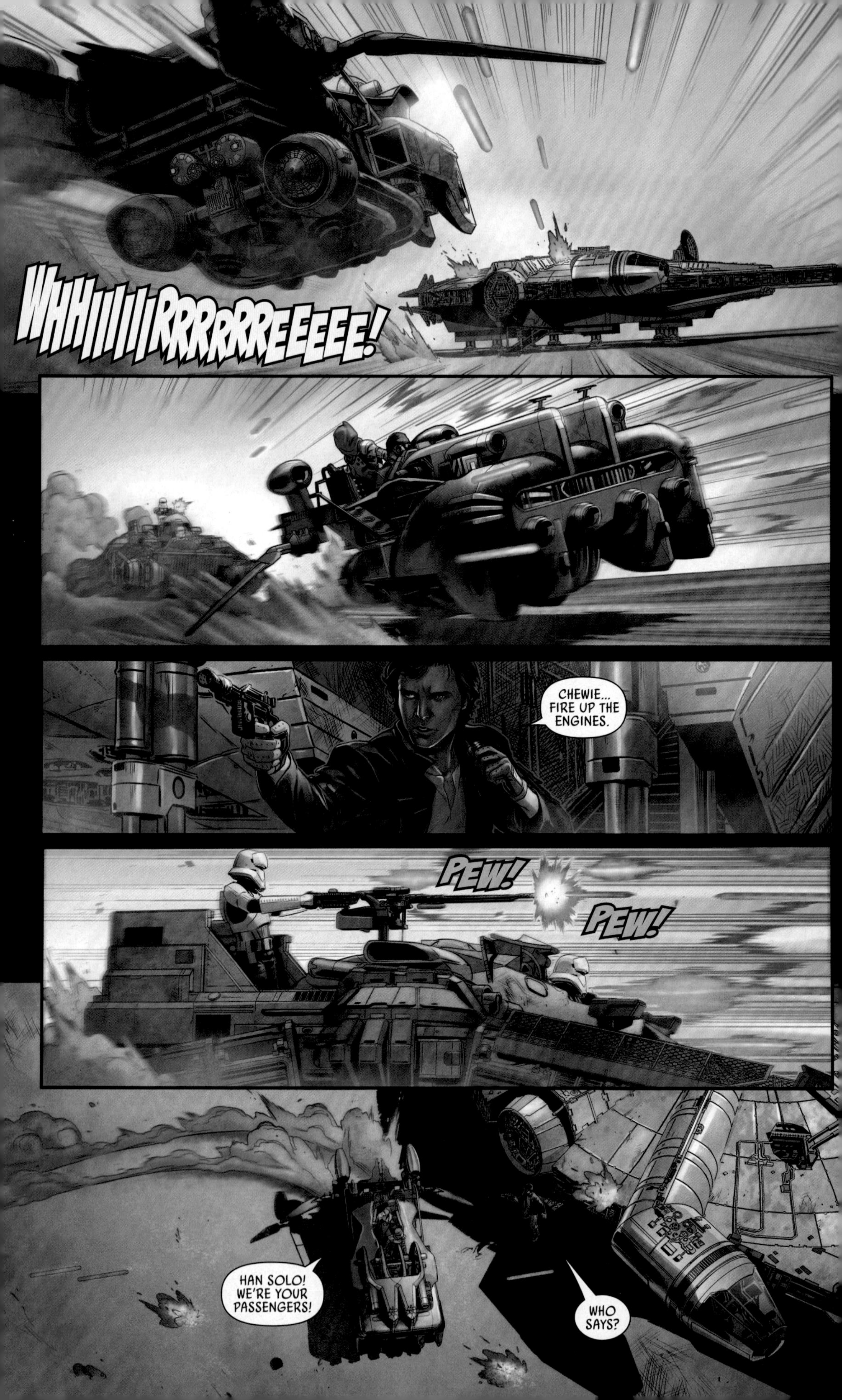

WHHIIIIIIRRRRRREEEEE!
CHEWIE... FIRE UP THE ENGINES.
PEW!
PEW!
HAN SOLO! WE'RE YOUR PASSENGERS!
WHO SAYS?

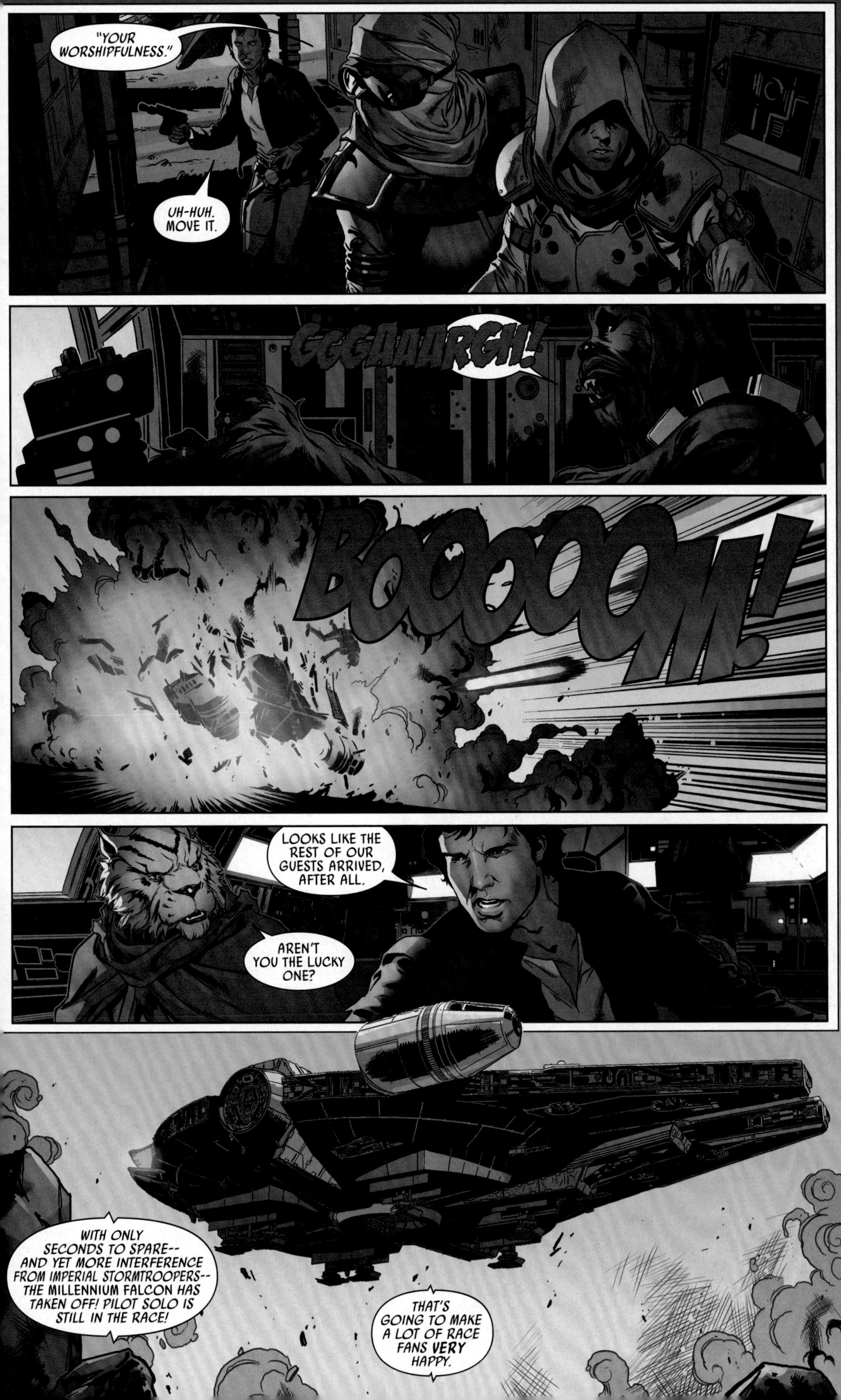
"YOUR WORSHIPFULNESS."
UH-HUH. MOVE IT.
GGGAAARGH!
BOOOOOM!
LOOKS LIKE THE REST OF OUR GUESTS ARRIVED, AFTER ALL.
AREN'T YOU THE LUCKY ONE?
WITH ONLY SECONDS TO SPARE-- AND YET MORE INTERFERENCE FROM IMPERIAL STORMTROOPERS-- THE MILLENNIUM FALCON HAS TAKEN OFF! PILOT SOLO IS STILL IN THE RACE!
THAT'S GOING TO MAKE A LOT OF RACE FANS VERY HAPPY.

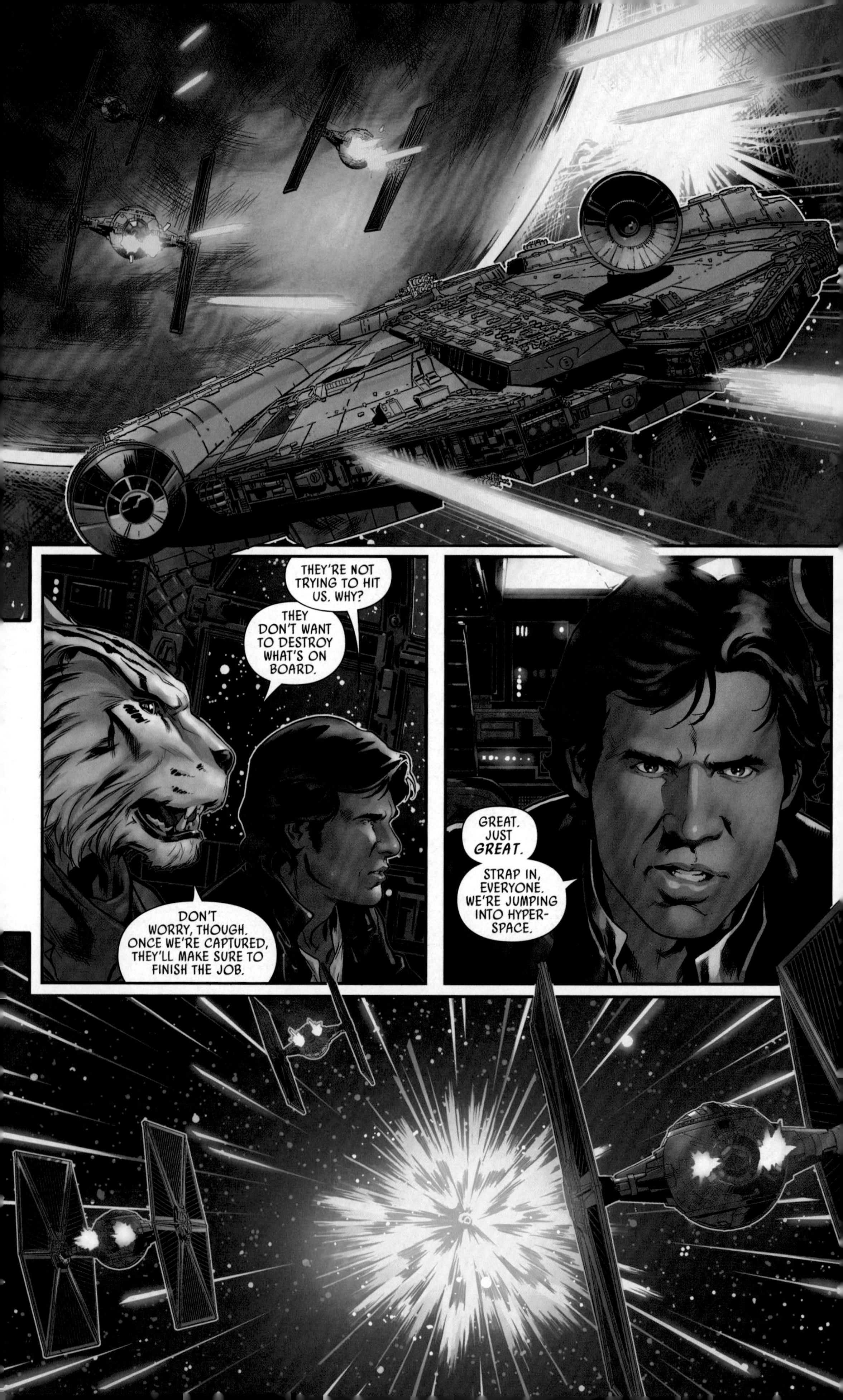
THEY'RE NOT TRYING TO HIT US. WHY?
THEY DON'T WANT TO DESTROY WHAT'S ON BOARD.
DON'T WORRY, THOUGH. ONCE WE'RE CAPTURED, THEY'LL MAKE SURE TO FINISH THE JOB.
GREAT. JUST GREAT.
STRAP IN, EVERYONE. WE'RE JUMPING INTO HYPER-SPACE.

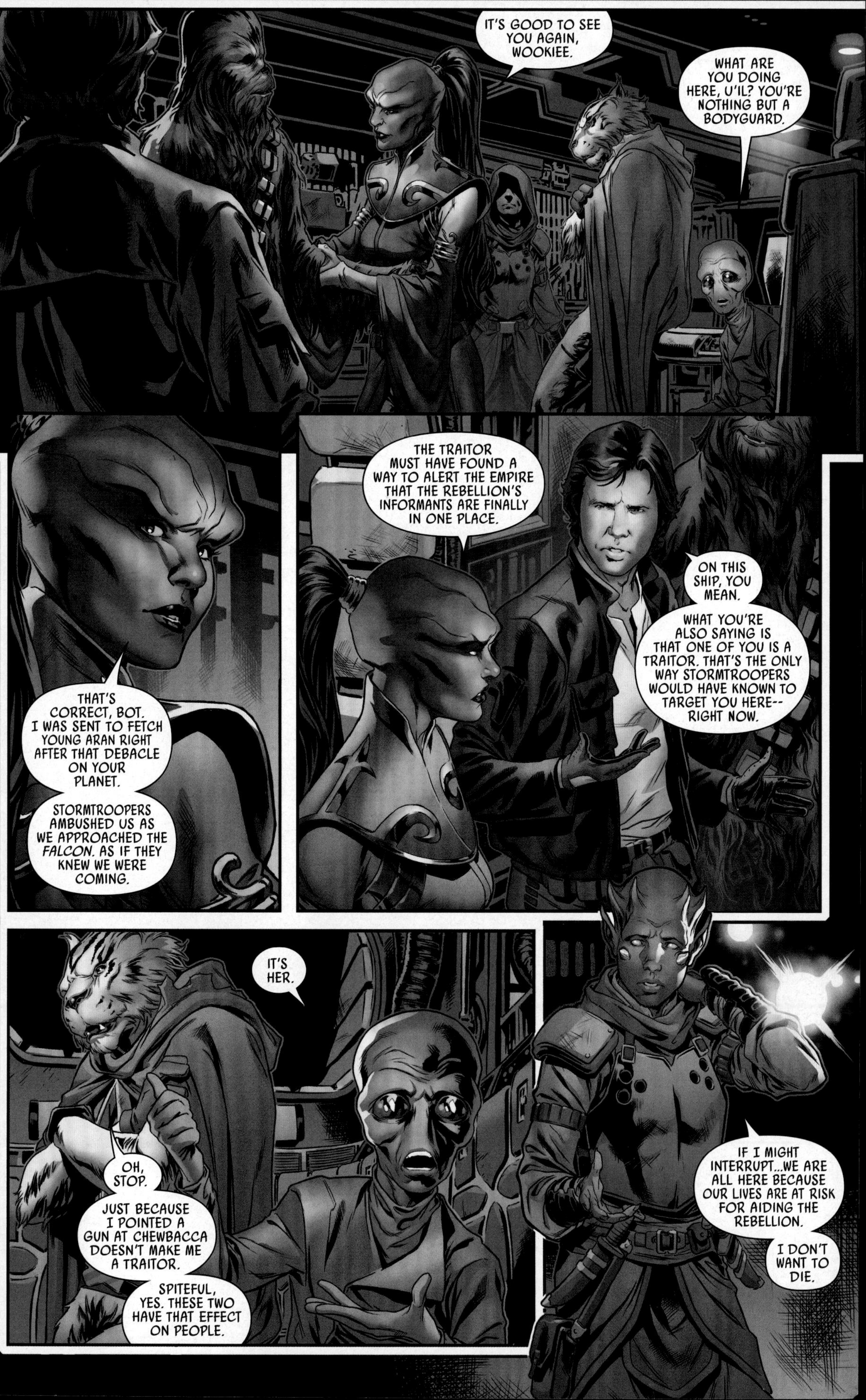
IT'S GOOD TO SEE YOU AGAIN, WOOKIEE.
WHAT ARE YOU DOING HERE, U'IL? YOU'RE NOTHING BUT A BODYGUARD.
THAT'S CORRECT, BOT. I WAS SENT TO FETCH YOUNG ARAN RIGHT AFTER THAT DEBACLE ON YOUR PLANET.
STORMTROOPERS AMBUSHED US AS WE APPROACHED THE *FALCON*. AS IF THEY KNEW WE WERE COMING.
THE TRAITOR MUST HAVE FOUND A WAY TO ALERT THE EMPIRE THAT THE REBELLION'S INFORMANTS ARE FINALLY IN ONE PLACE.
ON THIS SHIP, YOU MEAN.
WHAT YOU'RE ALSO SAYING IS THAT ONE OF YOU IS A TRAITOR. THAT'S THE ONLY WAY STORMTROOPERS WOULD HAVE KNOWN TO TARGET YOU HERE-- RIGHT NOW.
IT'S HER.
OH, STOP.
JUST BECAUSE I POINTED A GUN AT CHEWBACCA DOESN'T MAKE ME A TRAITOR.
SPITEFUL, YES. THESE TWO HAVE THAT EFFECT ON PEOPLE.
IF I MIGHT INTERRUPT...WE ARE ALL HERE BECAUSE OUR LIVES ARE AT RISK FOR AIDING THE REBELLION.
I DON'T WANT TO DIE.

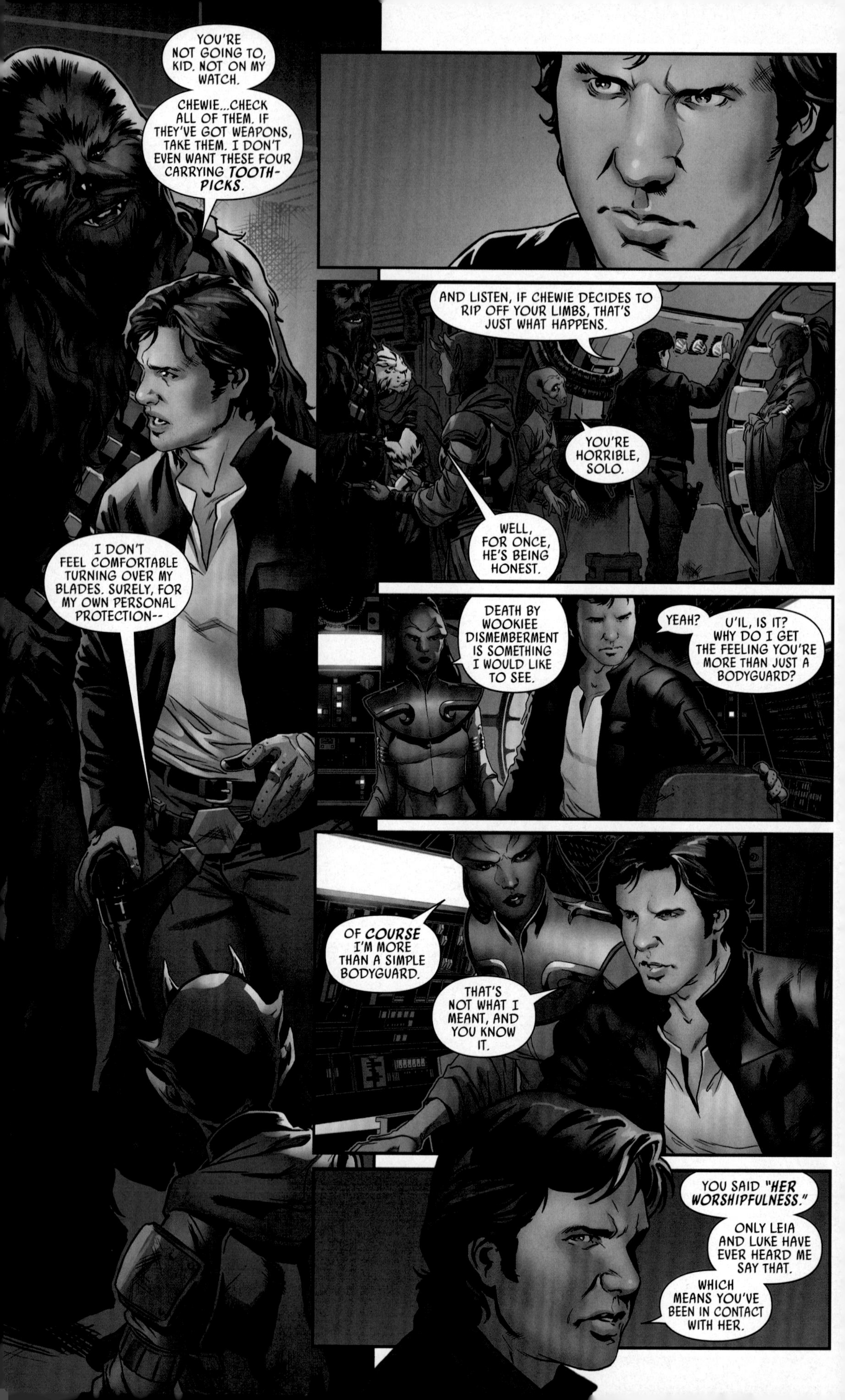
YOU'RE NOT GOING TO, KID. NOT ON MY WATCH.
CHEWIE...CHECK ALL OF THEM. IF THEY'VE GOT WEAPONS, TAKE THEM. I DON'T EVEN WANT THESE FOUR CARRYING TOOTH-PICKS.
I DON'T FEEL COMFORTABLE TURNING OVER MY BLADES. SURELY, FOR MY OWN PERSONAL PROTECTION--
AND LISTEN, IF CHEWIE DECIDES TO RIP OFF YOUR LIMBS, THAT'S JUST WHAT HAPPENS.
YOU'RE HORRIBLE, SOLO.
WELL, FOR ONCE, HE'S BEING HONEST.
DEATH BY WOOKIEE DISMEMBERMENT IS SOMETHING I WOULD LIKE TO SEE.
YEAH?
U'IL, IS IT? WHY DO I GET THE FEELING YOU'RE MORE THAN JUST A BODYGUARD?
OF COURSE I'M MORE THAN A SIMPLE BODYGUARD.
THAT'S NOT WHAT I MEANT, AND YOU KNOW IT.
YOU SAID "HER WORSHIPFULNESS."
ONLY LEIA AND LUKE HAVE EVER HEARD ME SAY THAT.
WHICH MEANS YOU'VE BEEN IN CONTACT WITH HER.

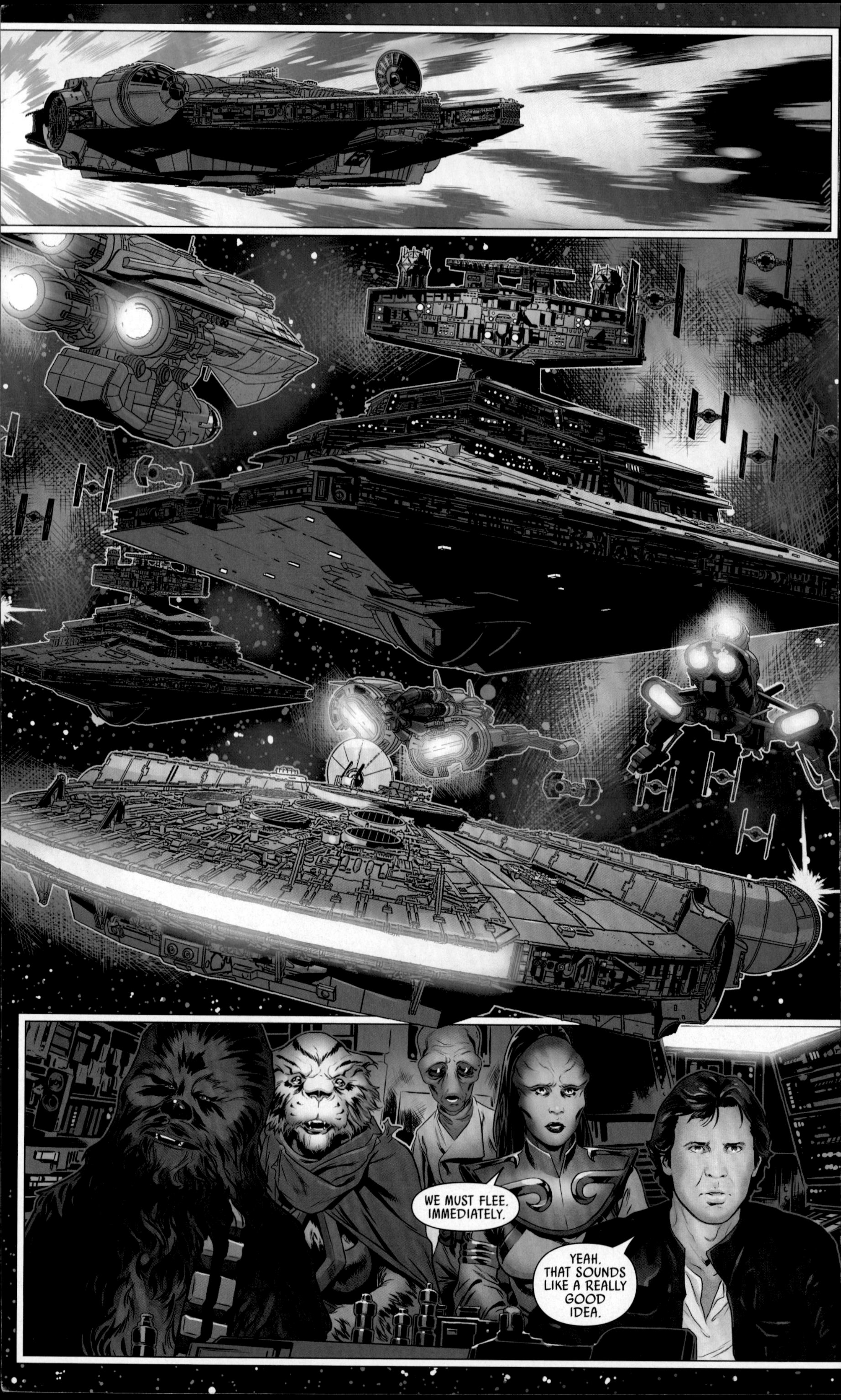
WE MUST FLEE. IMMEDIATELY.
YEAH. THAT SOUNDS LIKE A REALLY GOOD IDEA.

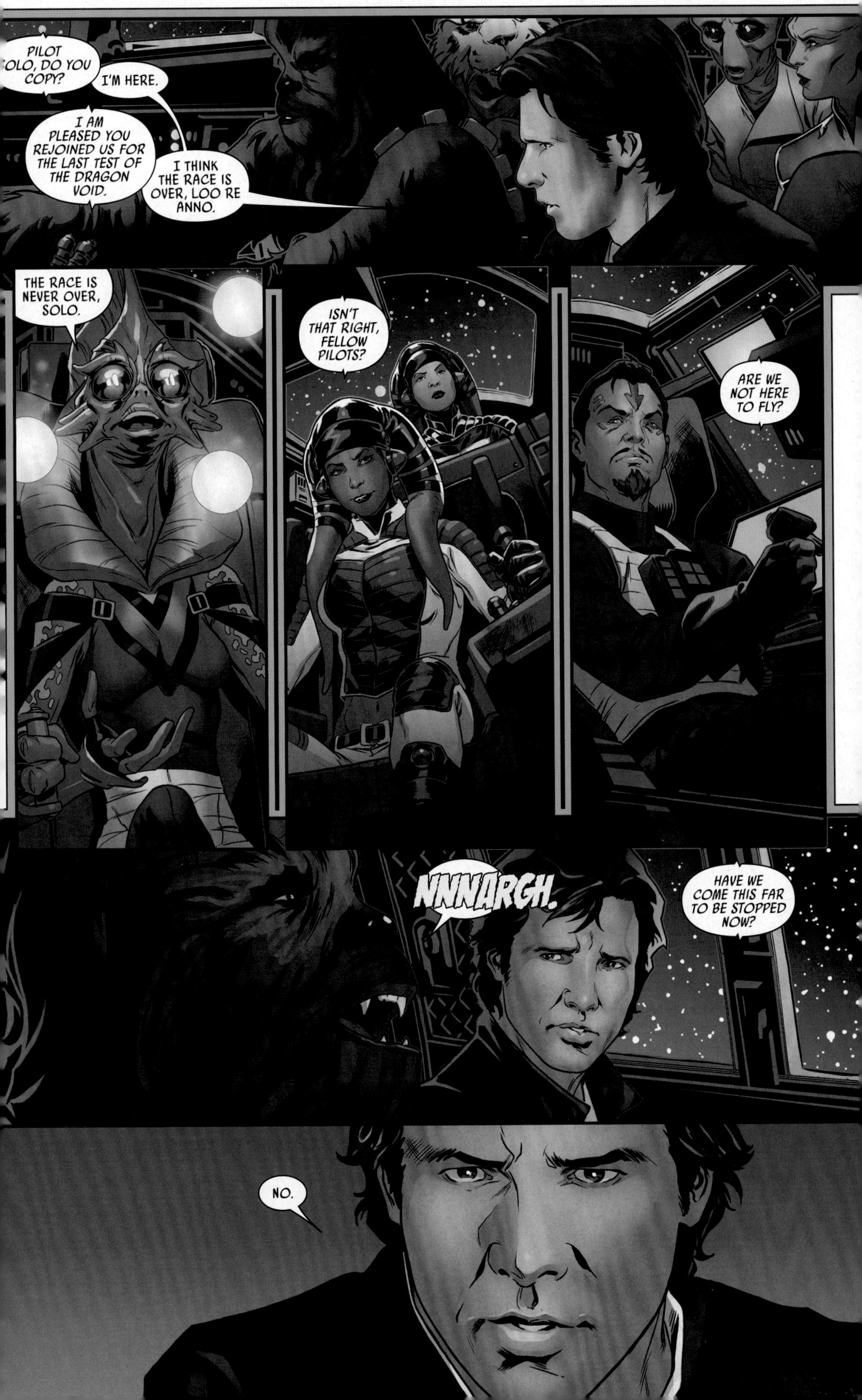

PILOT SOLO, DO YOU COPY?
I'M HERE.
I AM PLEASED YOU REJOINED US FOR THE LAST TEST OF THE DRAGON VOID.
I THINK THE RACE IS OVER, LOO RE ANNO.
THE RACE IS NEVER OVER, SOLO.
ISN'T THAT RIGHT, FELLOW PILOTS?
ARE WE NOT HERE TO FLY?
NNNARGH.
HAVE WE COME THIS FAR TO BE STOPPED NOW?
NO.

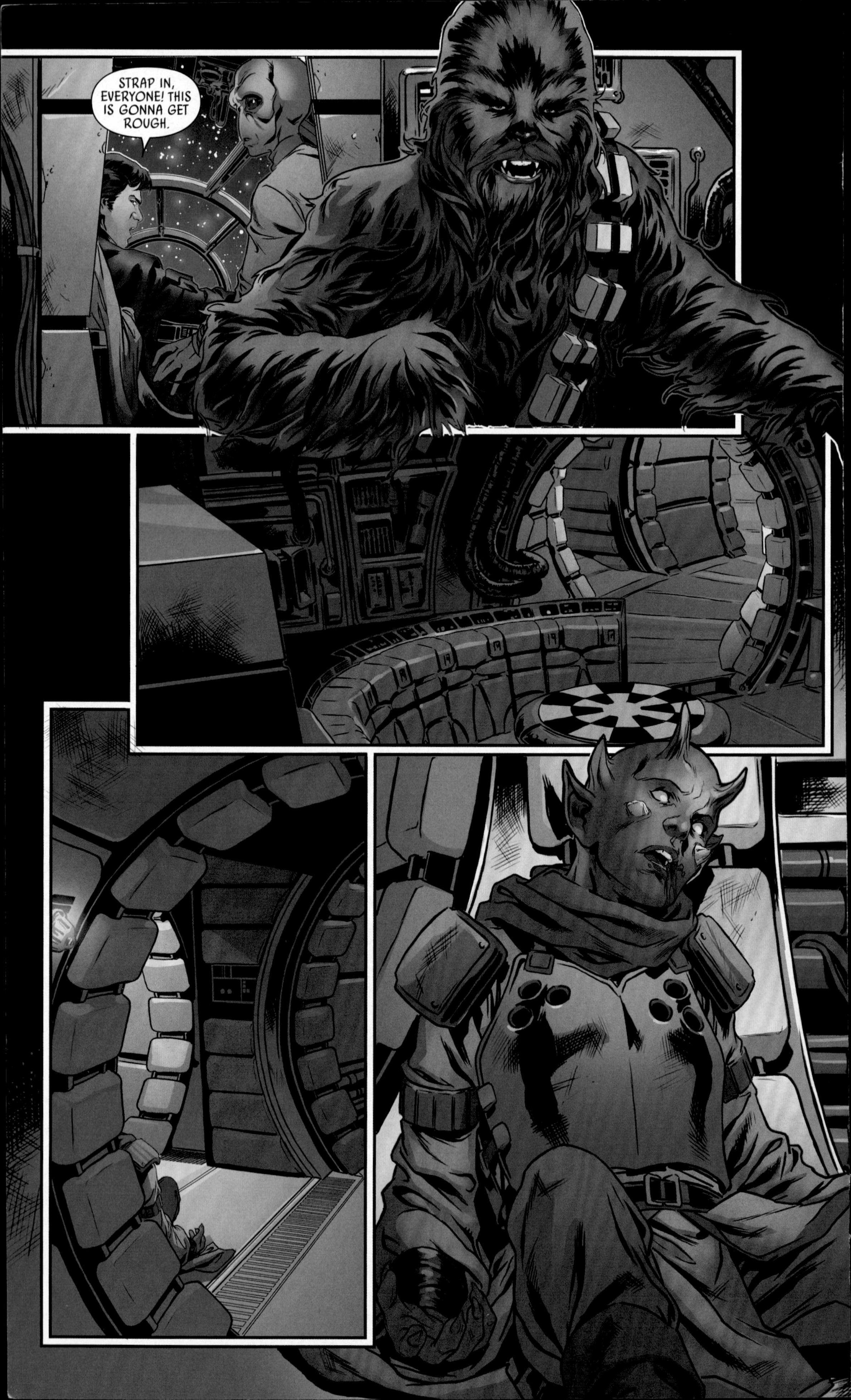
STRAP IN, EVERYONE! THIS IS GONNA GET ROUGH.

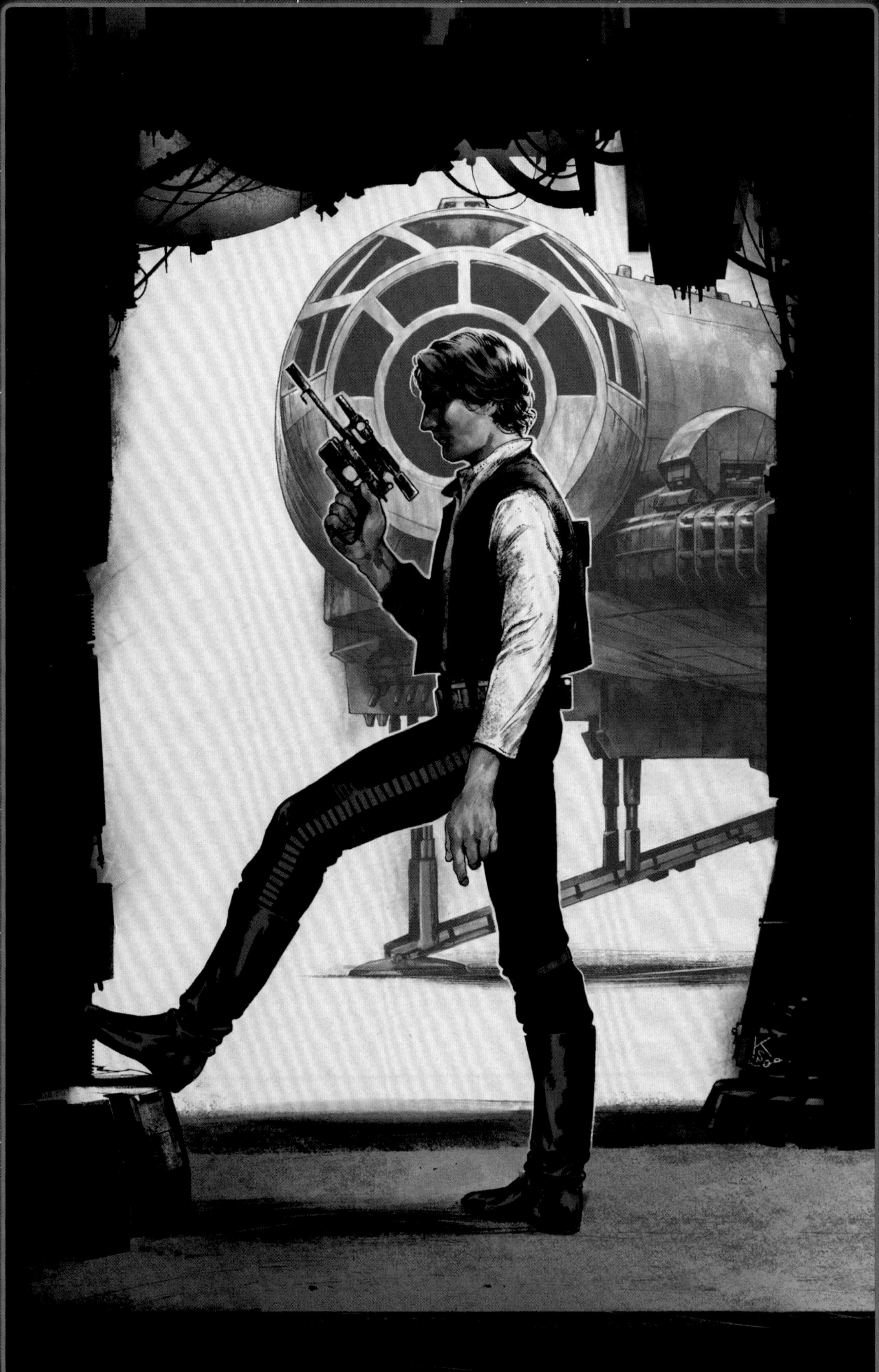

5

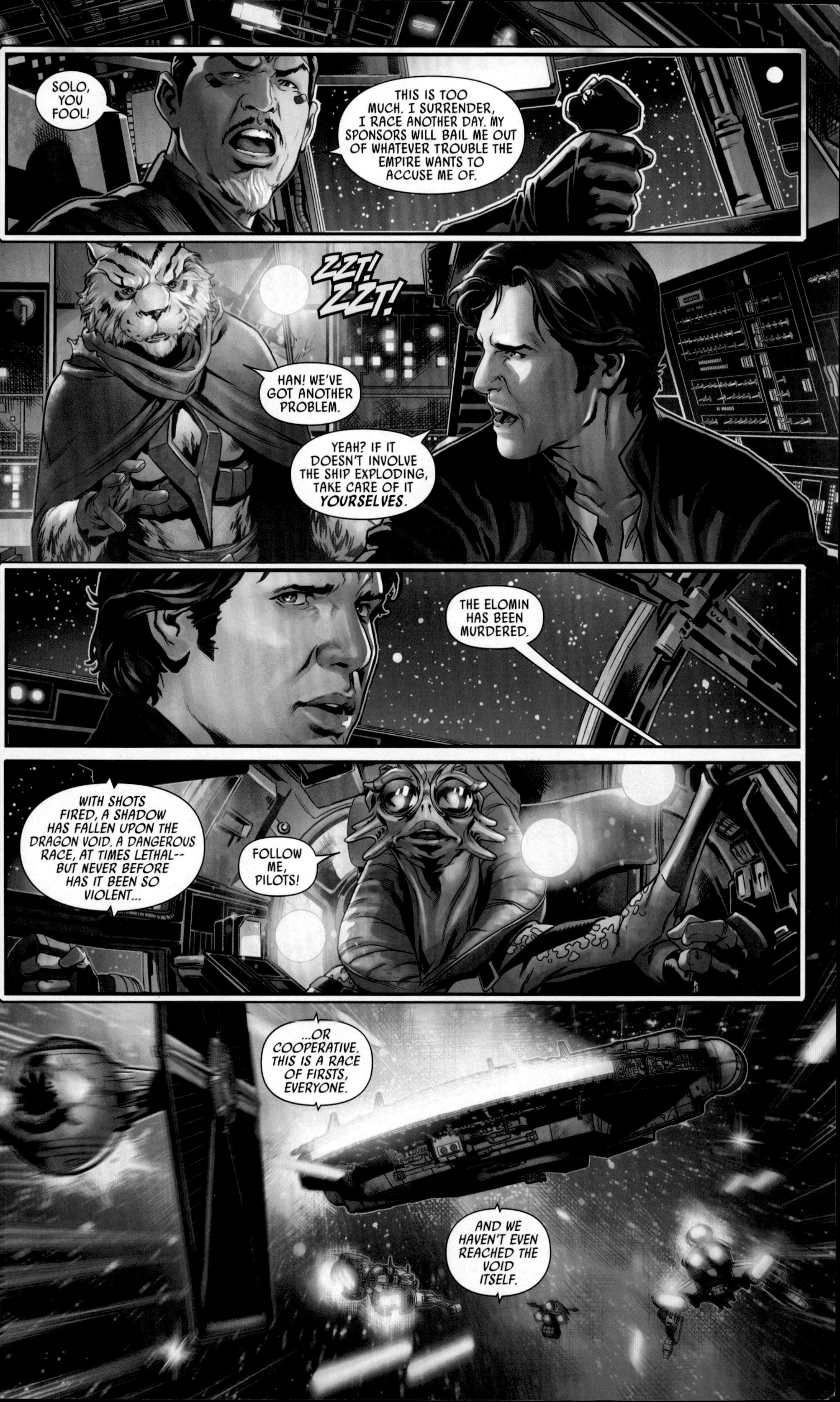
SOLO, YOU FOOL!
THIS IS TOO MUCH. I SURRENDER, I RACE ANOTHER DAY. MY SPONSORS WILL BAIL ME OUT OF WHATEVER TROUBLE THE EMPIRE WANTS TO ACCUSE ME OF.
ZZT! ZZT!
HAN! WE'VE GOT ANOTHER PROBLEM.
YEAH? IF IT DOESN'T INVOLVE THE SHIP EXPLODING, TAKE CARE OF IT YOURSELVES.
THE ELOMIN HAS BEEN MURDERED.
WITH SHOTS FIRED, A SHADOW HAS FALLEN UPON THE DRAGON VOID. A DANGEROUS RACE, AT TIMES LETHAL--BUT NEVER BEFORE HAS IT BEEN SO VIOLENT...
FOLLOW ME, PILOTS!
...OR COOPERATIVE. THIS IS A RACE OF FIRSTS, EVERYONE.
AND WE HAVEN'T EVEN REACHED THE VOID ITSELF.

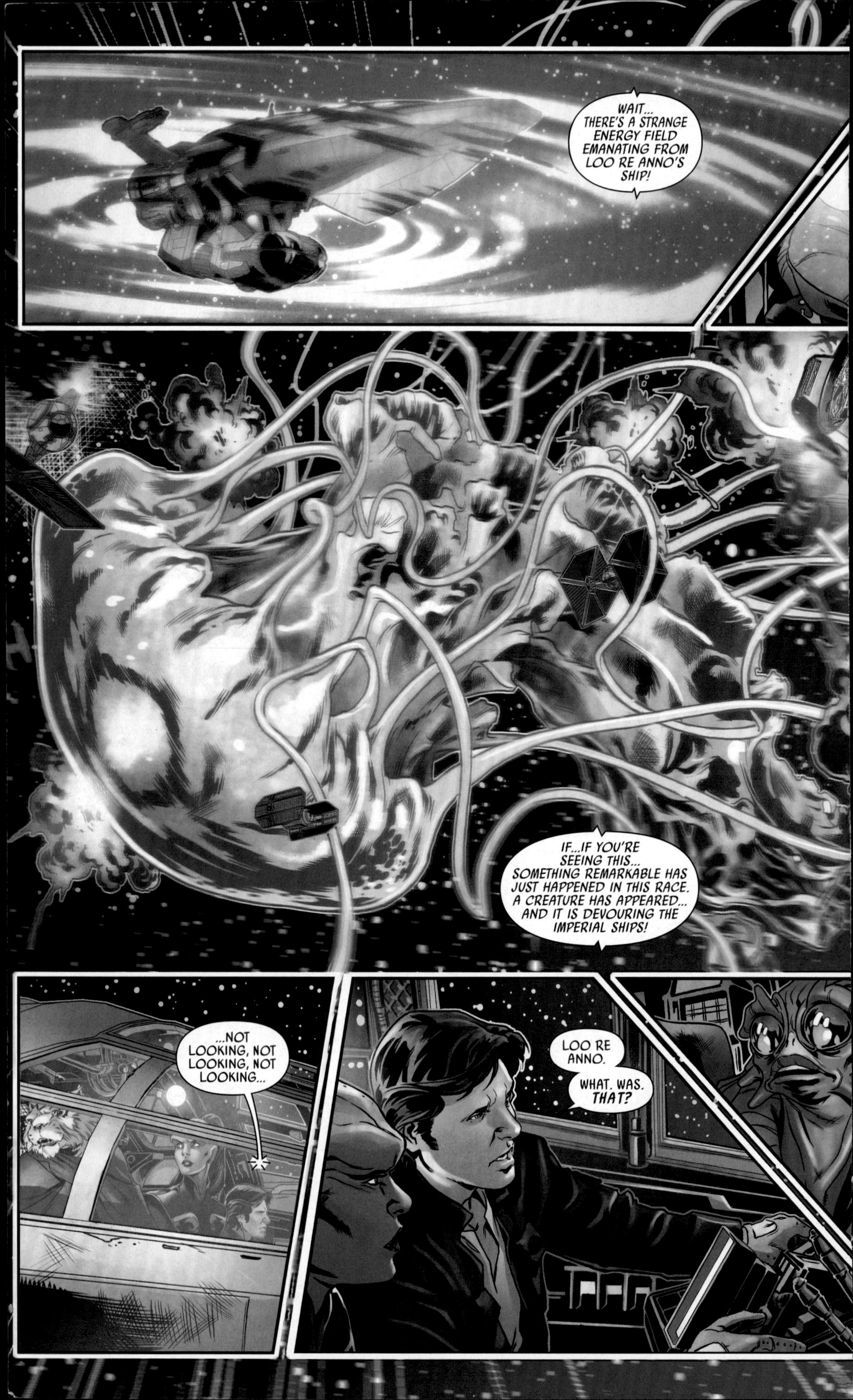
WAIT... THERE'S A STRANGE ENERGY FIELD EMANATING FROM LOO RE ANNO'S SHIP!
IF...IF YOU'RE SEEING THIS... SOMETHING REMARKABLE HAS JUST HAPPENED IN THIS RACE. A CREATURE HAS APPEARED... AND IT IS DEVOURING THE IMPERIAL SHIPS!
...NOT LOOKING, NOT LOOKING, NOT LOOKING...
LOO RE ANNO.
WHAT. WAS. THAT?

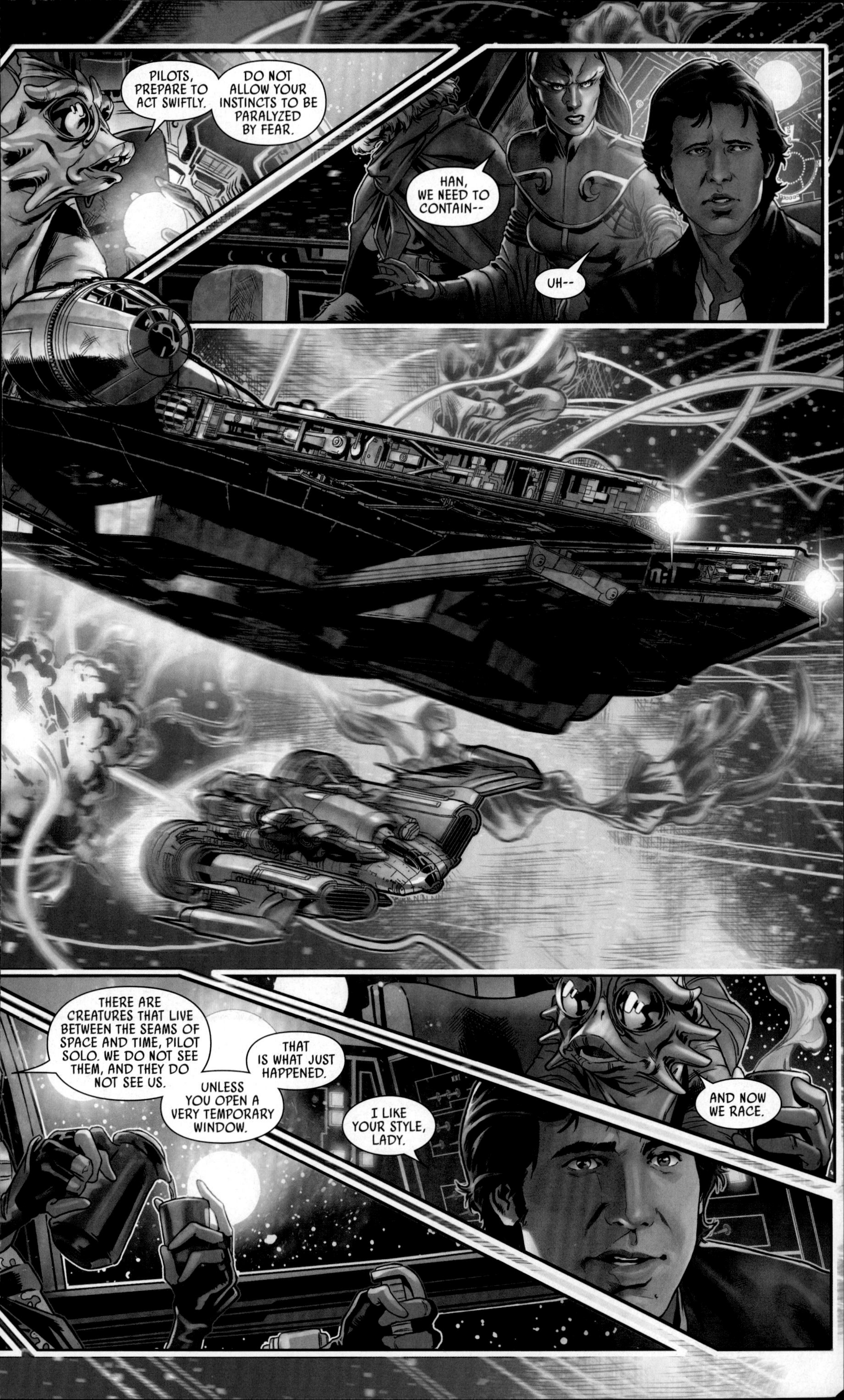
PILOTS, PREPARE TO ACT SWIFTLY.
DO NOT ALLOW YOUR INSTINCTS TO BE PARALYZED BY FEAR.
HAN, WE NEED TO CONTAIN--
UH--
THERE ARE CREATURES THAT LIVE BETWEEN THE SEAMS OF SPACE AND TIME, PILOT SOLO. WE DO NOT SEE THEM, AND THEY DO NOT SEE US.
UNLESS YOU OPEN A VERY TEMPORARY WINDOW.
THAT IS WHAT JUST HAPPENED.
I LIKE YOUR STYLE, LADY.
AND NOW WE RACE.

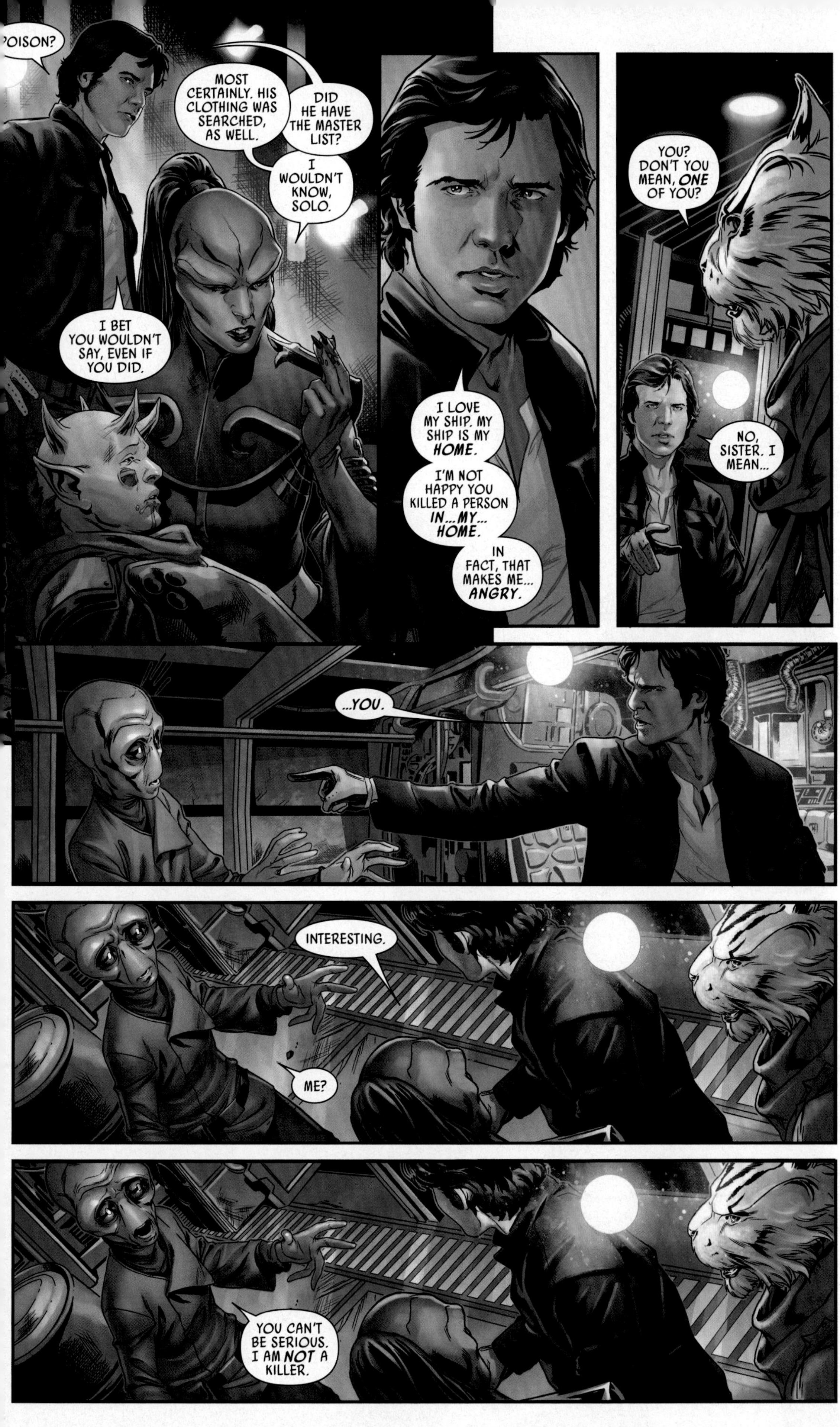
POISON?
MOST CERTAINLY. HIS CLOTHING WAS SEARCHED, AS WELL.
DID HE HAVE THE MASTER LIST?
I WOULDN'T KNOW, SOLO.
I BET YOU WOULDN'T SAY, EVEN IF YOU DID.
I LOVE MY SHIP. MY SHIP IS MY HOME.
I'M NOT HAPPY YOU KILLED A PERSON IN...MY... HOME.
IN FACT, THAT MAKES ME... ANGRY.
YOU? DON'T YOU MEAN, ONE OF YOU?
NO, SISTER. I MEAN...
...YOU.
INTERESTING.
ME?
YOU CAN'T BE SERIOUS. I AM NOT A KILLER.

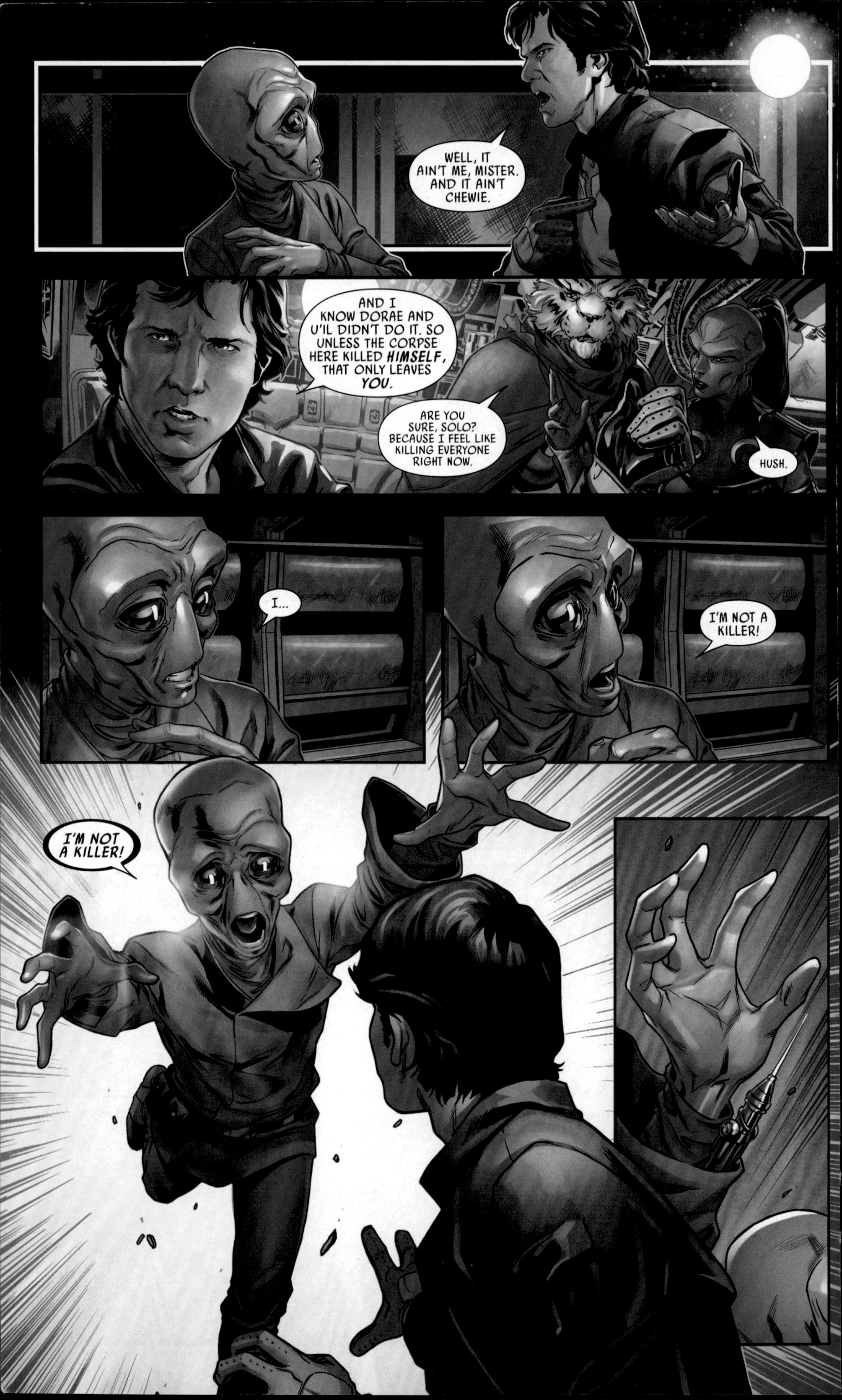

WELL, IT AIN'T ME, MISTER. AND IT AIN'T CHEWIE.
AND I KNOW DORAE AND U'IL DIDN'T DO IT. SO UNLESS THE CORPSE HERE KILLED HIMSELF, THAT ONLY LEAVES YOU.
ARE YOU SURE, SOLO? BECAUSE I FEEL LIKE KILLING EVERYONE RIGHT NOW.
HUSH.
I...
I'M NOT A KILLER!
I'M NOT A KILLER!

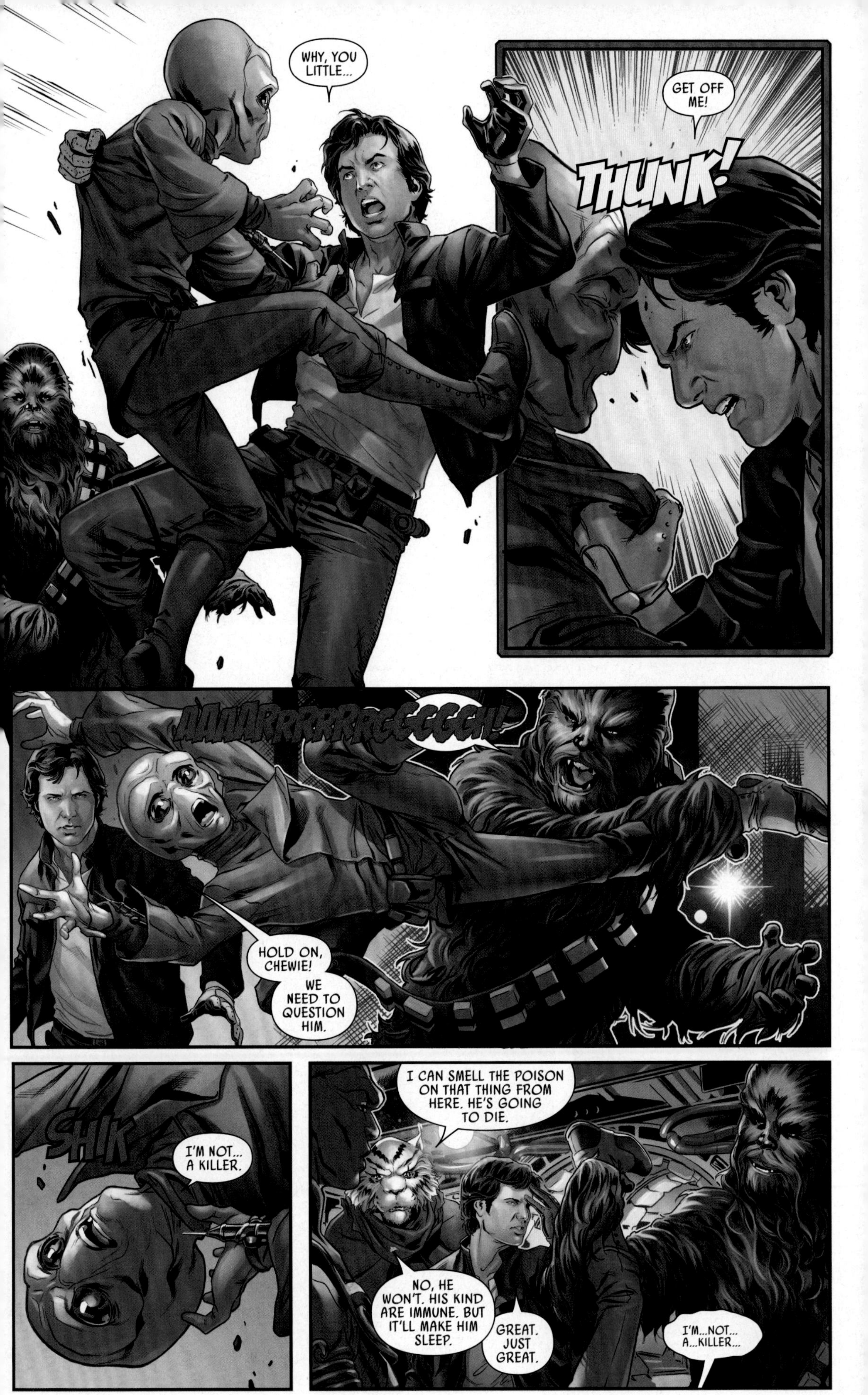
WHY, YOU LITTLE...
GET OFF ME!
THUNK!
AAAARRRRRRRGGGGGH!
HOLD ON, CHEWIE!
WE NEED TO QUESTION HIM.
SHIK
I'M NOT... A KILLER.
I CAN SMELL THE POISON ON THAT THING FROM HERE. HE'S GOING TO DIE.
NO, HE WON'T. HIS KIND ARE IMMUNE. BUT IT'LL MAKE HIM SLEEP.
GREAT. JUST GREAT.
I'M...NOT... A...KILLER...

HARRGH?

YEAH, YEAH, I'M FINE. THANKS, BUDDY.

I'M... NOT...A... KILLER...

WHY DOES HE KEEP SAYING THAT?

BOT DIDN'T BETRAY US BY CHOICE. HE WAS COMPELLED.

PROGRAMMED. BRAINWASHED.

BOT MUST HAVE BEEN COMPROMISED, AND THIS WAS THE PRICE HE PAID. HE'S THE ONE WHO LIKELY KILLED THE OTHER INFORMANTS.

YEAH? WELL, I'VE HAD ENOUGH. IF BOT WAKES UP, MAKE SURE HE CAN'T CAUSE ANY MORE TROUBLE.

KRRAAGH!

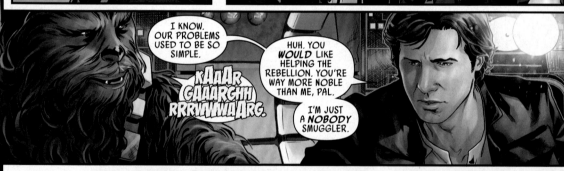

I KNOW. OUR PROBLEMS USED TO BE SO SIMPLE.

KAAAR GAAARGHH RRRWWWAARG.

HUH. YOU *WOULD* LIKE HELPING THE REBELLION. YOU'RE WAY MORE NOBLE THAN ME, PAL.

I'M JUST A *NOBODY* SMUGGLER.

AND I LIKE IT... THAT... WAY...

MY SHIP IS MY HOME. THE STARS, MY HOME.

UH...PILOT LOO RE ANNO, DO YOU COPY?

I DO, PILOT SOLO. HOW CAN I HELP YOU?

WHAT ARE YOU GOING TO DO AFTER THIS RACE IS OVER? WHAT DO YOU... I DUNNO...GO HOME TO?

BUT AS FOR THE RACE, PILOT SOLO...

...I WILL EITHER WIN...

...OR I WILL DIE.

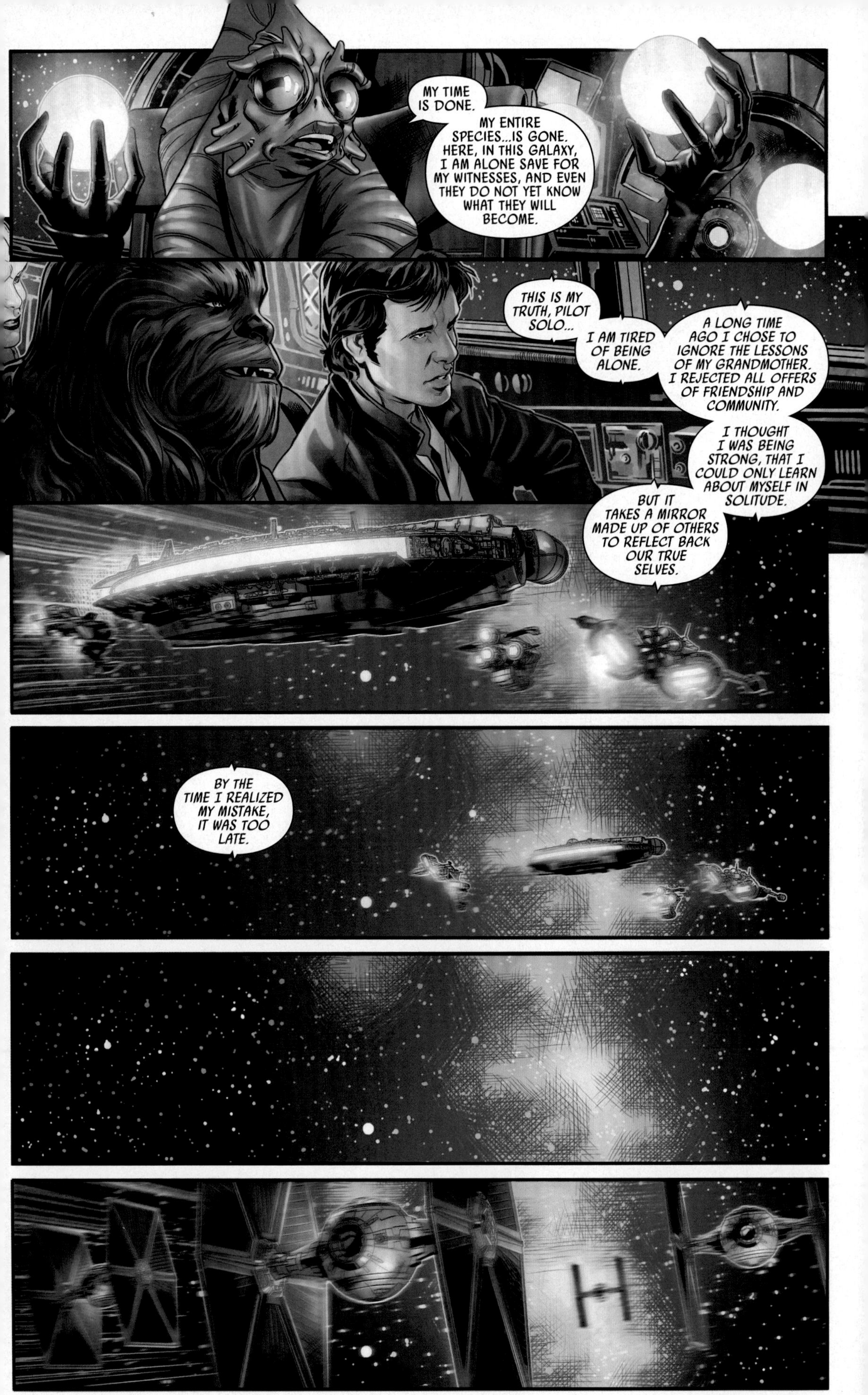
MY TIME IS DONE.
MY ENTIRE SPECIES...IS GONE. HERE, IN THIS GALAXY, I AM ALONE SAVE FOR MY WITNESSES, AND EVEN THEY DO NOT YET KNOW WHAT THEY WILL BECOME.
THIS IS MY TRUTH, PILOT SOLO...
I AM TIRED OF BEING ALONE.
A LONG TIME AGO I CHOSE TO IGNORE THE LESSONS OF MY GRANDMOTHER. I REJECTED ALL OFFERS OF FRIENDSHIP AND COMMUNITY.
I THOUGHT I WAS BEING STRONG, THAT I COULD ONLY LEARN ABOUT MYSELF IN SOLITUDE.
BUT IT TAKES A MIRROR MADE UP OF OTHERS TO REFLECT BACK OUR TRUE SELVES.
BY THE TIME I REALIZED MY MISTAKE, IT WAS TOO LATE.

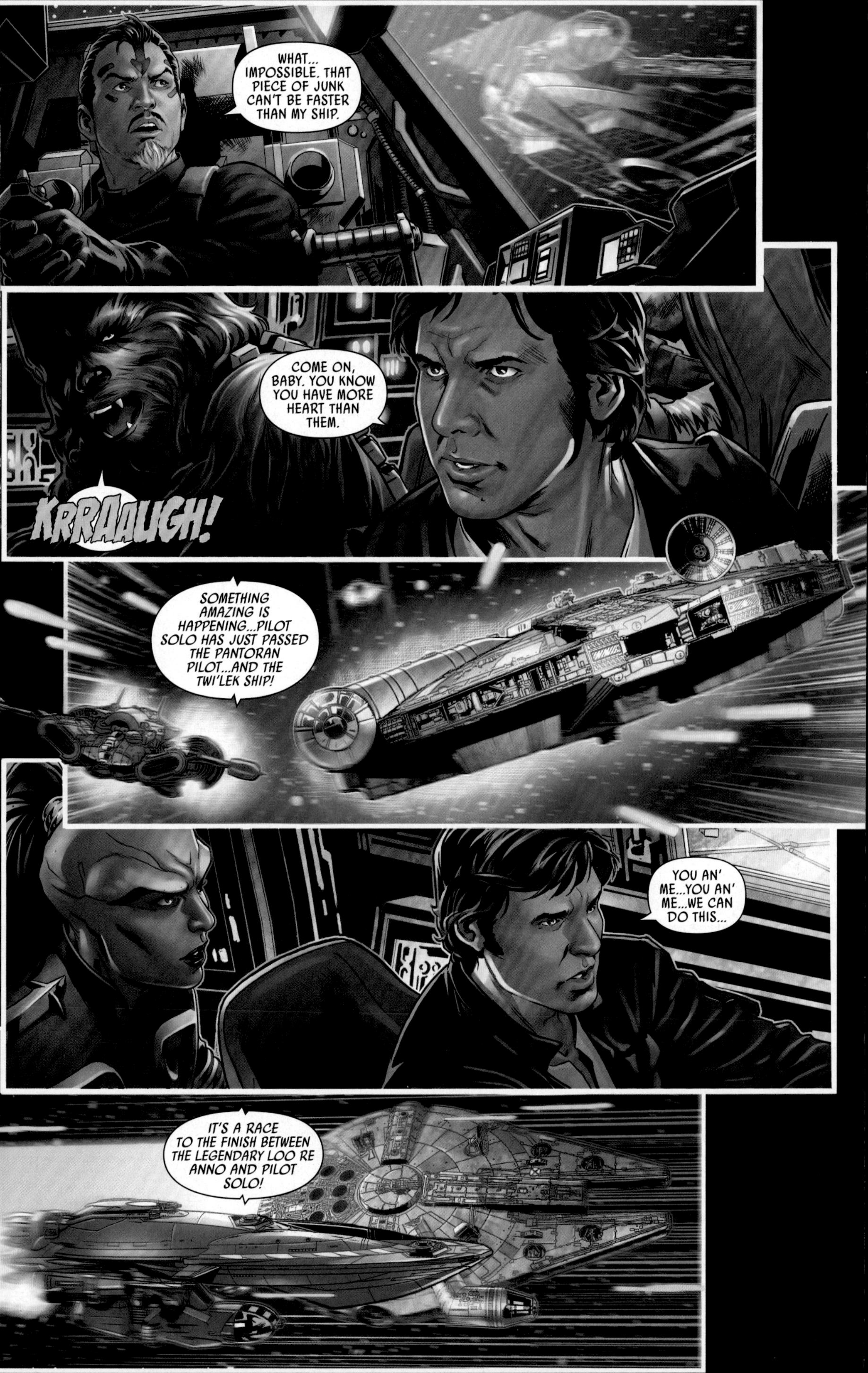
WHAT... IMPOSSIBLE. THAT PIECE OF JUNK CAN'T BE FASTER THAN MY SHIP.
COME ON, BABY. YOU KNOW YOU HAVE MORE HEART THAN THEM.
KRRAAUGH!
SOMETHING AMAZING IS HAPPENING...PILOT SOLO HAS JUST PASSED THE PANTORAN PILOT...AND THE TWI'LEK SHIP!
YOU AN' ME...YOU AN' ME...WE CAN DO THIS...
IT'S A RACE TO THE FINISH BETWEEN THE LEGENDARY LOO RE ANNO AND PILOT SOLO!

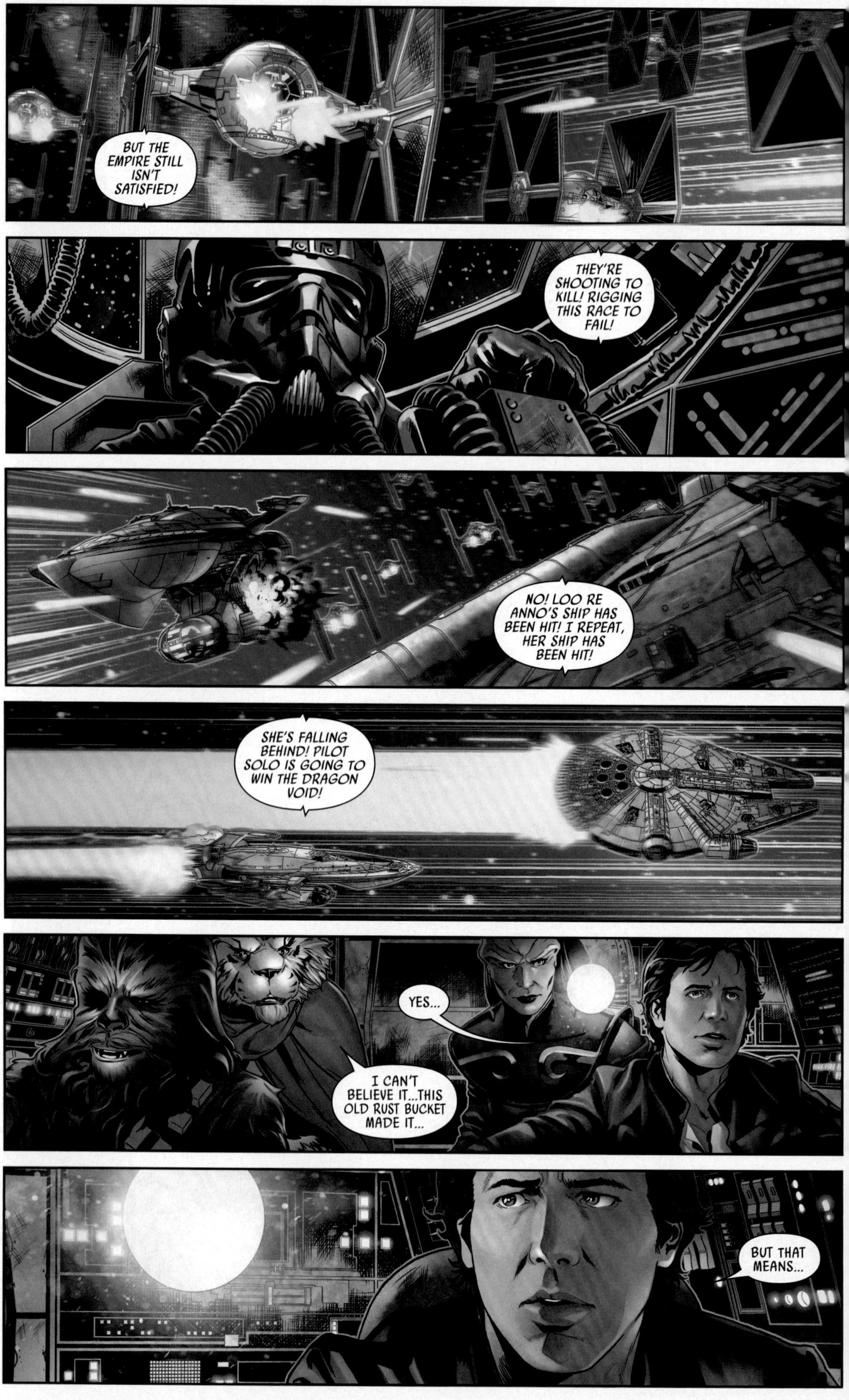
BUT THE EMPIRE STILL ISN'T SATISFIED!
THEY'RE SHOOTING TO KILL! RIGGING THIS RACE TO FAIL!
NO! LOO RE ANNO'S SHIP HAS BEEN HIT! I REPEAT, HER SHIP HAS BEEN HIT!
SHE'S FALLING BEHIND! PILOT SOLO IS GOING TO WIN THE DRAGON VOID!
YES...
I CAN'T BELIEVE IT...THIS OLD RUST BUCKET MADE IT...
BUT THAT MEANS...

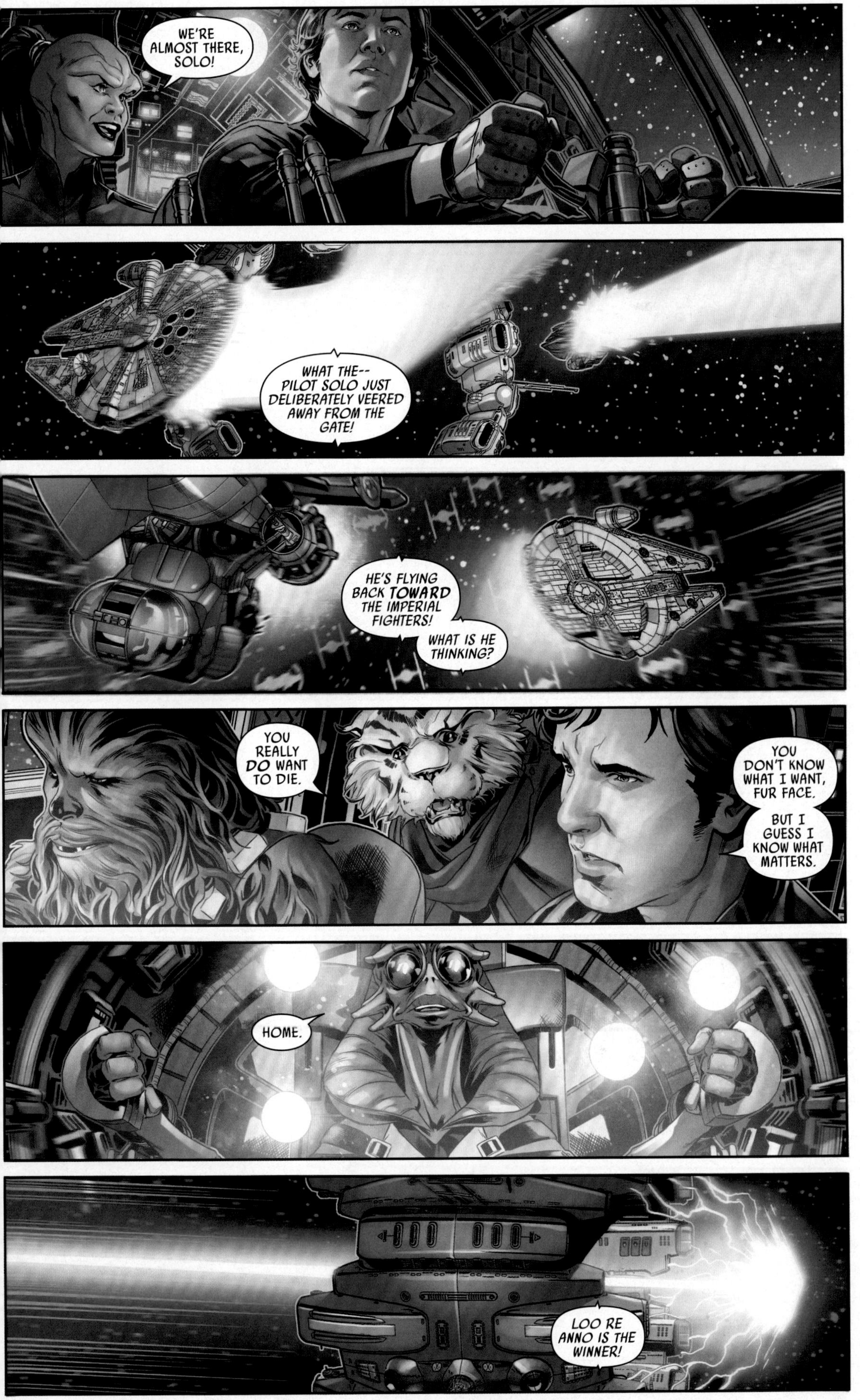
WE'RE ALMOST THERE, SOLO!
WHAT THE-- PILOT SOLO JUST DELIBERATELY VEERED AWAY FROM THE GATE!
HE'S FLYING BACK **TOWARD** THE IMPERIAL FIGHTERS!
WHAT IS HE THINKING?
YOU REALLY **DO** WANT TO DIE.
YOU DON'T KNOW WHAT I WANT, FUR FACE.
BUT I GUESS I KNOW WHAT MATTERS.
HOME.
LOO RE ANNO IS THE WINNER!

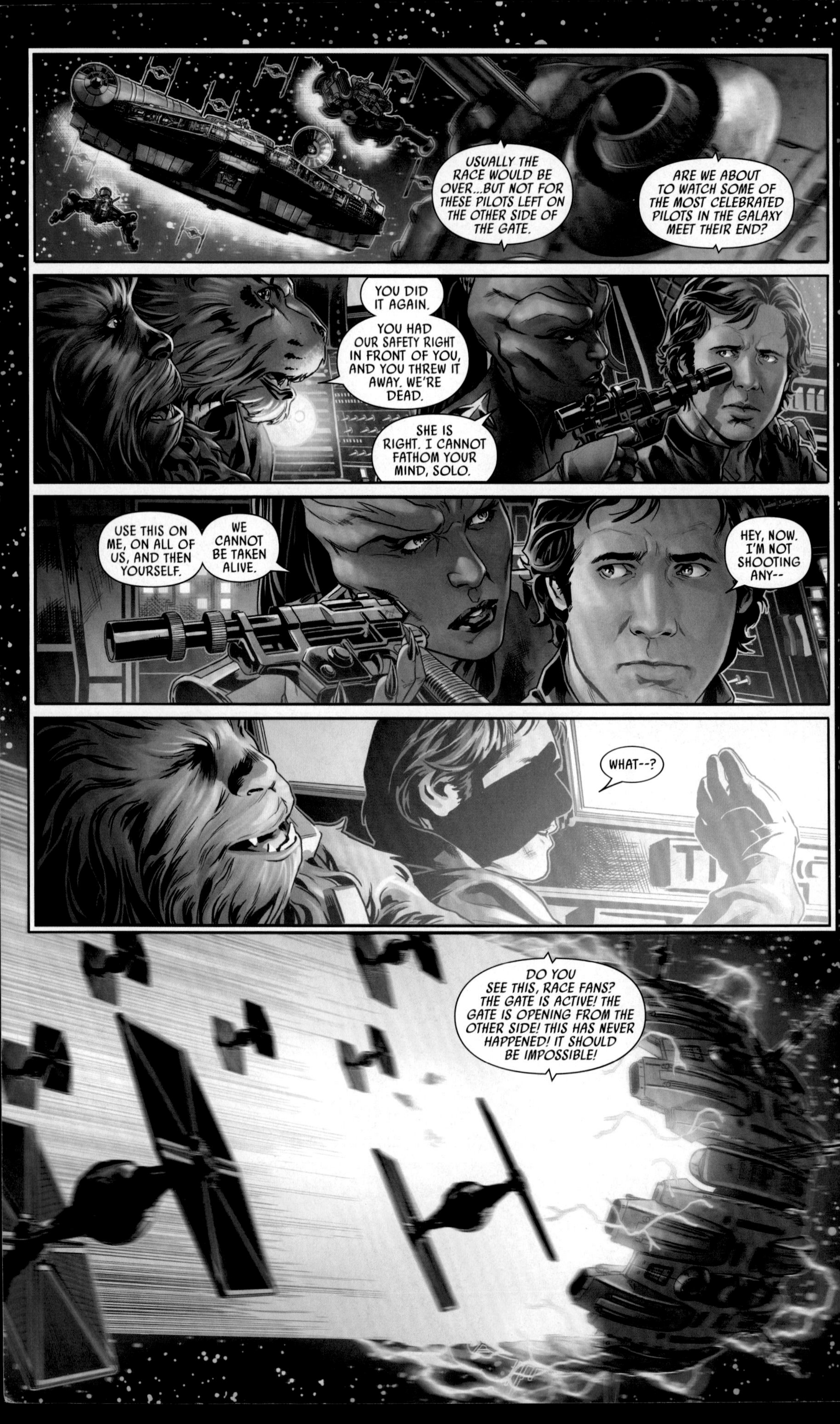
USUALLY THE RACE WOULD BE OVER...BUT NOT FOR THESE PILOTS LEFT ON THE OTHER SIDE OF THE GATE.
ARE WE ABOUT TO WATCH SOME OF THE MOST CELEBRATED PILOTS IN THE GALAXY MEET THEIR END?
YOU DID IT AGAIN.
YOU HAD OUR SAFETY RIGHT IN FRONT OF YOU, AND YOU THREW IT AWAY. WE'RE DEAD.
SHE IS RIGHT. I CANNOT FATHOM YOUR MIND, SOLO.
USE THIS ON ME, ON ALL OF US, AND THEN YOURSELF.
WE CANNOT BE TAKEN ALIVE.
HEY, NOW. I'M NOT SHOOTING ANY--
WHAT--?
DO YOU SEE THIS, RACE FANS? THE GATE IS ACTIVE! THE GATE IS OPENING FROM THE OTHER SIDE! THIS HAS NEVER HAPPENED! IT SHOULD BE IMPOSSIBLE!

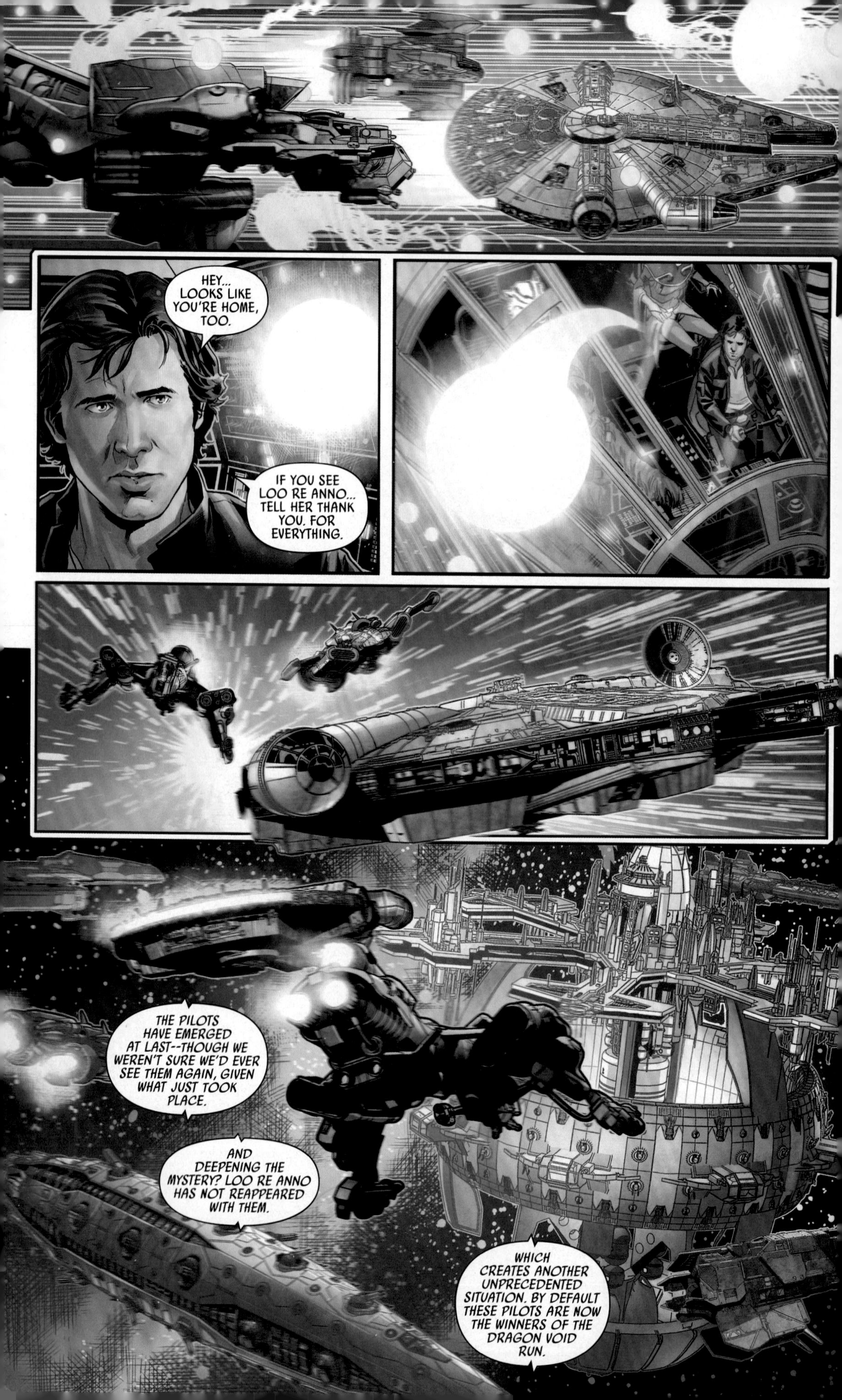
HEY... LOOKS LIKE YOU'RE HOME, TOO.
IF YOU SEE LOO RE ANNO... TELL HER THANK YOU. FOR EVERYTHING.
THE PILOTS HAVE EMERGED AT LAST--THOUGH WE WEREN'T SURE WE'D EVER SEE THEM AGAIN, GIVEN WHAT JUST TOOK PLACE.
AND DEEPENING THE MYSTERY? LOO RE ANNO HAS NOT REAPPEARED WITH THEM.
WHICH CREATES ANOTHER UNPRECEDENTED SITUATION. BY DEFAULT THESE PILOTS ARE NOW THE WINNERS OF THE DRAGON VOID RUN.

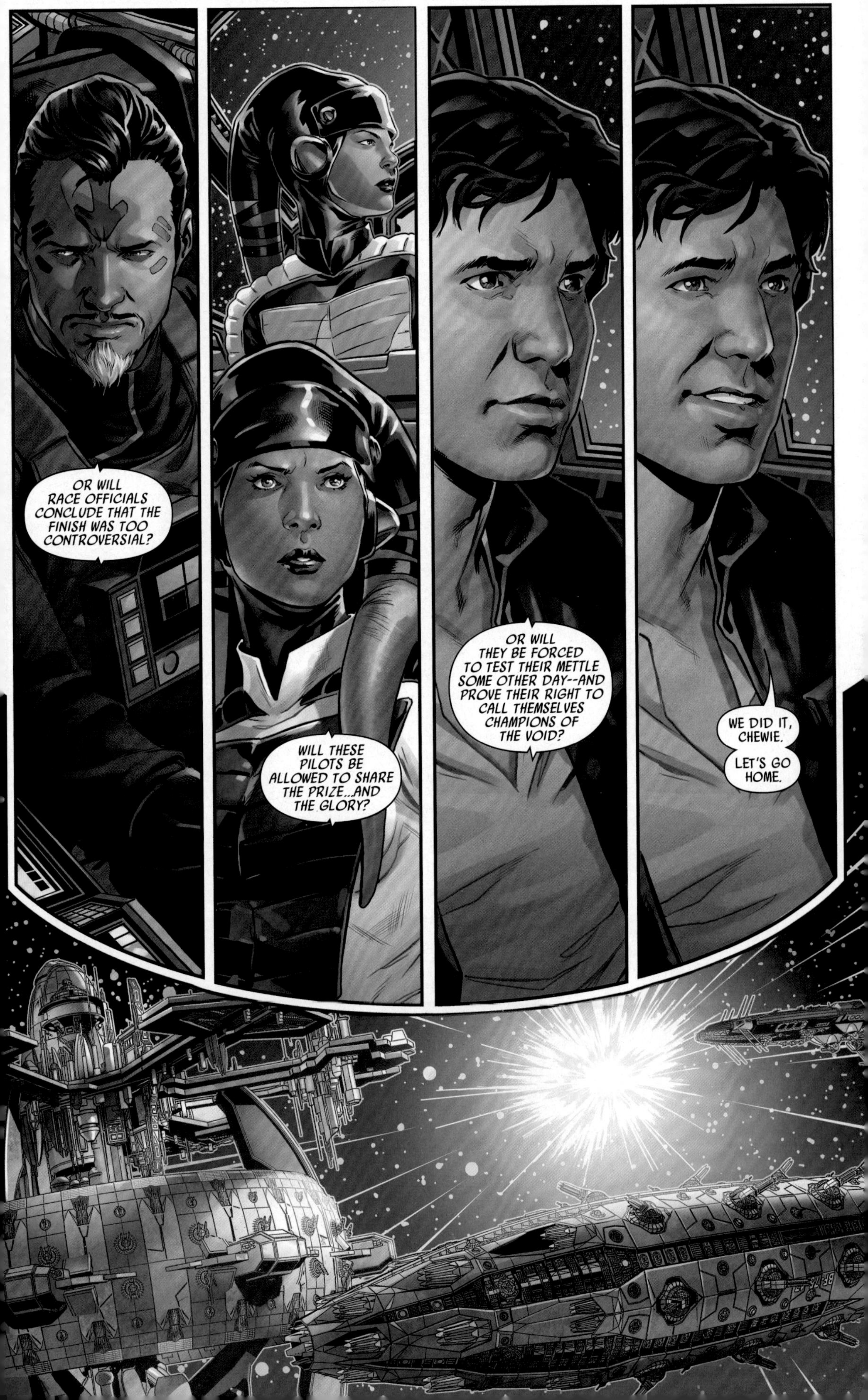
OR WILL RACE OFFICIALS CONCLUDE THAT THE FINISH WAS TOO CONTROVERSIAL?
WILL THESE PILOTS BE ALLOWED TO SHARE THE PRIZE...AND THE GLORY?
OR WILL THEY BE FORCED TO TEST THEIR METTLE SOME OTHER DAY--AND PROVE THEIR RIGHT TO CALL THEMSELVES CHAMPIONS OF THE VOID?
WE DID IT, CHEWIE.
LET'S GO HOME.

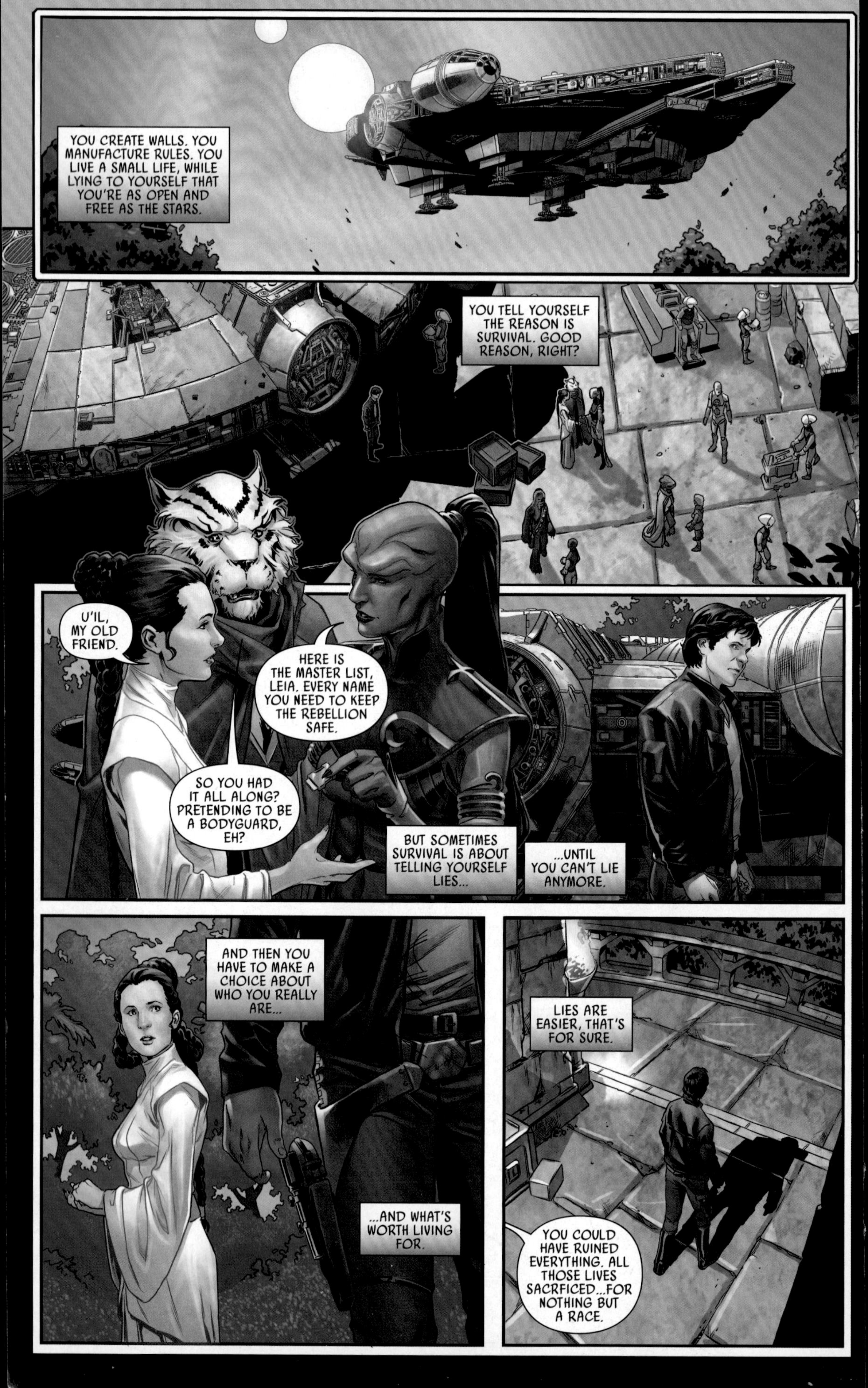
YOU CREATE WALLS. YOU MANUFACTURE RULES. YOU LIVE A SMALL LIFE, WHILE LYING TO YOURSELF THAT YOU'RE AS OPEN AND FREE AS THE STARS.
YOU TELL YOURSELF THE REASON IS SURVIVAL. GOOD REASON, RIGHT?
U'IL, MY OLD FRIEND.
HERE IS THE MASTER LIST, LEIA. EVERY NAME YOU NEED TO KEEP THE REBELLION SAFE.
SO YOU HAD IT ALL ALONG? PRETENDING TO BE A BODYGUARD, EH?
BUT SOMETIMES SURVIVAL IS ABOUT TELLING YOURSELF LIES...
...UNTIL YOU CAN'T LIE ANYMORE.
AND THEN YOU HAVE TO MAKE A CHOICE ABOUT WHO YOU REALLY ARE...
...AND WHAT'S WORTH LIVING FOR.
LIES ARE EASIER, THAT'S FOR SURE.
YOU COULD HAVE RUINED EVERYTHING. ALL THOSE LIVES SACRFICED...FOR NOTHING BUT A RACE.

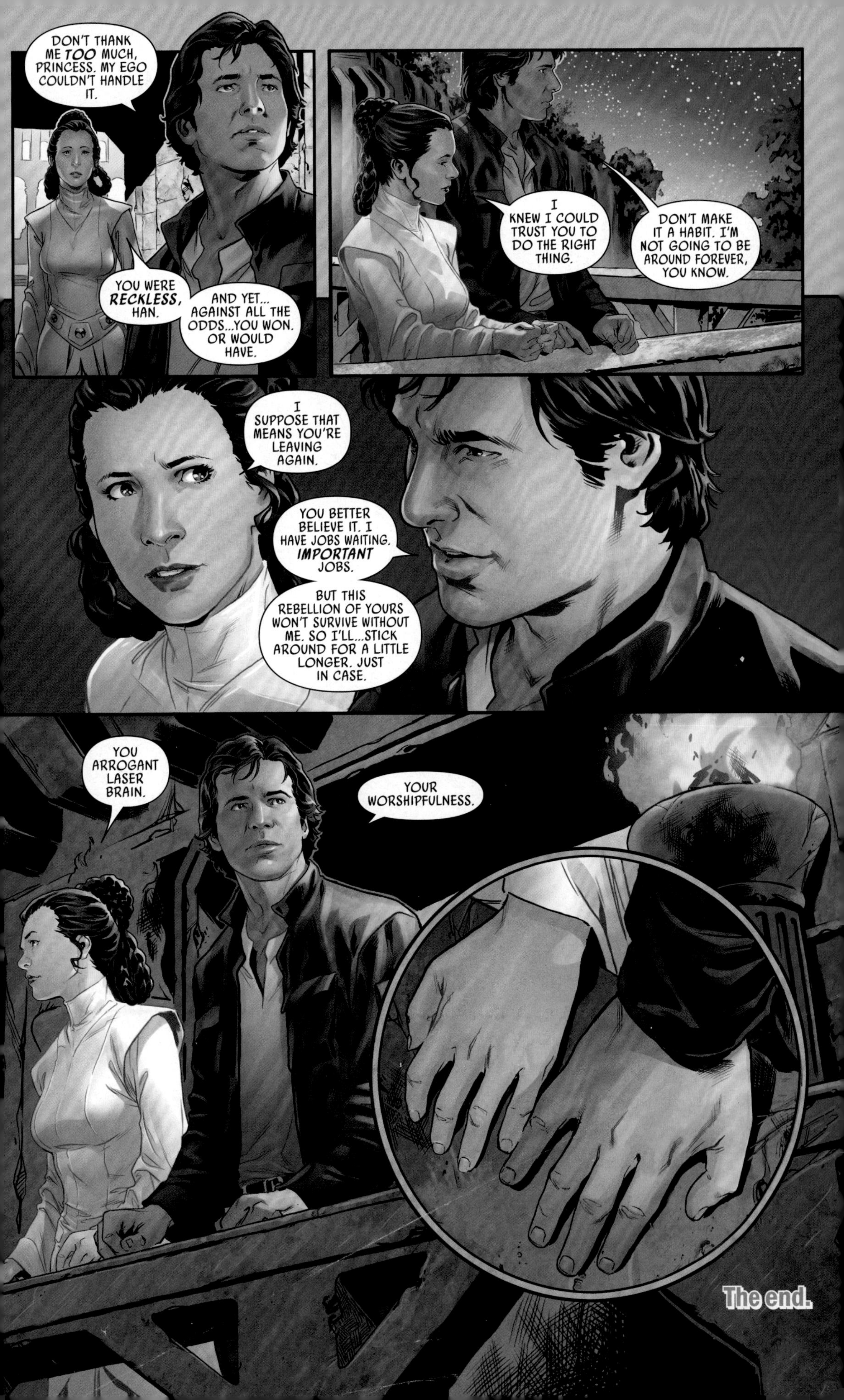

DON'T THANK ME *TOO* MUCH, PRINCESS. MY EGO COULDN'T HANDLE IT.
YOU WERE ***RECKLESS***, HAN.
AND YET... AGAINST ALL THE ODDS...YOU WON. OR WOULD HAVE.
I KNEW I COULD TRUST YOU TO DO THE RIGHT THING.
DON'T MAKE IT A HABIT. I'M NOT GOING TO BE AROUND FOREVER, YOU KNOW.
I SUPPOSE THAT MEANS YOU'RE LEAVING AGAIN.
YOU BETTER BELIEVE IT. I HAVE JOBS WAITING. ***IMPORTANT*** JOBS.
BUT THIS REBELLION OF YOURS WON'T SURVIVE WITHOUT ME. SO I'LL...STICK AROUND FOR A LITTLE LONGER. JUST IN CASE.
YOU ARROGANT LASER BRAIN.
YOUR WORSHIPFULNESS.
The end.

WHAT IS A PRINCESS WITHOUT A WORLD?

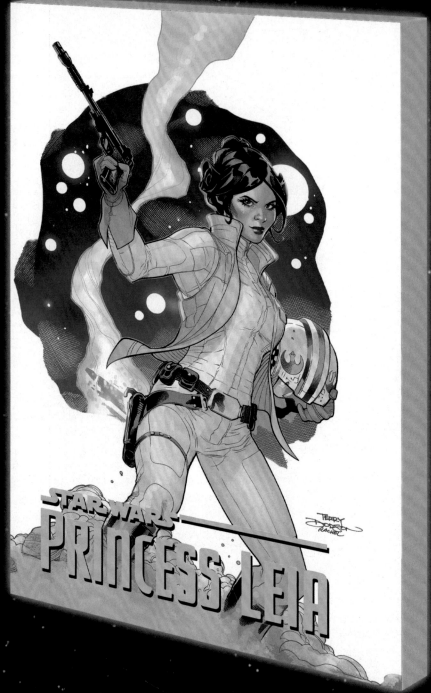

STAR WARS: PRINCESS LEIA TPB

978-0-7851-9317-3

ON SALE NOW!

CHARACTERS YOU KNOW.
STORIES YOU DON'T.

STAR WARS: LANDO TPB
978-0-7851-9319-7 • $16.99

STAR WARS: CHEWBACCA TPB
978-0-7851-9320-3 • $16.99

ON SALE NOW
IN PRINT & DIGITAL WHEREVER BOOKS ARE SOLD.

JOURNEY TO **STAR WARS: THE FORCE AWAKENS**

AFTER **RETURN OF THE JEDI**, AN EMPIRE LIES **SHATTERED**.

JOURNEY TO STAR WARS: THE FORCE AWAKENS
STAR WARS
SHATTERED EMPIRE
MARVEL
Disney
LUCASFILM
© & TM 2015 LUCASFILM LTD.

Journey to Star Wars: The Force Awakens – Shattered Empire TPB
978-0-7851-9781-2

ON SALE NOW
Wherever Books Are Sold

MARVEL Disney LUCASFILM

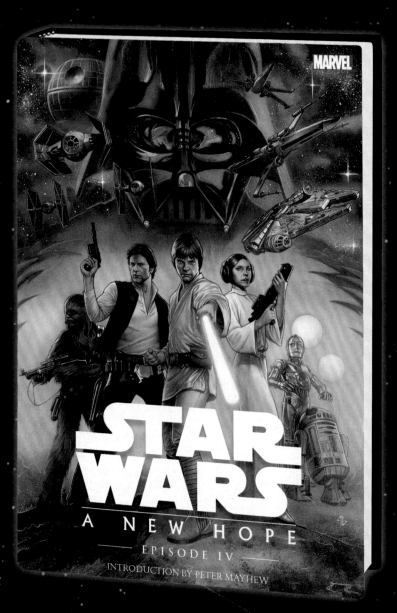

Y FAR, FAR AWAY!

F THE BIGGEST MOVIES IN HISTORY,
ERED INTERIORS!

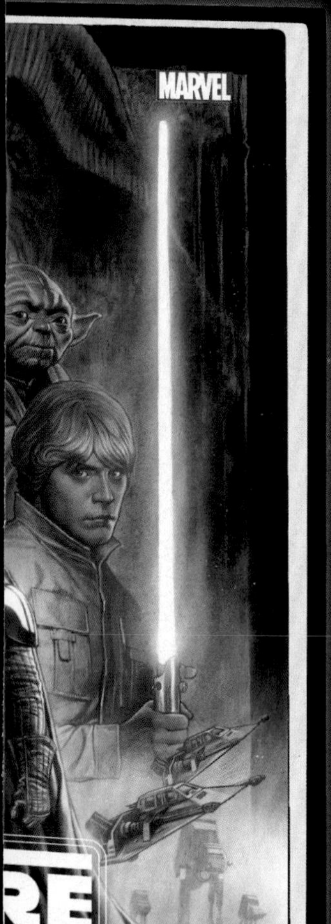
MARVEL
E WILLIAMS

PIRE STRIKES BACK HC

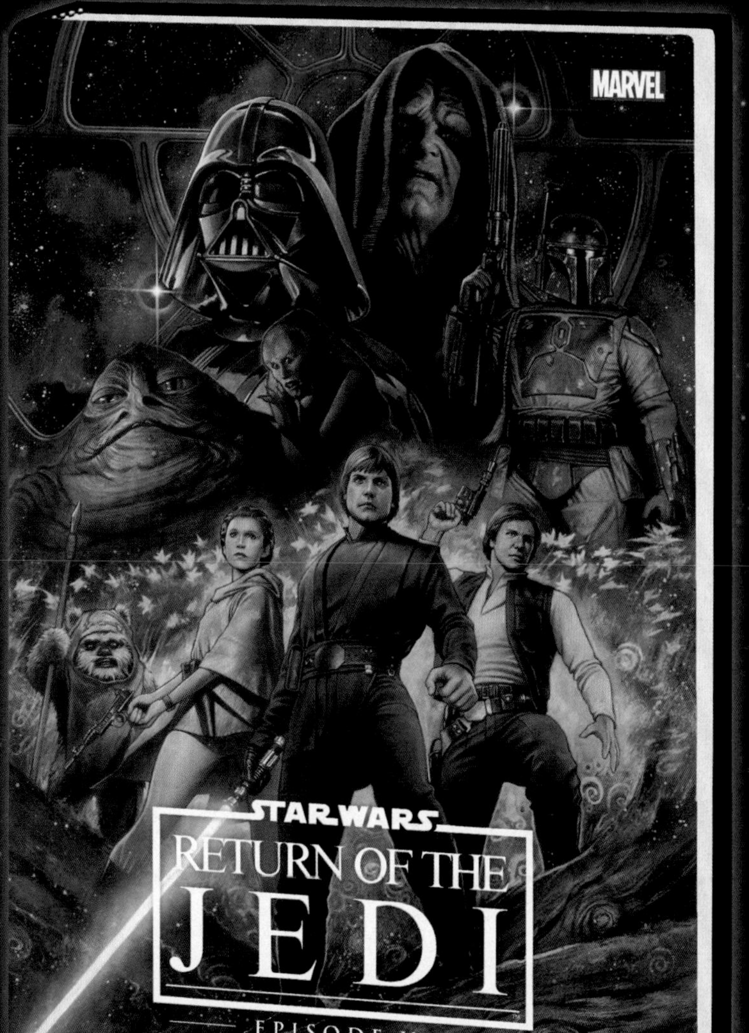
MARVEL
STAR WARS
RETURN OF THE
JEDI
EPISODE VI

STAR WARS: EPISODE VI – RETURN OF THE JEDI HC
978-0-7851-9369-2

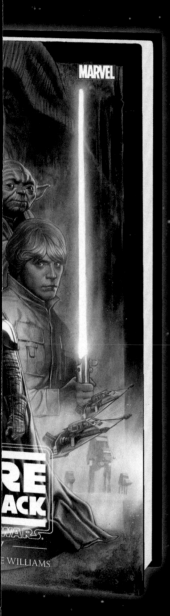

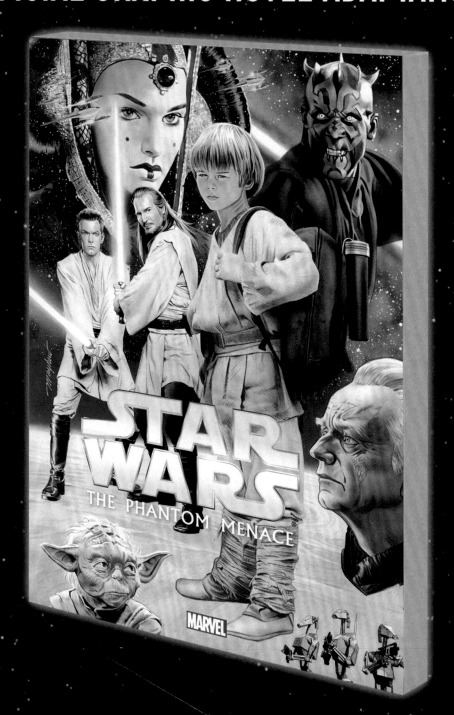